Papa — A Life Remembered

Papa—A Life Remembered
A Fictionalized Memoir

Philip J. Formo

Printed in the United States of America

Library of Congress Cataloging-in-Publication Data
Formo, Philip 1946–
Papa–A Life Remembered: a fictionalized memoir/Andreas Helland

ISBN: 978-1-4929-5623-5
ISBN: 1492956236

1. Helland, Andreas 1870-1951—Memoir
2. Authors, Norwegian
3. Clergy immigration—19th and 20th century
I. Title

Cover design by Jean Formo

Pecan Pie Press
6616 Chadwick Drive
Savage, MN 55378-4037

Available on www.createspace.com/4396079
or Amazon.com/DP/1492956236

Dedication

I dedicate this book to Andreas' parents, Bertha and Anders,
to his wives Clara, Helen and Anna
and to his children—Petra, Melvin, Bernhard,
Irene, Beatrice, Maurice and Winifred.

I also dedicate this book to my immediate family—
Jerry Formo, Winnie Formo, David Formo and Kay Formo.
One day I pray I will join all of these saints.

Introduction

Dear Papa,

Mom told me that when you came to live with us I had to stop running around the house and stop making so much noise. When you moved into our bedroom, David and I moved upstairs into a new bedroom Dad had built just for us. Looking back, I remember Grandma helping Mom in the kitchen, but you spent all day in your room in bed. I didn't know you were sick; I thought you were just tired.

On my first day of kindergarten, Mom told me to go and say "Goodbye" to you. When I walked into your room, you smiled and patted the bed and so I jumped up on it. Was I surprised when you pulled from under the bedspread a dollar bill, and then gave it to me and told me to have fun in school. You gave me a great big kiss. Your bushy white mustache scratched my face. I remember running home and telling you and Grandma Nanny all about my first day at Bancroft School in south Minneapolis. I wish you could have lived with us longer. I would have kept quieter if I had known you were so sick.

Now, 62 years later, I am sitting at my writing desk with your typewriter proudly displayed on it. I have been told you would type late into the night. I am writing this introduction at the other end of the day, and on something that did not exist in your day—a laptop computer.

Following in your footsteps, I became a teacher. Rather than teaching at a seminary, I taught in the Minneapolis Public Schools. That was until I made the mistake of raising my hand once too often and offering to become the chair of a call committee at Bethel Lutheran Church—you know, the same church at which my dad had directed the choir and where I was baptized. After our first candidate turned us down, the senior pastor offered me the position of lay pastor for education and youth. I told him I had just finished my master's degree in education and was done with schooling, and certainly was never going to seminary. Well, God had another idea.

Although I did not take the position, within six months I was attending seminary and enjoyed serving four churches during the past 31 years. I retired in 2011 and am spending my time writing, traveling and continuing to raise my hand for one committee or another.

Now, Papa, and anyone else reading this book, the general story line is accurate, but imbedded in the writing are additional events or information. Today this is referred to as creative nonfiction. You thought a memoir was something written by someone with a large ego, yet I am thankful you wrote as you did. I am so very proud of you.

Your loving grandson,
Flip

Contents

Chapter 1

Troubled Waters

Forty miles southwest of Bergen, off the coast of Norway, people lived as they had for centuries. In the late 1800s, the fishermen worked their trade while the farmers raised meager crops in the rocky soil, tending their milk cows, sheep and workhorses. And yet, by 1870 everything seemed to be changing. Families were being separated not only by disease and death but also by a new challenge known simply as "Amerika Feber" (America Fever).

Everything had been changing, even for the small, tradition-bound state church just up from the village dock in Fitjar. The new wooden sanctuary was a disappointment to those still stuck on the memories of their former centuries-old stone church. Over the years, as the ancient building deteriorated and the faithful were placed to rest in the church's cemetery, sacred memories were crumbling right before their eyes. The summer sun, already high in the sky, shown on the cross of the wooden steeple that accompanied their new sanctuary. Evergreens cast their shadows on the gravestones that stuck out of the ground as if resurrection day had already arrived. Dotting both sides of the wooden building, newer tombstones stood among the ancient ones. Those still living in this small island community had stubbornly chosen to survive the plague of the late 1800s known as America Fever. It seemed every family had said the long goodbye to a son, daughter or another family member who had caught the fever of hope and had emigrated to a foreign land.

On a Sunday morning, the faithful remnant could be found in the local church. Before the first congregant would arrive, Johan, the longtime usher and lay leader, stood at the wide-open door. His personal liturgy began as he stood motionless, facing the white wooden altar. His eyes locked on the painting of Mary as she looked up at her son hanging from the cross. Her grief-stricken face echoed Johan's own anguish as he thought of his wife's suffering from leprosy in a home for lepers in Bergen. Her funeral, some six years earlier, had been the very last service conducted in the old stone church.

An hour passed before Johan finally welcomed the first congregants as they made their way to worship. His warm, calloused hand swallowed up the hands of those he greeted. As he released his grip, the worshippers faced the traditional chasm known as the center aisle. Women and children would find their pew on the left while the men and their sons, nearly reaching manhood, would make their way to the right. Each family sat in the very pew their ancestors had occupied for centuries.

But on this day, the separation was even more defined. Some had responded to Johan's greeting with a typical smile and pat on the shoulder, while others belligerently pulled their hands away, giving their old friend nothing more than a cold stare. With the doors closed and the organ music filling the sanctuary, people were expected to prayerfully prepare their hearts for worship. But their best intentions failed as their thoughts drifted to the traumatic events of this particular Sunday.

As Johan took his place next to the aisle in the last pew, his mind was flooded with the images of the young pastors who had once served this little parish. While some had been gifted ministers, others were cut from a different cloth. This small, low-paying congregation received only new graduates just trying out their skills, or older pastors who had proven to be failures in larger parishes. Yet, deep within these rural people was a respect for the sacredness of someone called by God, assigned by the bishop and acting on behalf of the head of the Norwegian Church, King Carl IV.

Unlike other painful farewells, on this sunny July morning the majority of the congregation had gathered to wish God's speed to someone whose ministry had been in question and whose future was as choppy and uncertain as the sea lapping up against the Fitjar shore. For some time now, the bishop had received complaints regarding Pastor Olson's conduct. Johan stood in the back of the sanctuary, imagining the meeting where he would formally present to the bishop the congregation's charges. Johan's hands shook as he named in his mind those longtime friends who on this day had offered him only a cold stare.

Pastor Olson had given these island people the first three years of his hoped-for lifelong profession. While he was growing in his skills as a preacher, his personal habits were less than stellar. Instead of eating the typical breakfast of porridge or rømmegrøt, the pastor chose to break the fast with only high-proof aquavit, the people's favorite homemade brew. Following many a parishioner's strenuous boat journey across challenging sea currents and wind-tossed waves, too often the faithful would read a sign posted on the church door announcing that the worship service had been canceled. On the Sundays the pastor was able to maneuver the narrow path from his parsonage to the church, his heavy, woolen robe filtered the effects of his lack of bathing. His alcohol-laden breath not only offended the pious Haugean teetotalers, but also those accustomed to their own drink. His reddish face and alcohol-scented skin only served as an exclamation of the young man's troubles.

The sanctuary was not the only place life-changing drama was being played out. It was on this very same morning, a short distance from the assembled congregation, that Andreas Helland was slowly making his way into this world. The arrival of Bertha and Anders' sixth child was surprisingly a long, drawn-out affair. Labor had begun the day before, and as it ravaged the mother's body, hourly she grew weaker and weaker. While mother, father and midwife were predisposed, the Helland children had been sent off down the narrow path to the rocky coastline on which sat their parish church. Too young to be cognizant of the politics of the day, they were warmly greeted by Johan. As the four children walked in train-like fashion down the aisle, with their shoes clapping against the wooden floor, Helga, now a gangly 13-year-old, had to stop at every pew, whispering answers to inquisitive women.

With a worried look that betrayed the innocence of a child her age, she kept saying, "It hasn't come yet, not yet."

Almost every woman took her hand and simply said, "We pray 'Soon,' my dear, we pray 'Soon.'"

After a long and difficult pregnancy with weeks of bed rest, there would be a communal sigh of relief once the baby was safely delivered. Behind Helga walked Martha, the more verbal ten-year-old redhead, followed by their seven-year-old brother, Kristen. As he tried to kick the heels of Martha's shoes, he dragged behind him his five-year-old straw-haired brother, Kristofer Peder. Even at this early age, he had been schooled in the sacredness of his given name. Just 12 months prior to his birth, another Peder had been born to his mother but had survived only a few days. Bertha, Anders and their children were still wrestling with the haunting visits of grief and the stinging pain that accompanies this type of loss. As the service began, every mother was focusing not on a farewell or the fight within the membership, but rather a pleading for God's mercy on behalf of Bertha and a child coming into the world.

The service customarily ended with a prayer that urgently pleaded God's mercy on the grieving and deathly ill. Although news spread much quicker than the words of a prayer, this petition often served as the village health report or local obituary. Everyone's ears were attentive to this last petition.

"Our loving heavenly Father," Pastor Olson began, "I ask your blessing on this parish and every faithful member as I leave them this day. I pray your blessing on King Carl and our bishop. And, I pray for Bertha Helland and her family in this hour of extreme trial."

As Bertha's name was mentioned, every woman's eyes sprang open as Martha, fearful of the worst, let out a scream, jumped up from her pew and ran back down the aisle. Quickly, Helga followed as the congregants raised their heads and turned toward the commotion. By the time the two sisters arrived at the entrance, they were swept into Johan's arms as he quietly said, "Come, dear children, come now." Standing next to Johan was Borghild, an elderly neighbor, who had arrived late for worship only after visiting the girls' mother.

She took Martha from Johan, while pleading, "Don't worry girls, I have good news." Taking Martha's face into her fleshy, calloused hands, she looked her straight in the eyes, wiped away a tear and announced, "Hush now, hush now, poor little one; everything is fine. Don't worry. You have a baby brother, just born an hour or so ago. Mama is fine, just fine. And your baby brother is crying up a storm." She looked over at Helga, stroked her tear-stained cheek, and smiled. Still breathing hard, the sisters began to smile as this adopted grandmother figure shared the good news.

The pastor, now staring at the commotion, was waved on by Johan to continue his prayer. With confusion on the faces of the pastor and many a parishioner, Pastor Olson finished, with everyone chiming in with an "Amen."

Borghild wrapped her arms around Martha and repeated, "Poor little one, poor little one."

The closing hymn began as Martha escaped from Borghild's hold and retreated back down the aisle to whisper the news into the ears of her siblings. The last verse was hardly finished when the women left their pews and hurried back for Borghild's welcome news.

And thus a sixth Helland child was welcomed into this world, to the excitement of four siblings and two relieved parents. On July 31, 1870, in front of the very same people who had experienced the drama three weeks earlier, a joyous baptism took place, officiated by a visiting pastor who sprinkled water from a centuries-old baptismal font on the infant's bald head and announced, "I baptize you, Berndt Andreas Helland, in the name of the Father, and of the Son and of the Holy Ghost. Amen."

Chapter 2

School Bound

While Andreas' first name was popular all through Norway, his last name came not from some long genealogical line but from the piece of land that would become the home place on this rocky island of Stord, a good walk from the town of Fitjar. Ever since the 17th century, this small property had been referred to as the Helland Gaard. Thus, Bertha and Anders, and later their offspring, would inherit the last name of Helland.

For the first 14 years of marriage, the challenge to survive was nothing new to poverty-stricken Anders. For his young wife, it was a struggle from the very day of their wedding. Many a wedding was a lavish, multi-day affair with baskets of gifts received by the lucky couple. The tradition was for the couple to respond in kind by sending their guests home with baskets overflowing with local delicacies. If the bridal couple was not to be branded stingy, a certain quantity of hard liquor was to be served along with plenty of strong, homemade beer. Rather than a light lunch, substantial meals of pork, beef and both fresh and salt fish were commonly served. In this case, Bertha's father considered his daughter's marriage to Anders as a disappointing affair, a situation commonly referred to as marrying *down*. Thus, he was unwilling to pay for a typical bridal celebration.

There was, however, an honorable way out of this difficulty. If you were fortunate, as Bertha and Anders were, to have friends who were to be married in the proper manner, then the less-fortunate couple could be invited to the wedding, receive the same blessing and from that day be considered married. So, the couple celebrated their wedding at Bertha's childhood friend's home. While her friend Sylvia stood in her living room in the traditional red- and black-braided gown with a large, silver belt, Bertha wore a simple, white everyday dress. Following the short ceremony, the reception began with both couples seated at the wedding table. By custom, only the bride and groom hosting the wedding were to receive gifts. Thus, Bertha and Anders began their married life written out of her father's will, lacking the gifts received by a typical wedding couple and holding only onto their love for each other, the clothes on their backs, a small rowboat, two oars and a wooden chest that held their personal belongings.

Empowered by a stubborn sense of hope, an adventuresome spirit and an unbridled love, the young Helland couple began their lives together on a lonely island, missing friends and relatives, while attempting to survive on the one meal a day they could gather. As they struggled during their first year as farmers, Bertha not only questioned the decision she had made but wondered if the first year's failed crop had anything to do with the former use of their rented plot, the site of a pagan temple. Failing to produce even one potato, their survival depended on Anders' long hours of labor for his landowner, the owner's gracious understanding and additional work unloading fish at the local fishery. By the second year, after picking and piling endless rocks and plowing a small field using only Anders' strength and a borrowed hand plow, Bertha was able to dig her first potatoes. Thirteen years later, by the time of Andreas' birth, his father had cultivated most of the plot, leaving the rest for a small cabin with a loft for the children, a lean-to storage room and a stone summer kitchen.

Relying on his self-taught carpentry skills, the most difficult challenge of farming was finding the necessary wood to build adequate fencing. Anders smiled proudly as he inspected his most recent work. To Bertha's pleasure, it separated their one cow and a few sheep from their front door. Although his other fencing projects were usually adequate, he had learned from experience that his skills were always challenged by the neighbor's bull or the persistent nudging of the horns of a stray ram.

During the colder months, the family huddled together in the one room with a wider bed for Helga and Martha, a narrow one for Kristofer Peder and Kristen, and a third bed for Mama, Papa and little Andreas. Under the cabin, a small cellar had been dug for the storage of potatoes, milk and cheese. By now their hard work had produced small crops of barley, oats and carrots as well as eggs from a few loyal chickens. More often than not, eggs were used as tender for rye flour, sugar and other provisions.

No matter how successful the crops, the size of their small plot forced them to continue to rely on other income. In addition to the chores of milking and weeding, Bertha sheared, spun, wove and sold woolen clothing while Anders found work in the local iron mine.

As Andreas grew from a toddler to a young child, his health became a topic of hushed conversation between his parents. His coughing, fevers, earaches and general weakness created a fear that permeated the household. Reaching school age, he was still considered too fragile to attend. His sickly manner prevented Andreas from ever leaving his mother's sight. He would sit at the door waiting for his brother, Kristofer Peder, to return home.

"But Mother," he would cry out each day as his siblings walked out the door with lunch pails in hand. "But Mother, I feel good, I feel good." To his constant plea he would only see his mother shake her head.

When school was out of session, he overheard his brothers and neighbors playing their games in front of their home. He was not only forced to remain inside, but oftentimes sentenced to bed rest. At dinnertime, while his family ate, Andreas could be heard and seen shaking from yet another coughing spell. His condition struck terror in his parents as they were reminded of Anders' brother's earlier bout with a black plague that had visited Norway—the deadly disease of leprosy. Burned into both Anders' and Bertha's memories were the sights, smells and suffering at the Bergen home for lepers where Anders' brother, Jens, had been sent. Along with that fear, the grief of losing their first Peder continued to consume them.

Death·was not the only reason for painful farewells. Once confirmed in the church, most sons and daughters were ready to enter the work force as farm helpers, maids or even a sailor's hand. By the time Andreas reached the age of four, his sisters Helga and Martha had already finished their schooling, had said their tearful, long goodbyes and had left for service in local homes. The pain of separation was comforted only by a rare weekend at home, the few coins they had saved and the limited drain on the family's food supply caused by their absence.

Another difficult day arrived when a letter was received from Bertha's brother, Kristen Meling. Along with a warm greeting came the offer for 13-year-old Kristofer Peder to be trained as a baker's apprentice many hours away in the larger city of Sunmore. Bertha struggled with her brother's request and diligently prayed for God's will. In the midst of the decision, she began to grieve the fact that Kristofer would not confirm his faith in his home church.

Kristofer Peder was both excited about the possibility of learning a trade and yet hated to leave his younger brother behind. "Who is going to tell me stories? Who will play with me? Don't go, please Kristofer, don't go," Andreas pleaded. During the weeks of deliberation, Andreas was not only quick tempered but more often sullen and unwilling to speak. Finally, Kristofer agreed to accept his uncle's offer and Andreas' pleading was to no avail.

It was on a cloudy Wednesday in the middle of August 1878, with fog still in the air, that Andreas and the rest of the family bid Kristofer Peder a tearful farewell. Bending down, Bertha would wipe away Andreas' tears and assure him of his brother's return. But regardless of the promise, the eight-year-old only felt abandoned. The walk from their hilltop farm down to the Fitjar dock looked like a funeral procession. Leading the family, his father held tightly to the metal handle of the rose-painted chest he had built for his son. Kristofer Peder took hold of the opposite handle, while his other hand firmly grasped Andreas' shoulder. Behind Kristofer and Andreas walked their mother, carrying the box of sandwiches that would tide over the traveler during the journey. Behind her were Kristen, Martha and Helga, who had returned home for this solemn occasion. Once at the dock, they found the two neighbor men who had offered father and son a ride to Bergen. The neighbor's boat, known as a "half decker," was filled with a load of potatoes intended for market. Although the tall and strapping Kristofer thought his father's company was totally unnecessary, his parents insisted father would accompany his son to where the boy would board the steamer for Sunmore. While the two passengers sat in the stern, the neighbors pulled up a small sail and took in their hands the large, wooden oars. The light breeze and powerful rowing brought them to the end of the island and soon the boat was out of sight. The family was still wildly waving and hoping they might get just one more glimpse of father and son. As the family walked back up the hill, the only sounds heard were Andreas' constant coughs and the sniffling coming from Bertha and her daughters. Once out in the open water, Anders and son took a third oar and began to row. With every stroke, Kristofer's heart sank as the quiet was interrupted only by the sound of oars smoothly slicing the sea. Unaccustomed to talking about his daily tasks, Kristofer broke the silence by asking his father how he would get along without Kristofer's help. Not known for using any more words than necessary, Anders answered, "We survived before you were old enough to do chores and we will do the same now."

Fortunately a good breeze allowed them to arrive in Bergen in plenty of time to meet the steamer. Once father and son climbed the ladder to the dock above them, using ropes and the help of their neighbors, they raised the wooden trunk Bertha had so carefully painted and packed. The dirt road at the entrance to the dock was lined with waiting buggies and freight wagons. Kristofer's eyes registered surprise as he witnessed for the first time such an industrious port. Anders first shook his son's hand, but then, seeing the tears in his eyes, embraced him with the most powerful hug his son had ever received. With both of them quickly wiping away tears, Anders' voice broke as he said farewell. It was Kristofer's turn to wildly wave as his father made his way back down the ladder. Boarding the half decker, Anders stood and waved at his son as the boat made its way to the end of the dock and on to the city market where the potatoes would be sold.

When the steamer arrived, Kristofer handed the purser his ticket, asked another young man to help him with his chest and made his way to the large, general-passenger cabin. Soon the horn blasted three times and the ship slowly made its way out to sea and turned to the north. Rather than the adventure he had been looking forward to, Kristofer began to feel like a prisoner, condemned and sentenced to the unknown. As more and more passengers left the open deck and made their way into the cabin, a wave of loneliness and fear swept over him. Tired from the first leg of the journey, as the steamer

made its way north, Kristofer took his place on a bench and attempted to close his eyes. Every attempt at sleep was interrupted by the
blaring steam horn announcing their arrival at each stop along the
way. Finally, after a combination of sitting, standing and lying on his
side on the wooden bench, Kristofer heard the people around him
talking about the next stop, his own destination. This time when
the horn sounded, he was fully awake, anxious to debark and yet
wondering how his unknown uncle and family would receive him.

Once docked, another passenger with only a cloth bag in hand offered to help Kristofer with his storage chest. As they carefully made
their way down the wooden plank toward the dock, other passengers
hurried past them.

"Mange takk," Kristofer said as the man put down his end of
the trunk, tipped his hat and went on his way. Anxiously looking
around, Kristofer sought out someone who might have a family
resemblance. He was relieved to hear the comforting words, "You
must be Kristofer."

Kristofer nodded and said, "Uncle Meling?"

"Yes, son, and welcome. I will ask the livery man at the end of the
dock to deliver your chest since we have a walk ahead of us."

Nodding approval, the two of them walked quietly down the
dock where they found the carriage driver. Once the arrangements
were made, Uncle Meling looked again at his nephew and said very
deliberately, "Kri-sto-fer". "Kri-sto-fer," he repeated. "But, do you
have another name?"

Kristofer, looking puzzled, paused and finally said, "Well, I was
baptized Kristofer Peder."

"Peder, that will do. We will call you Peder. You see, we are a very
busy people in Sunmore and we cannot waste time pronouncing
unnecessarily long names. So Peder it will be."

As they walked up from the dock, Uncle Meling showed his
new trainee the various shops that lined the busy street. Arriving
home, he was introduced to his aunt and three cousins. That first
night, so far away from home, stripped of his preferred name, Peder
(Kristofer) soaked his pillow with tears, wiping them away with his
pajama sleeves.

August 14, 1878
Dear Family,
I arrived safely with a kind young man helping me with my chest. I am trying my hardest with Uncle Meling. I am up by 4 A.M. to learn the baking trade, off to school and then home again to work at the bakery. I have never slept so hard. I miss all of you. One troubling bit of news: Uncle insists on calling me Peder, rather than Kristofer. He tells me Sunmore is a busy city and there isn't time for long names. I miss you.
Your loving son,
Kristofer

Chapter 3

Back Home

The one-room wooden schoolhouse in Fitjar, with an apartment attached for the teacher, stood near the church. The elderly bachelor teacher had, like Pastor Olson, not only overstayed his welcome but, as if it were an epidemic, suffered from the same misuse of spirits. Overly friendly to the students, the children squirmed from his lap when confronted with his alcohol-laden breath. The lonely island life, limited facilities and low pay kept better-trained teachers from ever applying for this position.

As late summer grew into the cooler season of fall, excitement about Christmas began as early as the middle of October. Anders would butcher a sheep and the family looked forward to that one time each year when they could stuff themselves with mutton. From the animal fat, Bertha made tallow candles for the special occasion. Though every year seemed to be celebrated like the last, it still felt like a surprise. Close to the big day, with the equivalent of a dollar in hand, Anders would take the long journey to the country store close to the church to make the rare purchase of not what was needed but was actually wanted. For this one holiday, the family would enjoy store bread, sweet cakes, a bottle of syrup, a small bag of sugar and another of rice. Added to the celebration would be a few little gifts for each child. It was difficult in this small home for anyone to sleep through the preparations. With the holy day of Christmas Eve beginning at noon, Bertha was busy by 4 A.M., baking, boiling meat and heating water. The floor would be scrubbed and everything put in its place. For the Christmas Eve lunch, *Molje*, flatbread dipped in animal fat was the special treat. Finally, the best of all meals was ready. Tradition prescribed that the potatoes, newly salted fish and mutton be served on a big pewter platter on which was stamped the year 1770. Bertha would remind the family that the bowls holding the rice pudding had come all the way from Holland. Once the meal was eaten, the presents were brought out. Andreas would receive a new pair of wooden shoes, crafted by his father, a pair of woolen stockings carded, spun and knit by his mother's already misshapen hands, and a warm scarf. The extra store-bought surprise might be a one-cent clay cuckoo or a four-cent mouth organ. If the weather was calm, they would make the half-hour journey to the Fitjar church, but far too often the blistering cold winds kept the family nestled in their modest home, where they would sing their beloved Christmas hymns, pray and read the Christmas Gospel as a family.

For Andreas, this particular Christmas was even more exciting. His mother had told him that if he remained healthy, he would be able to begin school immediately following the Christmas break. Following a celebration of family games for New Year's Eve, Andreas went to bed counting the hours until he would join his friends. His mother had already taught this quick-witted redhead some reading skills as well as printing, but it was the exciting unknown that colored his imagination and fed his curiosity. He would have to go to bed only one more night before that long-awaited day would arrive.

On New Year's Day, as on most Sundays, the Helland family attended worship. As long as Andreas could remember, Johan was at the church door greeting each parishioner. Anders and his son took their places on the right side of the sanctuary while Bertha greeted her women friends on the opposite side. Eric, an older friend of Andreas, whispered that he looked forward to seeing him in school. As Andreas sat through the worship service, his mind drifted constantly to the events of the next day.

Following supper, Andreas announced, "Mama, if I go to bed early will tomorrow come faster?"

His smiling mother patted him on the head and said, "I think so, Son, I think so."

Off to bed Andreas went, looking forward to the next day, and more than ready for his first experience of formal education.

It was just a few hours after the kerosene lamp had been turned off that Bertha was awakened by a whimper that quickly grew into a cry, and then a loud shout.

"Mama, Mama," his whispering grew into scream, "Mama, Father."

"What is it?" Bertha whispered as she twisted her body to climb out of bed. "What is it, Son, what is it?" Stepping gingerly across the cold floor, she listened to her son's complaint.

"My ear, Mama. My ear," Andreas said.

Lighting a lamp, Father joined them at Andreas' bedside.

"It hurts, Mama, it hurts so much," Andreas cried.

"Is it a sharp pain or dull?" his mother asked. Still shivering in her nightgown, she heard her son moan and plead.

"It just hurts, Mama, it just hurts."

"Now, now, Son, I'll get something to help." As Anders held the oil lamp, his wife took a small stick, dipped it in the hot oil and carefully placed it in Andreas' ear.

"It might sting a bit, Son, but it will make it feel better," she said.

"Oh, ow. Oh," Andreas screamed, as he squirmed under his blanket and almost kicked the lamp out of his father's hand.

After removing the small stick, she walked over to the wood stove to heat the water in the kettle. Taking a clean cloth, she made a warm compress and laid it on his ear.

"This will help, Son," she said.

The warmth of the compress kept Andreas quiet for the night, but the next morning and the following days were spent trying other remedies generally known in the community. Along with the pain, the much larger disappointment was missing school. As days turned to weeks, it seemed nothing relieved the pain. A doctor's visit for something as simple as an earache was, in such a rural area, out of the question.

It was only a few weeks into this latest health scare that their money had again dwindled to nothing and mother was left to care for her patient while Anders, with a sleeping roll hanging from his shoulder and carrying a bag, returned to the only current site of employment, the iron mine on the south end of the island. Working two weeks at a time, he would go home every other weekend to catch up on the many chores his wife was unable to finish. Besides caring for Andreas, Bertha was busy milking the one cow, carding, spinning, weaving and knitting the wool from her favorite sheep and keeping the fire burning.

On Anders' first return to home, he encountered a son who not only was delirious but was unable to recognize him. Seeing Andreas still in bed and listening to his groans of pain, Anders, usually a stoic and quiet man, walked outside with head in hands, shaking his fist at God and sobbing. Thankfully by Sunday morning the boy's pain had begun to subside. Following the Sunday service and a simple dinner of potatoes, flat bread, homemade butter and dried fish, Anders began his lonesome march back to the mine.

Weighing him down, with every step he took, was his son's health and the prospect of long days in the cold, damp and dirty mine. Prayers for his son's healing matched the cadence of his walk. As often as Anders shook his fist at God, he would ask forgiveness for what he thought of as a lack of faith. Besides prayer, he passed his time on the journey calculating the funds he would need to purchase the next year's seed potatoes. Though at times tempted by the public help available through a local poor tax, his pride refused to allow the thought to linger very long.

Anders shook his head when he thought of better times, especially those of his father-in-law. The growth of shipping, agriculture, timber, mining and the fisheries had offered a robust life. But at about the time of his youngest son's birth, a downturn of the national economy and the subsequent lack of jobs had even extended to the small islands along the coast. Both the fisheries and the mines were often shut down.

The shipping industry's transition from sail power to steam was not only too slow, but in comparison to other nations, far too late to remain competitive in a new world market. It seemed that each and every week either a family from the island of Stord or a relative on the mainland was beginning their long journey across the Atlantic to what they believed would be a life of plenty. Instead of a small and rocky plot that could hardly feed a family, there were stories of acres upon acres of lush crops, freedom from the state church and from the rigid class system. Everything seemed better in America. But with the dream came the haunting fear that sons or daughters would never return to their homeland.

The seasons passed and it seemed every time Andreas was ready for school, something in his lungs would prevent him from starting.

It was finally at the age of 12, as the winter cold was exchanged by gentle spring winds, that his ailments began to subside.

By the beginning of summer, Andreas was again begging his mother and counting the days for school to finally begin. Like many island children, he had already learned basic reading and writing skills at the kitchen table with his mother serving as teacher. Along with excellent reading habits, Bertha had kept all the children up on their religious instruction, a common element of the school curriculum.

While waiting for school to begin, the Saterbo family, whose farm was at the highest elevation of the island, requested Andreas' help in shepherding their sheep. Given strict orders on what to do, Andreas was pleased to be treated like a man who could actually bring in a little income for the family. Lonely and cold at night, Andreas fervently prayed that in the morning light he would again find all of the sheep. Some nights he was accompanied by the eight-year-old son of the Saterbo family with whom he could talk. Thankful that all the sheep had been accounted for, the month-long assignment came to an end. A few coins were carefully counted out in his outstretched palm and he made his way back home. This experience, just a few miles from home, fed what would become a lifelong passion for adventure.

When the first day of the school term finally arrived, excited and curious, Andreas began the long hike down the rocky path that led to the school. As he approached the schoolhouse, noticing the size and age of children gathering at the door, Andreas was reminded of how far behind he was in his education. The teacher rang the bell, the door opened, and everyone ran in. Andreas slowly followed, towering over his classmates. The students were separated into two classes that met on alternating days. Andreas would continue to be the largest and oldest student in his class. Friends his age would attend on the days he was forced to remain at home.

"Andreas, you may place your things at this table," instructed Mister Olafson, as he pointed to a wooden chair and table that fit Andreas. He turned and hung his lunch pail on a hook behind him. On the table he placed his framed slate, pencil, pen, pen holder and the one sheet of paper he had brought. He sat at his desk, then quickly stood up, recognizing the younger children's proper etiquette of standing. On the front wall hung a large map of Norway and next to it a map of the world divided into two hemispheres. As Andreas stared at the map of Norway, he proudly looked for the town of Sunmore, where his older brother had moved to learn the trade of baking. Straining his eyes, he searched for the small circle representing this far-away place.

Mister Olafson's deep voice interrupted his search by announcing, "We begin each day with a Bible reading and a prayer. I will read from the beginning of the Bible, the book of Genesis."

The teacher slowly read the first verses from the creation story, said a short prayer and asked the students to be seated.

Though he was disappointed in attending school with such young children, Andreas was at least thrilled to finally be in the classroom. The first day sped by. At day's end, he picked up his lunch pail and assigned reading. While the younger children beat him out the door, running in every direction, Andreas made his way home via the same steep and rocky path.

Finally home, Andreas found his mother tending the garden. She met him with her kerchief on her head, a giant smile and a litany of questions about his first day. Bertha led him into the house and announced, "I have a surprise for you."

She turned to where their few books were stored and pulled out a letter from the end of the shelf, "A letter from Kristofer," she said.

"Oh, good! Let me see it," he said, grabbing it from her hand.

"Be careful," she scolded him.

He stared at the envelope and then, as if it was priceless, he opened it and began reading.

Dear Mama, Papa and Andreas,

I am so happy to hear that Mama is coming to visit. It has been so long since I have seen any of you. I am happy you will be here for my graduation from school. Uncle Kristen insists I show you the baking skills he has taught me over the years. All the family is excited to see you. I have told Uncle that I will continue to assist him at

*the bakery until I have saved enough money for school in Oslo. I
have decided to attend the university but have not chosen a course
of study. I am anxious for you to see how I have changed since I last
saw you. I think it has been five years now.*

*I miss Papa and, of course, my closest brother, Andreas. His letters
show how much progress he has made with your tutoring at home.
I hope he is enjoying his first days at school and hope that he is well
enough to attend.*

Love, and greet the rest of the family,
Peder

When he finished reading, Andreas realized his brother's signature
still made him feel funny, as if an uncomfortable distance—a strange
remoteness—had slowly occurred between the two brothers. After so
many years away, the family was accustomed to not seeing Kristofer
grow to the ripe age of 17. Andreas and his family were still adjusting
to Peder's name change.

As Andreas sat on the edge of his bed and read the letter a second
time, he questioned whether he would be able to recognize his brother
the next time they met. He wondered if Kristofer's voice had changed
like his own. Andreas read the letter again, this time even slower. The
memories of their childhood play flooded his mind as a few tears gathered at the corners of his eyes. Placing the letter carefully back in the
envelope, Andreas thought about sharing it with his father when he
returned from the iron mine on Friday. It was as if a gray cloud had
made its way right into the house as Andreas felt the pain of missing
both a father and a brother. Focused on Kristofer's handwriting on the
envelope, Andreas couldn't help dreaming of the day when he would
be able to join his mother on a trip to Sunmore. With Bertha back out
in the garden, Andreas carefully placed the letter back on the bookshelf and opened his schoolbook and began his first assignment.

The next day, Andreas went about his chores of picking eggs, milking the solitary cow and checking on the sheep. When he finished,
the young scholar returned to the book Mr. Olafson had given him.
Andreas loved the feel of the paper and spent time paging through

the thick volume. The first part was filled with fictional short stories and poems, followed by stories relating to hunting, forests, history and geography. These were Andreas' favorite topics and he lingered for a long time, reading as many words as he could. The last section reminded him of the hymnals at the church. He assumed these songs would be sung during the daily devotion time. Later, he placed the text on the shelf near the books his parents had collected. Treated as sacred objects, each book was in perfect condition without a stray mark on any page. Along with texts the rest of the children had used were *Luther's Small Catechism*, Sverdrup's explanation of the Catechism, and *Volrath Vogt's Bible History* book.

Early the next day, Andreas made his way back down the path toward the schoolhouse. When he arrived, he noticed a heavy cardboard sheet that had been placed on his desk. On one side was a penmanship exercise and on the other was a listing of Biblical proverbs.

He read them as he waited for Mr. Olafson to begin the class.

"The fear of the Lord is the beginning of knowledge. Fools despise wisdom and instruction." Proverbs 1:7

"A wise man will hear and increase learning. A man of understanding shall attain unto wise counsels." Proverbs 1:5

"When wisdom entereth into thine heart, and knowledge is pleasant unto your soul. Discretion shall preserve thee, understanding shall keep thee." Proverbs 2:10-11

Along with the card was the new bottle of black ink that had awaited his arrival on his first day of school. The teacher stood behind his desk and asked the students to stand. A short, redheaded girl slowly plodded through the assigned Bible text, followed by Andreas' neighbor, Eric, who was asked to say a prayer. Once seated, Andreas' spirit brightened when Mr. Olafson handed him one of the more difficult sheets to read. At his first try, Andreas was able to read almost every word. Usually Mr. Olafson was quiet and quite stern. Andreas was relieved to see a slight smile on the teacher's face when he had finished his first try at public reading.

All of the teaching done by his mother had paid off. Not only could Andreas read quite fluently, but his printing was clear and he had committed every word of the Catechism to memory.

Chapter 4

Mama's Visit

For years now, Bertha had received letters from Peder, pleading for a visit. Early on, they were signed only by Peder. As time went on, the entire family in Sunmore were encouraging her to come. None of his family members had seen Peder since his departure five years earlier. Bertha ached to see him, and every letter that arrived brought both an air of excitement and a reminder of how much he was missed. The end of each of Peder's letters included another invitation. Although he kept busy as a student and a baker's apprentice, the pain of missing his family could always be felt. It had been Peder's choice to expand his world in Sunmore, but living with that decision was a different matter.

Education, hard work and worship every Sunday were the values Peder was raised to respect in both Fitjar and in his new home. As the months grew into the first year, and that year passed on to the next, Peder grew more confident in his schooling and baking skills.

Following a number of letters back and forth during Peder's fifth year of absence, and now with him soon to graduate, Bertha announced her plans to visit her son. From the wool she had spun, woven and knit into scarves and caps, she hoped to save enough money for the journey. Like any mother, she was anxious to see what kind of young man her son had grown into.

Upon hearing the news, Andreas immediately begged to join her.

"You have just started school, Son. We cannot take you out now," she said.

"But Mama, I miss him so much. I must go, Mama, I must go. I don't even know what he looks like anymore."

"I'm sorry, Son, but I am going alone. Hopefully after graduation he will be able to return home to visit us."

Andreas' persuasiveness extended for some days, but to no avail. All he could do was write a letter and hope his brother would soon return home, as his mother suggested. He sat down at the kitchen table and began to write.

> *Dear Kristofer,*
> *I have finally started school but, as I told Mama, I would rather be with her on her visit. I hope you are having fun along with your school and baking. I wish you were here. I miss you very much. Mama said that you might return home when you graduate. I hope so. I miss the games we played and our country walks. I hope I still know who you are when you come home. Mr. Olafson is still our teacher. Did he ever smile when you were his student? He rarely does now. I don't like going to school with the smaller children but when I catch up I will join those my age. Please come back with Mama.*
> *Your brother,*
> *Andreas*

He carefully folded the paper and placed it in his mother's bag.

Island living had never calmed Bertha's fear of the waters that surrounded her. Before a joyful encounter with her son, she would endure both the warnings of finger-wagging neighbors and the actual rough-water journey. More than once she was forced to listen to the critical words of women who could not imagine leaving a husband and son behind, even for a short time. These words escalated the terror that woke her every night, and her neighbor's troubling questions exacerbated her fears of a maiden steamer voyage.

"Are you sure you will know which steamer to board? You know how difficult directions are for you. What if you fail to disembark and end up instead in Hamburg?" one of her neighbors pestered.

Bertha forged ahead making preparations, not only for her trip but for the care of her son left behind. What frightened her more was the possibility that Anders would have to be working in the mine, leaving Andreas alone. The day arrived when, like their farewell to Kristofer Peder five years earlier, Anders and his son led Bertha down the hill. At the dock they met Oscar, their neighbor with sun-darkened skin, and his muscular 20-year-old son. On their way to the market with a load of potatoes, they had offered to take Bertha on the sometimes-treacherous 40-mile voyage to Bergen and the mainland.

Before she boarded, Bertha gave her husband a peck on the cheek and then wrapped her arms around her son.

"Now Andreas, when Papa leaves tomorrow for the mine, Borghild will look in on you, but you will need to do the milking, pick the eggs, check on the sheep and keep the fire burning," she said.

"I know, Mama, I know," the 12-year-old politely answered.

Bertha continued her instructions. "Now Papa, be sure to get back as soon as you can on Friday. I am so relieved you have only five more days away."

"Yes, Mama, between Borghild and I, we will all do fine. Now get along in the boat."

Balancing on one foot and then the other, Bertha made her way down the ladder to the only vacant seat. With a cloth shoulder bag on each side of her, she snuggled amongst bags of potatoes.

Since their marriage some 30 years earlier, she had had to say farewell only when Anders left for the mine. As the two men began to row, she looked back, waved and began to wonder if she was making a mistake.

It wasn't long before the large swells of waves confirmed her fear of becoming sick. As they finally neared Bergen and the produce dock, Bertha saw in the distance the steamer she was hoping to board. Its size brought comfort to someone who had only ever endured the sea in a small dinghy. Once docked, thanking her neighbor, she picked up both bags and made her way between the piles of potatoes. She was given a hand as she climbed out of the boat, politely repeating, "Takk, Takk." Taking only a few steps, she turned back again, nodding with a smile on her face, and repeating her appreciation. With her typical rapid, short steps, and a carpetbag draped from each hand, she strode down the wooden walk toward the sign that read *Wilson Lines*. As she approached the dock, Bertha encountered the hoards of people who were suffering from a relatively new disease known as America Fever. Although this steamer was going north to Trondheim, people were in line purchasing tickets for the next Wilson Line steamer heading southeast toward Hull, England, and on to fulfilling their dreams in America. Neighbors had told her of the crowded docks of Bergen. On this day she found them suffocating. Her arms began to swing like pendulums as the passengers pushed past her, bumping her bags. Joining the ticket line, she awaited her turn.

Finally, facing a white-bearded, bald ticket agent, she had to scream over the noise of the crowd, "Return ticket for Alesund for tonight's sailing, please, returning four weeks from today."

"What class ticket?" he asked with a gruff growl.

"Steerage, please," Bertha responded.

The man passed the ticket through the window and impatiently waited as she counted out her kroner. Frightened by the crowds and the hurried pace, she hoped it wouldn't be long before she could board. Bertha slowly walked back to the peace of a nearly empty bench. A tired-looking mother of two children patted her hand on the bench, inviting Bertha to sit. The 40-mile boat journey and the crowded dock made her eyes heavy with sleep. Nodding off, she would awaken every time one of the children dropped a toy or jumped from the bench. As she thought of her neighbor's warnings, she was also reminded of Anders' comment, "The voyage home will be much more crowded with the steamer picking up the passengers along the coast on their way to America."

No matter how many exciting stories she had heard, even about her fellow island neighbors who had made the journey to America, she certainly had no desire to leave her homeland. Her thoughts quickly turned to the joy of seeing her beloved son again. He had not shared with her his immediate plans for the future, but she certainly dreamed of him returning home before attending university in Oslo.

As she waited for the steamer to arrive, her gentle smile and positive disposition was erased as she endured an aching back and joints that seemed to freeze in place. Her sitting was interrupted by slowly pacing back and forth between the bench and the end of the dock. Finally, along with the welcome sound of the ship's whistle, her mood changed to a sense of relief and excitement. The steamer arrived in port, bumping the dock as it slowed to a stop. Looking up at the side of the ship, Bertha saw the welcome letters *SS Argo*. She remembered her neighbor's warning not to get to her feet too early since she had to await the leisurely boarding of the first- and second-class passengers prior to the steerage class. Thankfully, the lines had shortened and the earlier crowds had dispersed by the time she reached the narrow gangplank.

Once she had given up her ticket, Bertha was directed to what was commonly known as "the area between the decks." When not needed for passengers, this area was used to carry cargo of all kinds. Unlike the other classes, there was no one to help with the luggage and so she dragged her two carpetbags down the narrow staircase to a dark hallway lit only by a few kerosene lamps. Finding a crudely built cabin for four with only wooden bunks, and no mattresses, Bertha placed her bags on the first vacant space. In all of their warnings, her neighbors had failed to tell her of the need to provide her own mattress. Exhausted from the day, she placed one bag at the end of the bed to use as a pillow. Lying down on the hard surface, she kept warm by wrapping her coat around herself. Once the ship had backed out, its motion lulled the tired traveler to sleep. Hours later she awoke startled, fearing she had missed the Port of Alesund. Without even washing her face, she grabbed her belongings and climbed the stairs where she found a sailor to ask about their location. She sighed when he informed her that they were within an hour of her destination. Reminded again of her neighbor's warnings, Bertha sat on the deck bench feeling quite proud of herself. Shivering from the cool spring wind, she nestled herself into her coat and took in the towering mountains and narrow waterway. Bertha walked into the lounge where she treated herself to a cup of coffee. Holding the large ceramic cup, she began to warm from both the inside and outside. With the blast of the steam horn came the captain's announcement.

"Prepare to disembark if your ticket reads Alesund."

Bertha went to the deck where she strained her neck to see a small town in the distance. Growing closer to shore, she could make out waving arms on the land below. When the steamer finally docked, Bertha struggled to keep her balance as she climbed the stairway. Once her feet landed on the dock she heard a familiar voice calling, "Mother, Mother, Mother!"

For the first time in five years she witnessed a boy grown into a young man towering over her.

"Oh Kristofer, Kristofer, Kristofer!" she yelled as she put her short, fleshy hands on his cheeks. A look of surprise came across her son's face as he realized that for the past five years he had only been called *Peder*.

"They call me Peder here, Mother," he responded.

"Oh," she said, "I forgot." She thought to herself, "What I call my son we can deal with later." Standing behind Peder were his surrogate parents and mentors, Uncle Kristen and Aunt Borghild. Following warm greetings, they climbed into a carriage and began their journey to a part of Alesund that lay inland a few miles.

When they finally arrived at the Meling home, Peder humbly served up his own rye bread, of which he was quietly proud. Even during the first day of his mother's visit, she could tell that he had not only learned the art of baking but had also claimed an interest in the current political scene in his homeland. It was a time of political strife with the conservative Rightist Party being led by a Fredrick Stang and the leftist Liberals led by Johan Sverdrup. His mother was surprised not only at his interest in local politics, but also at his talk of the very recent events in France, where the Royalists had lost to those supporting a more powerful parliament. Bertha politely listened to her son's concern about the events in the United States just a few months earlier when the Democratic Party nominee, Samuel Tilden, won the popular vote but lost the election to Rutherford Hayes in the Electoral College. On and on, Kristofer wondered about how a democratic country could allow this to happen. Not even interested in such matters on his island home, Kristofer had become quite the conversationalist when it came to the current political landscape. Along with his agreeing with Sverdrup's views, he liked the spelling change of the name of the capitol city from Christiania to Kristiania. As Bertha witnessed her son's skills as a baker, and heard of his new interests in Norway as well as the world, she realized how much he had changed from being the shy little boy she once knew.

During the next few days, while Bertha was getting reacquainted with her son and her brother's family, she tried to cover up the resentment she felt in missing so much of her son's life. She went between excitement and deep sadness. "Why couldn't they call him by his baptized name?" she thought. Carefully being polite with the other family members, when Bertha and her son were alone she peppered him with questions about the schooling, his surprising interest in foreign political views and his plans for the future. The more she learned, the more she grew to dislike some of his answers and resent her brother's influence on her son.

> *April 17, 1882*
> *Dear Anders, Andreas, Helga, Martha and Kristen,*
> *I am writing to let you know that I arrived safely and, unlike what Mildred had warned me about, was on time and did not get lost. Mildred had failed to tell me that I needed to bring my own mattress on board and so I had a very difficult sleep on a wooden bunk with only one of my bags for a pillow. Except for the hard berth, the SS Argo was a fine ship. I finished the lunch I had brought along and bought a hot cup of coffee. Brother Kristen and Kristofer, known here as Peder, were standing directly on the dock awaiting my arrival. I have tasted Kristofer's excellent baking, and have been told about his new interest in our country's politics, and am very saddened to hear he is soon leaving Uncle Kristen to begin schooling in Oslo. I am hoping and praying that he will decide to stop in Fitjar on his way to school. He has grown a good six inches and is quite a good-looking young man. I sit and am thrilled to simply look at him. From early in the morning he is so busy with his school finals and his baking. I feel sad that we have not been able to witness his growing into a man. He showed me the Bible we sent him for his confirmation, and it looks like it has been well used. I hope to write again before I begin my journey home. I pray Andreas is doing well in school and that you were able to return home from the mine on Friday.*
> *Love,*
> *Mother*

It may have been the constant warnings of the neighbor that caused Bertha to have a premonition that some accident would take place in her absence. With father tending to his chores, Andreas was left to playing on his own. Running across the rock-laden field, he forgot the open well that served as the secondary supply of water for the family. Unable to stop in time, he fell into the very cold water. Although the water and mud cushioned his fall, it was too deep a hole to find his way out by himself and so he began to scream. His cries were not only muffled by the depth of the well but also by the distance between the well and field in which his father worked. Finally, walking home from Fitjar, it was his neighbor, Rungvold, who heard his cry. Rungvold ran toward the well and found Andreas, still screaming and shaking, like a willow tree in a windstorm. His first response was to laugh and suggest that Andreas be left where he was found. But then, seeing the tears in the boy's eyes and hearing the fear in his voice, Rungvold said, "OK, OK, let me help you." Rungvold fell to his knees, reached down and pulled as Andreas tried to crawl up the cold, damp side of the well. Together, they did not have the strength to free the boy.

"Let me get your father. Don't worry, just let me get your father." Leaving Andreas in tears, Rungvold finally found Anders in his field and told him what had happened. Both men rushed back to the well and, with each taking one arm, they pulled a shivering, crying young lad to safety. It wasn't long before Andreas was sitting next to the hot stove, with his wet clothes replaced by a warm blanket. As father and son sat down for their evening meal of fish and potatoes, Andreas admitted that it was the first and last time he would ever go swimming. It was long after mother's return from her four-week journey that she heard of this mishap.

That spring and summer passed quickly and it was again time to begin the eight-week-long fall school term. Andreas was still disappointed that class was only every other day and that he was still attending with much younger children. Until he would be able to join students his age, his walk to school was a lonely one.

Mr. Olafson greeted the class with his typical Bible reading and a seemingly endless prayer. Again, when attempting to help Andreas with a reading or arithmetic problem, the teacher's bad breath was hard to stomach. Mr. Olafson, the only trained tailor in the area, would mend garments while the students studied. Although, among the parents, there was talk of his sour breath, there seemed to be no complaint about his merger of teaching and tailoring. The community was just happy to be able to employ a teacher for the low wage they offered.

Andreas' mother and father had not had many years of formal schooling but in some ways were wise beyond their limited education. As time went on, it became evident that Andreas needed to be challenged by better teaching and a more advanced curriculum. Many a night Bertha tossed and turned while realizing this dilemma. Her greatest fear was losing yet another child to the mainland. Besides the grief of missing her children, there was the practical realization that every time one left home the chores multiplied for those left behind.

As Andreas grew, his father realized his son's physical and intellectual gifts. With very little direction, Andreas possessed an innate ability to build and fix whatever was broken. At a tender age, he was able to visualize what was wrong. With little guidance from his father, he took steps to repair anything from a simple gate to the wind-up kitchen clock.

With the 1870s and a couple years of the 1880s behind them, a cloud of despair hung over the lives of many in Norway, and especially the island farmers. Mining was in less demand. The fisheries had difficulty selling their catch, and the small rocky fields failed to produce enough to even pay the rent. Every season seemed to bring more work, greater debt and fewer rewards. During these years of Andreas' middle childhood, it seemed the only words of hope came from the Sunday sermon or his mother's encouragement.

It was into these difficult times that King Carl IV and the bishop sent yet another pastor to Fitjar. Being served leftovers and has-beens in the past, the suspicion of the church members regarding the quality of the next pastor was rampant. Andreas overheard his parents discuss this topic at length. To their surprise, once Pastor Fryknell arrived, the talk in the village centered on the new pastor's excellent preaching and his ability to teach the Catechism. Yet, as time went on, it was the pastor's personal comments that served as fodder for the community's conversation. Many thought his jokes were unbecoming a to clergyman, and his everyday conversations seemed stilted or uneasy, as if he were searching for words or fearful of visiting with the commoner. Many women had taken up the full-time position of matchmaker for the middle-aged bachelor. As parishioners got to know him, the general consensus was simply that he wasn't the marrying type.

Besides preaching and teaching, a third redeeming feature was the new pastor's passion for the Biblical great commission, and the work of missions. Andreas was excited when he heard that the local mission society would hold their annual meeting in his home parish. Prayers for missions were always part of the grace prayed at mealtime in the Helland home. For months, plans were made for an influx of people the island had never before seen. Along with many others, Andreas was excited to take part in the preparations. Keen of mind, and with a natural building talent, he helped his father construct the preaching platform that would stand at the bottom of the amphitheater-like hill on which everyone would gather. To check for its correct placement and sturdiness, Andreas stood behind the lectern and began to speak as loudly as he could, while his father walked across the hillside checking for volume. With a father not known for speaking up, Andreas was amazed when Anders announced, "Son, you look good on that stand. Your voice is strong and it just might be where you belong."

Following supper that night, Andreas and his friends sat on the hillside watching one boat after another anchor in the small harbor. Except for their rare visit to Bergen, the boys had never seen so many boats in one place. Shivering from the cool spring breeze, they sat spellbound as the sun began to set and boats continued to arrive. Common rowboats with sails attached, larger sailing vessels and even steamers were making their way to the only dock. Many of the islanders had seen steamers only from a distance as they sailed between the islands in route to England. For months, the talk of the community was all about the invasion of 9,000 souls for the two-day event. Sitting on the hillside or walking into Fitjar, Andreas and his friends had never seen such a mass of humanity. Finally, left alone,

Andreas sat and stared at the boats and visitors as the sun set in the west. Looking down with pride at the platform and lectern, Andreas imagined what it would be like to speak to such a number of people. With only enough twilight to see the path, he returned home. Sleep did not come easy that night.

Early the next morning, with chores completed, the Helland's found their spot for the day on the hillside, awaiting the music and preaching. With blankets laid out on the wet grass, they sat wrapped in shawls. There were still many standing in their boats and on the harbor dock, while hundreds of others made a ribbon-like procession toward the hill. With no building large enough to hold such a crowd, everyone had been praying for the kind of sunny day that greeted them. Finally the song leader of the church in Fitjar took his place on the podium and stepped toward the lectern. He announced the name of the hymn, raised his arms and the crowd stood and broke into song, briskly singing every verse. Hearing the music, those still standing on their boats and dock joined the chorus. The service included a round of hymns, interrupted by an impassioned sermon, followed again by more singing. This went on all morning long with a break for lunch. The afternoon and evening were filled with the same joyous music and heartfelt preaching. Just prior to each sermon, a guest vocalist or instrumentalist would sing or play. Immediately following each sermon, baskets were passed to collect mission gifts. Once the first day's program was completed, people slept in the visiting boats, the island houses and barns. Some were fortunate to have a bed, while most slept on fresh straw. While brother, Peder, had to stay behind to tend the bakery, it was the Meling relatives from Alesund who filled the extra beds in the Helland's small house and barn.

The next morning was filled with sunny skies. Bread, cheese, dried fish and coffee nourished family and visitors alike prior to the closing service. By mid-morning the hillside was dotted with blankets and the chatter of voices. The music leader came to the podium and announced the first hymn. The accordion began to play and the crowd sang as they had on the previous day. Few had ever heard such music made by so many. Following the closing service, the ships began to sail mostly to the north and east. Talk of this event went on for months as members of the congregation and the community spoke of their plans to attend next year's mission society meeting in Bergen.

While family, neighbors and friends continued to reminisce, Andreas was surprised by his father's invitation to join him on a boat trip to Bergen. This was Andreas' first visit to a city of any great size. It took hours to fill the boat with their potato crop. Early the next morning they were on their way. His excitement turned to disappointment when Andreas was asked to use only one oar to assist with the rowing. Friends his own age were not only allowed but expected to use both oars while crossing the waters. With every stroke, Andreas' resentment grew. As they neared the end of the 40-mile trip, Andreas was embarrassed every time he noticed a father entrusting a son with two oars. Closing in on the end of their voyage, Anders pointed toward the Bergen harbor and the dock at which they would disembark. Men and boys looked down at the two of them and offered a hand with the line to secure the boat. More embarrassed than ever, Andreas quickly took charge of the ropes as if he was the most experienced sailor and tied them to the bow. Both Anders and Andreas were tired from the trip, ending the day with a supper of cheese and bread. They sat on their small deck and watched the flickering lights shine on the gentle waves of the harbor. As darkness came, they laid out their blankets to get some rest. Between father and son there was nothing but silence. It was only once they were settled for the night that his father surprised Andreas by complimenting him on his rowing.

"Son, I especially appreciate your hard work with only one oar and let me tell you why. I don't think you knew that a few years ago, while working in the mine, I suffered an accident with my left hand. Look here," Anders said, as he showed his crooked and stiff middle finger. "I'm afraid it has caused my entire left arm to be less useful than my right. That is why I needed extra help and someone strong to row on the left side of the boat. I know it is more difficult to row with only one oar but I knew that with your help we would be able to stay in a straight line." As the sun fell into the sea, Andreas' anger evaporated with a smile of accomplishment taking its place.

The early morning sun and the constant traffic of fishing boats awoke them both. Once the boat was untied, the two of them made their way to the market where Anders' merchant did business. Anders would sell some of his potatoes to the man from whom he would buy rye, barley and other winter necessities. Andreas was assigned to go door-to-door among the houses near the sea to sell the rest of the load. With a lighter boat, they rowed back to the original dock to spend one more night in Bergen before returning to Fitjar. Again they faced the setting sun and were about to lie down when, to their surprise, they heard a familiar voice from behind.

"Father, Andreas, Father, Andreas!" Quickly, turning toward the lights of the city, they saw Peder running toward them.

He simply said, "Come along, as I run to catch my steamer." The three ran to the steamer dock where Peder's ship to Oslo was boarding. As they grew closer to the depot where Peder was to buy his ticket, he explained that a neighbor from Fitjar had told him that Anders and Andreas were in town. Not knowing exactly where they might be, Peder had spent the day searching the harbor docks and asking merchants along the way. He told them of the letter he had sent home explaining his reason for not visiting family on his way to his future schooling. By the time they arrived at the pier, the steamer was boarding and Peder had to wish them farewell. They stood at the end of the dock waiting for the steamer's departure as Peder looked over the railing and Andreas and his father yelled their goodbyes.

After returning to their boat just as the seemingly endless summer sun was setting, they ate some of the leftover cheese, a piece of dried cod Anders had purchased at the entrance to their dock and bread Bertha had sent with them. Although room on the boat was still scarce, trading a load of potatoes for bags of grain made a more comfortable bed and quickly the two of them fell asleep. They awoke early the next morning to the relentless summer sun and a brigade of fishing boats going out for a long day of work. Anders woke his son and they prepared to cast off for their lengthy trip home. Once out of port, Anders was able to raise the sail and give them both some rest from constant rowing. Later in the morning the wind suddenly died down and again they took their places to row. This time Andreas was happy to be left with only one oar.

As they rowed through the channel, it was not the sore muscles that caused concern but Andreas' relentless coughing. His father grew very concerned and insisted on turning east toward the shore. The doctor assigned to their island of Stord had moved and a replacement had not yet arrived. Thankfully, Anders knew of the small community to which their doctor had been reassigned. While Andreas rested, his father rowed as fast as possible and raised the sail when it seemed advantageous. The further they went, the worse Andreas' cough became and his father began to question if they could get to the shore in time. With the increased wind came waves that became more and more difficult. Water splashed against the gunnels and Andreas' coughing was replaced by moaning and frequent screams. Again, the fear his father had felt a few years earlier invaded like a painful enemy. For what seemed like hours Anders fought waves while trying to keep up a steady speed. Looking out into the late afternoon sun, they noticed another boat coming their way and as it approached, both father and son were relieved. It wasn't long before they noticed that the other boat contained their very own doctor who had been making an emergency call. Anders explained the situation and the doctor carefully climbed aboard to check his next patient. The doctor advised Anders to head straight for the shore. Knowing the doctor and his sailor friend were following right behind felt like a miracle had visited father and son.

Arriving safely, they made their way to the small home in which the doctor had his office. There he asked Andreas to place his finger on the source of his pain. Not able to do so, the doctor gently put his finger on Andreas' back just below the right shoulder and everyone heard Andreas' curdling scream.

"I thought it might be there," the doctor announced with a confident smile on his face. Doctor Olson was familiar with all of the health challenges the boy had faced throughout his yet short life, the most painful being Andreas' chronic earache and its constant drainage. Checking that his hearing now seemed normal, and that the drainage from the ear had stopped, the doctor wrote a prescription for this latest crisis. He confided to Anders, "You were wise to bring him now. If you would have waited much longer, I do not think he would have lived."

The doctor's ominous words caused both Andreas and Anders to fall silent, holding their heads down and saying a silent prayer of thanks.

"Each evening," said the doctor, "you are to put a Spanish fly plaster over his right lung and keep it there for 12 hours, no matter how painful it might become. When you remove it you will find a sack filled with a yellowish liquid. Cut a hole in the sack and allow the liquid to run out. Soak a rag in melted tallow and again place it on the sore. That will help relieve the pain."

Taking a bottle of medicine in his hand, he instructed Anders to mix two drops with a tablespoon of water. "Repeat this three times a day," he insisted.

Dr. Olson then picked up a bottle of cod liver oil and instructed Anders to give his son one tablespoon daily. "Also have him drink a glass of sweet milk each day." Anders wondered how he was going to carry out the last instruction since the aging family cow was drying up.

Known on the island of Stord for his sympathy toward struggling families, Doctor Olson made arrangements for Anders to receive the next prescription at a reduced price.

It was still daylight and Anders and Andreas were anxious to get home. At the boat, Andreas lay down on the pile of grain sacks as his father took both oars. The doctor pushed them off the rocky shore and waved farewell. Daylight was fading once they arrived at the dock in Fitjar. Just finishing the nightly chores, Bertha saw them in the distance and ran to greet them both. Anders explained to his wife the necessary extra stop they had to make and told of how fortunate they were to literally run into the doctor while on the water. Late into the night, husband and wife sat at the table sharing recent news. As Andreas fell asleep, he overheard his mother and father whispering a prayer of thanksgiving.

The next morning, before the boy awoke, his mother was busy making arrangements with a neighbor to provide the daily glass of sweet milk the doctor had prescribed. Andreas' health slowly improved as the summer light dimmed and early fall arrived. The breezes grew colder and Andreas' coughing lessened as his strength returned. Carefully, not mentioned in the presence of any of the Hellands, the local wisdom wagered that young Andreas would never live long enough to become a grown adult.

Chapter 5

Farewell to Fitjar

Among other qualities of the Norwegian people, philanthropy was exhibited by many. An example was Lars Oftedal, a noted politician and pastor. Born to a teacher and his wife, Lars was ordained a pastor and served as the "Seaman's Priest" in Wales, when the Cardiff Port was one of the busiest in the world. A man of many talents, he served in the parliament for the Liberal Party. As an author, his book on the Psalms proved to be wildly popular, selling more than 200,000 copies. Besides his theological and political interests, Pastor Oftedal founded a number of social welfare agencies such as homes for orphans, a hostel for sons of professional men and another hostel for boys from the rural areas of Norway. The hostel provided a Christian setting while the boys attended school away from home. It was in the spring of 1884 that a letter arrived, addressed to the parents of Kristen Helland.

March 6, 1884
Dear Mr. & Mrs. Helland:
Through your son, Peder, it has come to my attention that your son, Kristen, might do well in a school with more students and an enriched curriculum. As the owner of a residence for country boys and a member of the board of the Stavanger Cathedral School, I am offering Kristen a full scholarship to the school as well as room and board at the Country Boy's Home. Your son Peder's strong recommendation has aided me in my decision.
If you choose to accept this offer, I will need to know in a very short time since these positions are not often available.
Yours sincerely,
Pastor Lars Oftedal

Home from his job as a farm hand, his parents sat Kristen down at the kitchen table and showed him the letter.

Kristen read it carefully between sips of his mother's coffee. Anders and Bertha sat quietly and waited. Kristen looked up at them, smiled and looked down to read the letter a second time. Folding it up, he said, "I know this is a wonderful offer, Mother, Father, but I am happy at the farm and I wish to stay here for now."

Overhearing them talk, Andreas realized he would love to take advantage of the opportunity. Once Kristen started back toward his employer's farm and Anders and Bertha returned to their chores, Andreas found a piece of stationery in his mother's writing box and wrote a quick note to his brother Peder.

> *April 1, 1884*
> *Dear Peder,*
> *I know that Kristen has refused the offer for school and housing from Pastor Oftedal. Would you please write again and ask our parents if I could be given the same offer? I have been doing very well in class and am feeling quite fine. I know I would have to catch up on some subjects but I can do that. Please write soon.*
> *Your brother,*
> *Andreas*

He placed the letter in an envelope from his mother's writing box, carefully addressed it, stuck it in his pocket and began his journey to the post office. If he came upon one of his parents they would ask where he was going. Guessing his father was working in the field, and his mother was in the chicken coop, he quietly set out. Once past the farm place, Andreas began to run toward the post office to get there before the closing hour. Panting like a sheep dog, he opened the post office door just as the postmaster was to lock it.

"Mr. Jensen, could I please buy a stamp for this letter to my brother?" He pulled out an old coin he had saved from his short stint as a shepherd.

The postmaster, with disgust in his voice, answered, "I am ready to be closed, you know."

"Oh," Andreas said, bowing his head. Almost in a whisper he added, "I want to get this letter to my brother."

The postmaster let out a deep sigh, took a stamp from his tray behind the counter and handed it to Andreas with his palm held out waiting for payment, "Well?" he said.

"Thank you," Andreas answered as he handed him the coin. He grabbed the stamp, licked it and gave the letter back to Mr. Jensen. With a scowl on his face, the postmaster announced, "I am closed now, so on your way."

Andreas breathed deeply, walked out of the small building and walked on to the schoolhouse. Needing a reason to be gone so long, he was fortunate to find his teacher, Mr. Olafson, still in the building mending clothes.

"Well, Andreas, aren't you a bit late for school?" the teacher joked.

"Mr. Olafson, I am wondering if I could borrow the history book you showed me yesterday?"

"Of course, son, of course. Look for it on the bookshelf under the window."

Andreas took it from the shelf and walked back out the door with both a book and an alibi in hand. Returning home, he found his parents so busy they had not noticed his absence. He turned up the wick of the kerosene lamp and began to read.

Two weeks later, Andreas anxiously checked to see if there were any letters in the Helland box at the post office. Every day it was empty. Andreas spent one sleepless night after another hoping and praying Peder would write and plead on his behalf. At last, one day, an envelope appeared in the Helland box. Andreas saw that it was addressed to Anders and Bertha Helland, Helland Gaard, Island of Stord, Fitjar, Norway. The return address was Peder's.

Rather than the usual leisurely walk up the hill toward home, Andreas ran as fast as he could, passing all the younger children.

As he arrived, he yelled, "Mother, Mother, you have a letter!"

Bertha, weeding the carrots and potatoes, rose to her feet, wiped her hands on her apron and answered, "Let me see now, Son, let me see."

She took the letter, walked into their house, sat down at the table and carefully opened the envelope. Sitting next to her, very quietly, was her anxious son.

She read the letter as if every word was a long-lost jewel.

"What does he say, Mother, what does he say?" She raised her hand as if to say *wait*. She read the letter again.

"But, Mother, what does he say? Can I read it?"

She carefully folded the letter and placed it in the envelope.

"What does it say, Mother?" Andreas begged. "Isn't it from Peder? What does it say?"

Bertha quietly announced, "Before we talk about it, I need to talk with Father. But Peder greets you, be sure of that. He is fine and he greets you."

Newly arrived letters were often the entertainment provided at the supper table, with the letter read over and over again. But, on this evening, everyone was quieter than usual. Afraid to ask about the content of the letter, Andreas simply ate his supper and awaited his mother's devotional reading and prayer.

Worried now that its content was not what he wished for, Andreas returned to his studies and undressed for bed. Bertha took the letter from the envelope and placed it on the table before her husband. Under the light of the kerosene lamp, Anders read it and, as if sharing a family secret, the two parents whispered to each other.

Pretending to be asleep, Andreas listened carefully to his parents' conversation, but was unable to decipher much of what they were saying.

The next morning, as the three of them sat with their oatmeal, Bertha took the mysterious epistle out of its envelope and passed it to Andreas to read.

> *April 13, 1884*
> *Dear Mama and Papa,*
> *I understand that Kristen has chosen not to accept the kind offer from the school in Stavanger. May I be bold enough to suggest that this gracious offer not be left to a less deserving student? If I have done something that is out of line, I am truly sorry, but I have taken it upon myself to ask Pastor Oftedal if this same offer*

could be extended to Andreas. The pastor has prayerfully considered this request and I have been asked to write and offer you the same opportunity given Kristen for Andreas. If you could spare his hands at chores, and were willing to see him off to what I humbly consider a better education, there is but one condition. Due to Andreas' late start in school, he would first need some tutoring by someone enrolled in the gymnasium prior to starting school with his class-mates. I believe this would be a wonderful opportunity for Andreas since even with his limited schooling he has proven to be an excellent student.

All is well here and I hope and pray for a positive answer from all of you.

Your son,
Peder

As Andreas carefully placed the letter back in the envelope, a quietness fell over the three of them.

His mother looked up and asked, "How did Peder know you might be interested in such an offer?"

With a sheepish grin on his face, he confessed that he had written to his brother.

His mother, the more talkative and decisive member of the family, said that she and his father would prayerfully consider the offer as they had for Kristen but confessed that she thought he was too young for such an adventure.

"Are you sure this is what you would like?" she asked.

With school to begin in the early fall, they knew they would have to make a quick decision on this most important opportunity for their youngest son.

A week later, following church services, chores and a dinner of chicken from the oldest hen in the flock, Anders announced a family meeting. Everyone, except for Peder, returned to the Helland farm. Brother Kristen and his two sisters were able to stay for two full days. It was the first time they had been able to gather like this since last Christmas. As they sat closely around the table, Bertha, who sat at the end of the table nearest the wood stove, spoke up, "It is so good to have all of you around the table today. It feels like Christmas."

"Yes," said Anders in his usual quiet manner. The father of the house continued, "We are gathered to talk about this special offer given to Andreas. It is a good opportunity, but..."

Bertha chimed in, speaking with her usual confident spirit. "What father is trying to say is this generous offer can be accepted, but only on two conditions."

Andreas' face quickly changed from a smile to a look of concern.

"I know you have been feeling better lately, but that must continue," his mother said. "And then, we must talk with the pastor to see when you might be able to be confirmed. If all of that works out, Father and I have agreed to let you go to Stavanger." There was silence, as everyone looked down at their plates, "Even so, we will miss you very much."

Andreas looked first at his father, then his mother. In a quiet, humble voice he said, "Thank you, Mother, thank you, Father. I will return home; do not worry, I will come home."

"Tomorrow I will see the pastor and ask for a meeting," Bertha said.

For the rest of the meal and into the afternoon, the family sat on their hillside, enjoying the sun and each other.

It was on the following Friday, a cool and rainy April day, that Andreas and his parents waited outside of Pastor Fryknell's study. Once the pastor arrived, the three stood. Anders tipped his hat and they followed him into his office. Inside there was a bookshelf, a few books, a dirty window and three wooden chairs across from the pastor's desk. "Have a seat, Helland," he said, failing to address them by their first names.

With a stern expression, the clergyman looked at Anders and said, "Now, what have you come for?"

"As you know, Andreas has been a sickly child and has missed a great deal of school. We have received an offer to help him with his future education. His older brother, Kristen, has been offered a scholarship to the Cathedral School in Stavanger but he has chosen to remain on the farm, in his current job. Last week we received another letter offering the same position to Andreas. We would miss him very much but think the schooling would be good for him provided he remains healthy and is able to be confirmed. He would be leaving us in August and so we are wondering if, well, if…"

Bertha chimed in, "We would like Andreas to be confirmed before next fall."

Pastor Fryknell stared at their son, looked over at Anders, and seeming to ignore Bertha, cleared his throat. With a stiff smile he said, "Well, I am sure that is a wonderful opportunity, Andreas. How old are you now, son?"

"I am 13 but will be 14 on July 10th."

"I see," the pastor replied.

The mood was heavy in the air and the silence was deafening.

The pastor wiped his hands together as if he were washing them. "You see, well, the problem is that registration for confirmation comes up next month, in May. I'm sure you understand that I have to go by the rules. My confirmation students must have reached the age of 14 by the time they register. This is a very important and sacred time of education for young people."

Bertha was about to speak.

The pastor put his hand up to stop her.

"You see," Pastor Fryknell continued, "we must be consistent with how we approach this."

Andreas hung his head and his mother countered with "But…"

Raising his hand once again, Pastor Fryknell promised, "I will pray about this and you can come to the registration on May 10th and I will give you my decision at that time."

The parents showed an expression of hope while Andreas could only look down at the floor, as if the world had fallen in on him. They thanked the pastor for his time, shook his hand and tipped their heads in respect as they walked slowly from his office back up the long and winding path to home.

A week later Andreas and his parents took the same path back down toward the church for the registration. There were two families ahead of them. The pastor seemed in a jovial mood as he visited in a friendly tone with the other two families. When Andreas, Anders and Bertha approached the pastor, his smile quickly faded and he looked down at the floor.

"Now, Anders, I have considered the situation you and your son have found yourself in but, as you know, like our Lord's Ten Commandments, a rule is a rule and must be treated as such. And, so, I think it best that Andreas wait until his appropriate age to complete his confirmation instruction."

"But," Andreas protested as he looked up at his father and then turned to hide his tears.

There was a lingering silence until Bertha piped up, "Well, but..."

Anders interrupted his wife, as he rarely did, with a stern look, and said, "Well, Pastor, a rule is a rule is a rule, but I certainly hope I do not find that you have failed to follow this rule with anyone else or, for that matter, any other rule you have made for this parish. I certainly hope not."

"Good day, Pastor," Anders said crisply as he tipped his hat. Andreas had already turned around, hiding his tears, with his mother following behind him.

On the way home, the silence was interrupted only with Andreas' lament, "It is not fair. It just is not fair."

At home, with the chores completed, supper eaten and a settled quiet permeating the living room, Andreas collected enough courage to begin his assault.

"Mother, Father, what if, instead of losing an entire year of schooling, what if, if I were in good health that is, what if, instead of putting my confirmation off, I get instruction in Stavanger and was confirmed there?"

"Think of your family, Andreas, your family! We could not be there. It is such a distance, we would miss this important day in your life. And this is the church in which you have been baptized and raised."

"I know, Mother, I know, but I do not want to miss school," he said.

There was a long silence at the table, as if the three were weighing the possibilities.

His father spoke up, "A rule is a rule. That is true."

Lingering silence followed Anders' words.

"But," his father continued, "but a rule is nothing so sacred that it cannot be bent when needed."

Andreas smiled and his mother shed tears of relief.

In comparison to past decisions, this one came as quickly as a lightning strike. Even so, it was not completely settled. Andreas had to continue to become stronger and healthier during the coming summer. While a compromise had been struck, Bertha watched carefully as her son approached the August departure date.

In preparation for his journey, Bertha had carefully packed the wooden chest that had been painted with the traditional red and blue rosemaling. As she carefully folded and packed each piece of clothing, she would stop and offer another prayer petition, most often begging that her son remain faithful to God and morally pure. Watching her pack, Andreas began to question what he had asked for in leaving his family.

Raised in a home as close knit as the woolen clothing his mother had provided for all of them, the children's socialization had come through school, church functions and the few cousins and friends who lived in the Helland Gaard.

Lucky enough to be in the best health he had ever experienced, on August 5th, 1884, Andreas and his father began their journey. With tears running down her face, his mother hugged him close, his cheek rubbing against her woolen sweater. She kept holding him until he finally pried her hands away, smiled and promised, "I will see you soon, Mother, I will see you soon."

His anxious father insisted they climb aboard their seaworthy rowboat to begin their trip to catch the steamer. It was 11 o'clock in the evening when his father, Andreas, and his belongings began the ten-mile journey toward Brandasund, the port where they would catch the steamer, *Karmsund*, on its way from Bergen to Stavanger. Anders pushed them from the dock and both began to row, Andreas with one oar on the left, making up for his father's weakened side. Looking back, they saw only a dark hill and a few lantern-lit homes. Mother slowly made her journey up the hill from the dock, praying a petition for safety with every step she took. As she sat at the only table the family had ever used, Bertha recounted the struggles Andreas had suffered during the first 14 years of his young life. She recalled her difficult pregnancy, his constant chest infections and all the long nights of coughing. She thought of the countless nights of worry, wondering if Andreas would go deaf and remembering the ugly puss seeping from his ear. As the night wore on, between her tears, she uttered a prayer of thanksgiving for his current good health. She begged for wisdom as her son began his life as a young man, not yet confirmed, but already away from home.

Chapter 6

Away at School

Anders, a man with a quiet spirit, was surprisingly talkative with his son about the future as they rowed the boat. He feared this would be one of the few times the two would be alone. Warning his son of the city temptations that might come his way, yet not listing what those might be, Andreas began to grow fearful of the unknown. He imagined that these must be events so terrible his father couldn't even speak of them. The warnings were punctuated by the splashing of the oars and the call of the gulls flying above them in the night air. By one o'clock the next morning, they drew closer to the shoreline. The moon-filled night illuminated the large fish storehouses and the accompanying nets that hung to dry. Steep fjord walls on both sides of the boat made the waterway look like nature had cut a slice into the mountain. As they neared the wharf, they were surprised by a shriek that sounded like a child's cry.

"It must be a group of gypsies fighting," Anders quickly concluded.

The shrill sound grew louder the closer they came to the shore. The boat bobbed on the waves like a bottle with a message in it. With the dim light from the summer sun, they could see the outlines of rocks, bushes and small trees. Slowly, as they rowed, they realized the screaming was coming from nothing more than two stray cats mating. The echo caused by the mountain walls made the affair sound more like a murder in progress. Laughter lightened the mood of the heavy hearts of a father and son and their pending separation. With the right oar, Anders slowly turned the boat toward their destination, now just a hundred meters from the commercial dock to which the boat would be tied. Looking up, they saw the weathered sign for the port town of Brandasund and the steamship dock. As the boat edged its way to the side of the pier, Andreas tossed a rope to the night dock man. Father and son unloaded the lovingly painted wooden chest that contained all of Andreas' worldly possessions. The weary travelers found a bench—a place to rest—and awaited the arrival of the steamer, which would carry Andreas to Stavanger. Finally the foghorn of the *Karmsund* jolted them both awake. They quickly checked to see that the trunk was still next to them. As the steamer docked, Anders' calm spirit failed to comfort his son's anxiety. He helped his son carry the trunk aboard. Anders looked him straight in the eyes, now that both were almost the same height, and wished his youngest son God's speed. Andreas' face was streaked with tears as his father gave him a bold hug. Anders tearfully said farewell and walked back down the boarding plank.

The rusted bow of the ship loomed ahead as Andreas slowly made his way into the large passenger cabin where he took a seat. Among the many passengers, some were lying on benches while others spoke quietly about what life might be like in America.

The ship slowly backed away from the dock and turned toward the south, continuing its journey in the early-morning darkness.

Andreas bought a cup of hot coffee and returned to his seat, next to two young parents and their three very active children. As the young mother cried, her children stood in front of her asking over and over again, "What's the matter, Mama; do not cry, Mama; what's the matter?"

The metal coffee cup warmed Andreas' chilled hands. He sat there quietly wondering if he should move. Not seeing another vacant seat, he simply looked straight ahead, sipping his coffee. Finally he gathered enough courage to turn and ask about the family's destination. Her tears wiped away, and with a surprisingly strong voice, the mother announced they were bound for America. It was a place they had only read about in their relatives' letters. It was called Wisconsin. Her husband was looking forward to work in the lumber mills. By this time her three children had joined their father, who was standing at the rail gazing into the dark, choppy waters.

Later, the parents and children began to doze off and rest on each others' shoulders or lie on the deck, using their small bags as pillows. Andreas, fueled with coffee, anxious nerves and excitement, took a place at the deck rail to enjoy the moonlit sights as he awaited the morning sun and his final destination. Switching between the cool night air and the more comfortable cabin, the five hours went by and before long he was looking for his brother, Peder, who had come to Stavanger to meet him. Only seeing his brother once in five years, Andreas paced back and forth, worried he might not even recognize Peder. With most on board continuing their journey to England and on to the "Promised Land," Andreas was one of the few to disembark. Once on the dock, with his wooden chest at his side, the boy sat and awaited a familiar sight or sound. Finally Andreas spotted Peder who was walking briskly down the street and onto the dock. First there was the polite handshake, immediately followed by warm embraces. Andreas took a good, long look at his now grown-up brother. "You came all the way from Oslo to meet me. Thank you, thank you."

"Well, Brother, it has been a long time and I wanted to get you settled. I think you will like it here. I have loved living in a larger city."

Following a quick "I hope so" from Andreas, Peder arranged for a drayman to deliver the precious chest to the Country Boy's Home.

As they began their way toward a friend's home to stay that night, Andreas kept on looking at his brother as if something was not quite right. Finally, with a questioning voice, he said, "Peder, you sure are taller, but you still look the same. Even so, you do not sound like yourself. What happened? You sound so different!"

Peder raised his eyebrows. "I don't know. What do you mean?"

"Well...what do they call it? The way you talk? You sound different," Andreas said.

"I guess I have been gone five years. Is my voice different?"

"Sort of. I think it may be how you say your words."

"Oh," Peder said, "maybe I sound more like I am from Sunmore than Fitjar."

"That must be it," Andreas conceded.

His older brother had lost his Fitjar accent. It felt strange listening to a different dialect from a family member. To Andreas, Peder's sophisticated talk made it sound as though he was being disloyal to his roots.

And so off they went, slowly climbing the hill toward the home of Peder's friend, where they would spend the night.

The next morning, earlier than Peder ever liked to be out of bed, he and his younger brother were again at the dock, this time with Peder's carpetbag in hand, ready for another farewell.

"I wish I could introduce you to Pastor Oftedal, but you will meet him the first day of school," Peder said.

"I hope I can come to Oslo sometime," Andreas said.

"I hope so, too. Money is short, so we will have to see," Peder responded.

And with that, Andreas said goodbye to his older brother and closest friend.

With Peder's directions tucked away in his memory, Andreas began the journey up the hill from the dock, hoping with every step that he would remember the way to his new home. The name of the street was Oslo and the number was his year of birth, 1870. He walked and kept looking around, turning to adjust to the crowds, with their voices and busy activity. After a few wrong turns, he discovered himself at the corner of Oslo Street and 18th. He looked up the gentle slope to find a row of the largest houses he had ever seen. He spotted a large, wooden home painted white with dark-blue trim. Next to the door were the numbers 1870.

He knocked on the door and before long a stout woman greeted him, her gray hair tied in a knot at the back. As she wiped her hands on her apron she said, "You must be Andreas."

He took off his hat, nodded politely and quietly acknowledged, "Yes, I'm Andreas Helland."

"I'm Miss Thomassen, the matron. Well, come in, come in," she said in a commanding voice while waving her arms.

Stepping back to get a better look at the new arrival, she added, "My, my, a skinny one aren't you?"

Andreas stood there with a puzzled look on his face, never having heard himself described by a stranger. He was used to being reminded of how sickly he had been. He wondered if every boy got this kind of inspection.

"I will show you to your room now. I know your chest has been delivered and put in its place. You can do your unpacking. You will meet the other boys a bit later."

"Thank you," he answered.

Andreas followed the older woman as she slowly and carefully climbed up the two flights of stairs toward a hall lined with bedroom doors. At the top of the stairway, two boys chased each other, and seeing the matron, slowed their pace to a walk.

"Boys," she chastised, "come back up here and introduce yourselves to our new student, Andreas."

Looking up, the redhead dutifully responded, "I'm Gunnar" and offered a handshake. The other boy, a blond, said, "I'm Olaf." Without another word, they turned and walked down the remaining steps. Once they reached the first floor, they ran through the front door as if they were escaping prison.

Miss Thomassen shook her head and continued to lead Andreas down the dark, tomb-like hall. She stopped at the last door. "This will be your room."

She turned the black, metal doorknob and the light from the sun-brightened room flooded into the hallway. The room was furnished with metal-framed beds in each of the four corners. "There, son," pointing to the only vacant bed in the back corner, "that one will be yours. You will meet the other boys at supper. If you like, when you have unpacked, come down and have a cup of tea."

Andreas threw his cap and jacket onto the assigned bed and thanked the matron as she left the room. He shut the door and looked around. The only thing that felt like home was his painted chest. As tears filled his eyes, he quickly wiped them with his shirtsleeve and sat down on the thin mattress. On a nearby wall hung an old, framed mirror. He looked at his reflection and wondered if everyone thought of him as weak and too thin. He walked to the end of the bed and opened the chest. It had the welcoming aroma of home. He knelt and surveyed its precious contents. There, neatly packed, were two suits, an overcoat, a light jacket, cotton underwear, three cotton shirts, a hat, a blue sweater and a cloth bag that held personal items. Looking around the room, he noticed how the other boys had hung up their trousers and shirts, leaving their books on their tables. They must have left the rest of their belongings in their chests. He sat back on the floor to admire the chest with his father's craftsmanship and his mother's artistic painting. He dug back into it, still enjoying its fragrance of home, and found his two textbooks and Bible. After he placed the books on the table, he took the blanket, pillow and the quilt his mother had made and carefully laid them out on the bed. Finally, sitting back against the pillow, a deep feeling of regret filled every cell of his body.

He lamented, "I don't want to be here. I wish I were with Peder. I really do not want to be here."

After a time, Andreas forced himself out of bed, down the two flights of stairs and through the swinging door into the kitchen in the back of the house. He sat at the old pine table. The teapot on the wood-burning stove was already humming. Miss Thomassen poured the brewed tea into a blue metal cup and pushed it toward Andreas.

"I have much to do," she said briskly. "Drink up and I will see you at the evening meal."

"Yes, Ma'am," he answered in a polite, quiet voice.

"When you arrive at school tomorrow you will meet your benefactor, Pastor Oftedal. The other boys will show you to the school." As the door shut behind her, Andreas finished his tea and wondered what to do with himself. Finally he returned to his assigned room to wait for supper. He lay on his freshly made bed and studied each corner of the room, wondering about the other boys. His eyes became heavy and he quickly fell asleep. Later he awoke to the voices of two boys entering the room. He quickly sat up and, to his delight, the two introduced themselves and shook his hand.

"I'm Gunner," the shorter one reminded him. "We met in the hallway when you arrived."

"I'm Eric," replied the taller, older-looking boy. His voice had a low, husky tone.

"I'm Andreas Helland."

"Where are you from?" asked Eric.

"I am from Fitjar," Andreas proudly declared as if everyone knew of the place.

"Where is that?" Gunner asked with quizzical look on his face.

Andreas explained, "Oh, it is on the island of Stord."

With even more of a confused look on his face, Gunnar repeated,

"So where is that?"

Andreas elaborated, "It is south of Bergen by about 40 miles."

"Oh," Gunnar replied. The two boys turned and walked back out of the room, leaving Andreas alone.

Gunnar popped back through the open door. "The matron, old Miss Thomassen, told us to tell you that supper is at five o'clock. A bell will ring when it's time to come down."

"Thanks," said Andreas. They were not like his friends at home. The only advantage of this place, he thought, was the indoor facilities he had never had the privilege of enjoying at home. Having missed two nights of sleep, he laid back on the bed and his eyes quickly closed.

"Didn't you hear the bell?" a boy yelled impatiently, startling the new student.

Quickly sitting up, Andreas rubbed his eyes, "I must have fallen asleep. I will be right down."

Throwing his mother's quilt aside, he ran to the door to find the messenger already gone. Still in a fog, Andreas descended the two flights and pushed open the swinging door to the kitchen. There he was met by Miss Thomassen and ten boys, most of them older.

"Sit over there," she commanded, pointing to the last open chair.

"Gunnar, please lead us in grace." After a short prayer, the boys grabbed for the metal plates piled with boiled fish, potatoes and bread. As everyone ate, conversations seemed to exclude Andreas. At home he talked freely at the table and here he was not given the chance to speak.

When supper ended, each boy brought his dishes to a sink filled with water. Three of the boys stayed to wash and wipe. Miss Thomassen took the leftovers to the root cellar out in the back yard. Everyone else migrated to the parlor, which housed an upright piano and a cluster of wooden chairs. The pine floor was covered with an oval braided rug. Eric sat down at the piano and began to play while the others stood and talked amongst themselves. Andreas sat alone, listening to the piano and thinking of home. Freckle-faced Gunnar came into the parlor, noticed the empty chair next to Andreas and sat down. He turned to Andreas and confided, "This is the part of the day I really hate. I like my studies and living here but I don't take to this devotion time. I can't understand why we do this every night; Sunday worship should be enough." Andreas, not knowing what to say, simply nodded.

Following the Bible lesson and prayer, the boys were dismissed for an hour of reading or homework in their rooms. Miss Thomassen reminded them that she would visit each room to see that everyone was doing their work. She asked Gunnar if he would take charge of getting Andreas to school the next morning.

"Yes, Ma'am," Gunnar replied as he ran up the stairs. The matron's futile order to "walk" echoed up the stairwell. Andreas followed the boy, careful to maintain the requirement to walk. Gunnar lit the gas lamp on his desk and began to draw. Andreas idly paged through his history book, wondering what he would face the next day. The boys kept opening and closing the bedroom door, ignoring the matron's instructions to study. If she discovered them in the hallway, their standard excuse was, "I need to use the bathroom, Miss Thomassen."

The hour passed quickly. Andreas heard the bell and waited to see what was next. Sitting on his bed, he wondered where the boys undressed. He certainly hoped it would not be done in front of everyone. At bedtime Gunnar began to take off his socks and trousers. "Andreas, aren't you going to undress?" Andreas saw Eric and Olaf undressing as well, with little attention to modesty. Andreas slowly took his nightgown out of the trunk, took off his shirt and slid his nightgown over his head. He turned away from the others and quickly removed his trousers. One boy had left for the bathroom while the other two had already crawled under their blankets.

"The new boy always turns off the lamp," Gunnar declared.

Accepting that fact, Andreas tiptoed to the door where there stood a small table and the oil lamp. As he turned the metal knob, the lamp wick descended and the room went dark. Carefully tiptoeing back to bed, he slipped under the quilt that still held the fragrances of home. Silently praying the prayer he had been taught as a child, he was interrupted by Gunnar who began to tell a joke. The roommates quickly laughed at the off-colored punch line while Andreas kept silent, wondering just when he would become the brunt of

Gunnar's humor. "What's wrong, Andreas? Haven't you heard that joke before?" Gunnar asked, still laughing. "Tell us one of your favorite jokes, Andreas, one from that place you came from, wherever that is."

"I can't think of any right now," admitted Andreas. "I have been up since 11 o'clock two nights ago and I am really tired."

"Well you'd better think of one for tomorrow night. It will be your turn. Do you know what happens to those who don't take their turn?"

The tension and homesickness made for a restless night. Andreas dreaded the coming day.

Sunlight shown through the window and flickered onto the wooden floor. The now-familiar bell was ringing again. While Olaf and Gunnar rolled over to catch a little more sleep, Eric swung his tall and lanky body out of bed and dressed. Andreas quickly did the same, not knowing exactly when he was expected at the breakfast table. Dressed and ready to go before Olaf and Gunnar had stirred, Andreas and Eric strode out of the room and down the two flights of stairs toward the smell of breakfast cooking.

"Andreas, we serve ourselves from the stove and table," the matron announced. Her wrinkled dress and apron, her unkempt hair and stern look suggested to Andreas that morning was not her favorite time of day. Between clearing her throat and using a hanky to blow her nose, she added, "I have a pot of oatmeal on the stove. Take what you would like from the table."

Andreas was relieved to see the toast, preserves and cheese sitting on the table next to the crackling wood stove. Andreas picked up a plate that had been placed at the table the night before. As soon as he picked it up, Eric warned him, "Andreas, I would not do that. That is George's plate and he doesn't like for it to be moved. George is not happy in the morning."

Picking up the plate next to George's, Andreas again heard, "That plate belongs to Gunnar."

Andreas looked at the chair where he sat the night before. No warning came as he picked up that plate. He scooped out a portion of oatmeal and picked up a piece of brown goat cheese and an already cold piece of toast. The eight other residents, all students at the

Cathedral School, soon joined them. They sat in customary seats and ate in a foggy silence. Not used to the crude jokes and the language used the night before, Andreas was thankful for the quiet. Finishing first, he waited to see what came next in the morning routine.

As if she could read his thoughts, Miss Thomassen told the new boy that everyone would leave at 8:30. When they arrived at the school, Gunnar would take Andreas to the office of Pastor Oftedal.

Eric got up from the table, and washed his plate and silverware in the galvanized metal sink. He laid his dinnerware on the towel set out for the dishes. Andreas followed his example and then returned to his seat. When everyone finished, the matron, using now her familiar, serious voice, prayed a prayer of thanksgiving and dismissed the boys to prepare themselves for school. After everyone had washed their faces, brushed their teeth and used the new luxury—for Andreas—indoor toilet, the boys gathered in the large parlor.

With some boys ahead and others straggling slowly behind, Andreas and Gunnar trudged up the hill toward the 12th-century church next to the Cathedral School. The wooden building, with a stone foundation, looked new compared to the church. In the wall next to the front door was the school's 1825 cornerstone.

Gunnar and Andreas entered through the heavy wooden doors, turned down the hall and into the vestibule of Pastor Oftedal's office.

Gunnar pointed to a bench. "You sit here and he will come out when he is ready." Andreas began to question just what to do next. On the door in front of him was written in black lettering, "Reverend Oftedal." As he sat waiting, he wondered if this was the place where he belonged.

He heard the loud ticking of the nearby grandfather's clock and watched its long hand creep past the 12. Andreas gathered enough nerve to leave the bench. He knocked just twice on the carved door.

"Come in," uttered a deep base voice.

Andreas opened the door to find a very heavyset man sitting behind an equally massive desk. The man rose wearing an encouraging smile. "Now, who might you be?" he asked.

"I am Andreas Helland," the new student answered, shifting his hat from one hand to the other.

Andreas had rarely seen anyone dressed with such splendor. Pastor Oftedal wore a gray suit and a black-velvet vest buttoned close up to the throat. A heavy, gold chain swung across his broad chest. His gold-rimmed spectacles, ruddy face and jet-black hair made him look even more distinguished.

As Pastor Oftedal sat back down, his chair creaked, bearing his full weight.

"I am Andreas Helland," the boy repeated, wondering if he had been heard the first time.

"Oh, you are Peder's brother. Is that right?"

"Yes, sir," Andreas said as the man shifted in his chair, causing it to creak once more.

"How is Peder doing?" he asked.

Andreas told of his brother's move from the bakery so that he could continue his schooling in Oslo.

As the jovial man smiled, his jowls shook and he said, "That is a fine idea. He is a bright boy, you know, and he will go far."

Also knowing of Andreas' father and mother, the pastor politely asked about them. Then, as if that was enough polite conversation, the man took on a more serious tone.

"Starting school as late as you have here at the Cathedral School, you normally would begin your studies with 11-year olds."

Immediately Andreas' heart sunk to the floor.

"However," Pastor Oftedal went on, "since that won't do, I have asked Peter Hognestad to serve as your tutor. Peter is in his middle year at the Gymnasium. If you work especially hard, by next year you will be able to begin either on the fifth or sixth level."

"Yes, sir," Andreas said with relief.

"Have you found your place at the Country Boy's Home?"

"Yes, sir."

"Well, I have built that home for boys just like you and I am very glad that you joined us. Now, have a seat out on the bench while I call for Peter."

Andreas passed his hat from one hand to the other, and bowed repeatedly as he backed toward the door.

As he waited, Andreas wondered how such a great man, in such rich surroundings, could talk so simply and be so kind. The boy would always recall the splendor of the office, the large wooden desk, the brown leather chair, the bookcases from floor to ceiling and the window overlooking the city and fjord.

Andreas heard the echo of footsteps down the hall in the person of a lanky, red-haired young man. His chin was slightly shadowed with red stubble. His plain brown jacket had been carefully mended here and there.

"Andreas? I'm Peter. Come with me and I will show you some books you can begin to read until I am able to meet with you later today."

He took Andreas to a small room, furnished with a table and two chairs. This was a far cry from the kind of office Andreas had just visited. Peter assigned him a story to read and some simple math problems. He added, "I will be done with my class by mid afternoon and then we can begin."

Peter's encouraging smile made Andreas feel a bit more confident. As the tutor left, Andreas eagerly set to work on the first assignment. Time passed and finally the door opened. Eric had come to say it was break time. As they walked down the hall, the noise of boys eating and talking grew louder. Entering the break room, Andreas copied his friend as he dipped a metal cup into a pail of cool water. With only one open seat at Eric's table, Andreas found a vacant seat and began to eat the cheese sandwich that had been sent with him that morning. Andreas was surprised when suddenly all the boys got up from their tables, placed their cups on a pile of used dishes and left the room. While the others returned to their classrooms, Andreas started back down the dark hallway toward his barren study room. The hinges squeaked as he opened the door. He crossed his arms, attempting to warm himself. From the small, simple table, he picked up a book, took his seat and returned to the chapter he had left earlier. After each paragraph, he would stare at the wall, thinking of his mother's words and dreaming of his return to the only home he had ever known.

It seemed like an eternity until the door opened. As promised, Peter had returned and took a seat next to his student. "Where are you from?" the tutor asked.

"My home is in Fitjar," Andreas said.

"Where is that?" Peter asked.

"On the island of Stord," Andreas responded.

"Where?" Peter said.

"Among the islands south of Bergen."

"Oh, yes, my uncle has fished in that area of the country." Peter smiled and rested his hand on Andreas' shoulder.

"Pastor Oftedal's office is the fanciest room I have ever seen," Andreas confided with a shy smile.

"Yes, it is a grand room. You know, he not only helps with this school but he has also built the Country Boy's Home and the Women's Home. He has been on the city council and is a member of parliament. He's an author, as well."

"What did he write?" Andreas asked.

"A book about the Psalms. You can find it in every home. Your mother and father might have it," Peter offered, "but, enough of that, let's get to work."

Andreas tried to imagine his parents having enough money to purchase more than the Bible and the few books that had been given to them by the local teacher.

He then summoned enough courage to ask, "Do you know the student, Eric?"

"I have not tutored him but, yes, I know of him," answered Peter.

"Do you know why his voice sounds different?"

"I have heard boys tease him. He had diphtheria as a child and it caused him to lose his voice."

"Oh," Andreas answered. "He seems to be very nice."

"That he is," Peter assured him. "And he would make a good friend."

With the school day coming to an end, Andreas followed his tutor down the hallway, past the other classrooms and out the front door where they separated. Andreas headed down the hill toward the Country Boy's Home. Seeing Gunnar ahead of him, he slowed his pace so that they would not meet before they arrived back home. As he climbed the white wooden stairway, he thought the place would never feel like home, never.

The welcoming smell of freshly baked cookies drifted out of the kitchen. Miss Thomassen wiped her hands on her apron. With a stern face and serious voice she admonished, "You know the rules— two cookies each. That's it until supper; two cookies."

Andreas was sorry to hear of the limit. At home there was always a larger meal at noon. Today's lunch was just the one cheese sandwich.

Quickly the boys grabbed the hot cookies and ran off. Andreas passed through the swinging door, and up the stairs, retreating finally into his room. There he found Gunnar snapping a towel at Eric. Not wanting to get into the middle of the towel fight, Andreas sat down, started his second cookie and tried to begin his homework. The other two boys had discarded the towels in favor of a spirited wrestling match. Andreas felt even more like a stranger. He turned back toward the window and watched a group of boys play hide and seek in the backyard.

"Too much study makes a boy boring!" Gunnar called out as he snapped a towel at Andreas' chair.

Surprised, Andreas turned away protecting his face with his folded arms.

"Yes, I suppose so, but I have a lot of catching up to do," he said, with a slight impatience.

Surprised at the tone of Andreas' voice, Gunnar was about to escalate the teasing when Eric countered, "Gunnar, let's go to the backyard to see if any of the pears or apples are ripe. I'm still hungry."

A few minutes later, Andreas looked up from his book and, through the window, saw them trying to grab an apple off one of the many fruit trees. Still hungry himself, he quickly got up from his table, ran down the stairs and out to join his two roommates.

Before the supper bell there was still time to write home.

September 12, 1884
Dear Mother and Father,
I have arrived in Stavanger and am well. I miss you very much. The steamship was fine, with a lot of people going all the way to

America. I was almost the only one who got off in Stavanger. Guess who was on the dock to meet me? Peder. He came from Oslo just to see me. We had fun for one day before he had to leave.

The boys here are nice. I have three roommates. Miss Thomassen, the matron, made us fresh cookies today. My tutor is Peter Hognestad.

My first day of school was today. I met Pastor Oftedal. He is a very big man. He is very important. His office has a big desk, a leather chair and more bookshelves than I have ever seen. They are filled with many books.

I hope everyone is well. Please greet Kristen, Helga and Martha for me. I hope to visit Peder sometime. I miss you.

Love from your son,
Andreas

He finished the letter, carefully excluding his roommate's jokes. He went to the kitchen where Miss Thomassen was scurrying around, preparing the supper.

"Do you have a stamp I could buy to send my letter home?" he asked.

"Yes, Andreas, but I don't have time now. Just leave the letter on the table and I will take care of it later." He felt a sudden urge not to let go of it, then placed it near his plate.

"Thank you," he said.

"Run and play now," she ordered in a scolding voice. "Get some fresh air. Supper will be coming soon." Waving a long wooden spoon, she repeated, "Run and play now; go, go!"

Andreas sped through the swinging door, wishing he had a friend in Stavanger.

Despite the questionable jokes and the words his father referred to as swearing, Andreas did his best to adapt to his new home. After a few nights of having to hide salty tears, he slowly settled into life away from Fitjar. As the nights passed, he was relieved that Gunnar had not renewed his demand for a joke from Andreas. He wondered if he had been raised in a humorless home.

Weeks grew into months. The only real excitement was the occasional troublemaking by one of the boys and the surprising announcement that Miss Thomassen was moving to Oslo to care for her elderly mother.

The pleasure of study seemed to replace those previous feelings of homesickness. It was on a Sunday evening that the boys were called to the parlor and warned to be on their best behavior. Andreas ran down the first flight of stairs, then quickly slowed as he saw from the landing Pastor Oftedal standing below. In the parlor, the boys took their places on the wooden chairs.

Rubbing his fleshy hands together, the pastor stood near the fireplace waiting for silence. Sitting to his right was a small, delicate woman who spread her smile around the room, eyeing each boy.

"Silence," he commanded. "I would like to introduce your new matron. This is Mrs. Fleum." While some boys politely clapped in unison, others remained silent. She placed her hat on the next chair and stood up.

"Hello, boys. I am so happy to be here with you. I know we will get along very well." Her words sounded more like a wish than a statement of certainty. She took her place next to Pastor Oftedal. He announced that Mrs. Fleum would begin her duties the very next morning.

Mrs. Fleum was a recent widow. She and her pastor husband had lived in Oslo. He had died from a stroke and she was left without a home. For the first few weeks, all of the boys tried to be quieter, but it wasn't long before their running and wrestling resumed. As with Miss Thomassen, worldly language had to be kept to quiet chatter at bedtime.

As the weeks grew into months, Mrs. Fleum's quiet nature evolved into one of confidence and joy. She seemed friendlier than the last matron, especially when someone would grab an extra cookie. Along with the ever-present cookies, she baked apple and pear pies. She filled the dining table with oatmeal, cheese and bread in the morning. The boys were also treated to fried eggs and her favorite hot cereal made of wheat, sprinkled with bits of apples or pears and a generous dose of sugar.

Never having had her own children, she lavished the boys with a motherly concern and attention. Everyone was treated the same, no matter their age. In the past the older boys had greater privileges. Now, privileges were meted out on the basis of equality and earned merit. Everyone agreed, she was a kinder person and a wonderful cook.

Mrs. Fleum would become especially helpful to Andreas and his need to be confirmed. His parents had allowed him to leave home to attend the Cathedral School provided that he would confirm his faith. Although first refusing to compromise his own set rules, Pastor Fryknell eventually sent a letter informing the Stavanger pastor of his permission for Andreas to attend confirmation outside of the home parish.

Following weeks of study, the first hurdle was the public catechism held at the church the week before confirmation Sunday. On a warm Sunday afternoon, seven boys and three girls lined up in front of the congregation, clothed in their Sunday best. The confirmands looked sheepishly down at the floor, switching their weight from one foot to the other. At the church in Fitjar, Andreas would have known everyone. Here, Andreas recognized only his housemates and Mrs. Fleum. Although nervous, he knew his *Barnelaerdom* (Catechism) from front to back and was confident he would survive this one last requirement. As he stood in line, third from the left, he listened to the first two girls flawlessly recite what was asked of them. When he was asked to recite the third commandment and its meaning, Andreas did so perfectly. The questions continued amidst sweating brows and shaking knees. Two girls perfectly recited the meanings of the petitions to the Lord's Prayer. With that completed, Andreas nervously wondered what the pastor would ask of him.

Expecting to be asked to recite the first article about God the creator, Andreas began to say it to himself. To his surprise, he heard the pastor say, "Now, Andreas, would you please recite for us the third article of the Apostles' Creed and its meaning?"

His memory flashed forward to the end of the creed, as if he were searching for help. He began to speak hesitantly.

"I believe in the Holy Ghost, the Holy Christian church...the community, no I don't mean that."

Some congregants nervously cleared their throats.

"I believe in the Holy Ghost, the Holy Christian church, uh...."

A student whispered, "You know it Andreas, you know it."

Following another lengthy silence, punctuated by the pastor's clues, Andreas confessed, "It is not coming to me, Pastor."

"You do know it though, don't you?"

"Yes, Pastor, I know it."

The pastor rescued him saying, "That will be enough," and went on to the next student.

With the ordeal of catechism finally over, Andreas worried about the following Sunday. Tradition required the boys to wear a similar black suit made of broadcloth, black stiff hat, black shoes, white shirt, white collar and a black bow tie. The girls must wear formal white dresses with matching white shoes. The clothes would be brand new. Regardless of their position in society, the students must all look alike. If Andreas had been living in Pastor Oftedal's boy's orphanage, he would have received a new suit of clothes from a local store. Andreas was caught in the middle. Although he did not suffer the disadvantages of being an orphan, his family was of very modest means.

Of course his mother had already thought of this important event in his life. Months before his farewell to Fitjar, his mother had presented him with a confirmation suit. This was his mother's hand-spun, hand-woven hand-sewn creation. Instead of stylish broadcloth, it had been lovingly made from his mother's hand-dyed, dark-blue woolen fabric. Wanting to be like the other boys, he worried about his blue suit.

And so it was that Andreas garnered enough nerve to share his predicament with Mrs. Fleum. A kindly lady, she listened carefully to his plight.

"What can I do?" Andreas pleaded. "I want to be dressed like the rest. It isn't fair; it isn't right. And my shoes, Mrs. Fleum, they are not new but have been used by my older sister, Helga."

Mrs. Fleum quietly thought for a moment and then offered her thoughts. She concluded, "Now Andreas, think for a moment about your mother and what she has done for you. She has first spun the yarn by hand. She has woven the cloth for an entire suit. She dyed it and then sewed it. She did this all for you."

This was not the solution that her young charge expected to hear. Andreas sat in silence on the kitchen chair, pondering what she had said. After a moment, he got up, excused himself and went to his room. He thought to himself, "There is no winning this argument. It still isn't fair, isn't right. How much simpler and less embarrassing it would have been if he had waited to confirm his faith in his home church where attire would have been less important." He was greatly disappointed.

The historic day finally arrived. St. Petri Church was down the hill from the Country Boy's Home, on a corner just three blocks from the harbor. It was a sunny day and a bit warm for the season. Standing in front of the congregation were six boys in matching black suits, three girls in white dresses and Andreas wearing the blue suit his mother had made for him. He kept looking at its color and comparing it with the beautiful fabric of the other suits. Following the service, which was honored by the presence of the bishop, the young people opened the gifts given by their families. To Andreas' surprise, his parents had remembered him with a hymnbook from home, a new Bible, letters and a few little tokens of remembrance. Once he had forgotten about his suit, the day of confirmation felt almost like celebrating Christmas.

As was the custom, the day after confirmation was a holiday from school. Andreas awoke feeling a great sense of relief. With breakfast out of the way, he and Eric decided to spend the day together rediscovering the places they liked to play. They climbed the hill behind the Country Boy's Home where they caught salamanders from an old pool, and went on to play in rock caves they had been warned about. Instead of returning for the noon meal, they picked ripe fruit from the parsonage apple tree. With the end of the afternoon closing in, they hiked back home, very tired, yet still smiling.

During the last months of the school term, Peter Hognestad continued to tutor Andreas in Norwegian grammar. Andreas had never studied nouns, adjectives, verbs and so on. When Andreas complained about the tedious study, Peter reminded him that all of it would be necessary in learning other languages.

As the spring term drew to a close, Andreas made an appointment with the president of the school, Rector Johannes Steen. A tall stick of a man, he proved to be very kind. After Andreas recounted his accomplishments of the past year, Rector Steen replied, "Even so, there are some large gaps in your schooling, son. You will need to work especially hard at history and geography."

Immediately, Andreas promised to study those subjects while at home during the summer break.

Looking again at the report Andreas' tutor had written, the rector said, "Well, we will have to try the sixth middle-school class in the fall."

Andreas was thrilled to hear that news. Not having seen his family since Christmas, he was also excited to make the trip home for the summer holiday.

Andreas bought his ticket for Brandasund where he would meet his father. He boarded the same steamer on which he had come to Stavanger many months before. From Brandasund, Andreas and his father would row the ten miles to their island home.

Leaving most of his possessions at school was a certain sign that Andreas had decided to continue his studies in Stavanger. The glad reunion of father and son happened at the Brandasund dock. The trip from there to Fitjar was filled with animated conversation. They finally docked at Fitjar and headed up the hill. As he walked over the threshold of the little house, his mother smiled, gave him a hug and welcomed him with a sort of measured restraint. Every Sunday during his six-week holiday, the whole family gathered together. Sunday meals were spent around the family table with stories being told and laughter drifting through the open front door. When bedtime arrived, Andreas was reminded of how awkward it was for parents and children to undress for bed. At night he would lie in bed, wondering just what had changed since he had been home for Christmas. Although his father had always been very quiet, he and his other children seemed overjoyed to see their youngest family member again. Adjusting his head on the fresh straw pillow, Andreas wondered about his mother. As he had told the story of his confirmation, the family listened to every word while his mother quietly busied herself preparing a meal.

As the summer sped by, Andreas spent much of his time in the fields working alongside his father. Outside, they repaired fences and gates. When the rain forced them inside, the young scholar read his assigned history and geography texts. On an especially rainy day, while reading his history book, his mother sat at the table and began to page through his geography text. After looking at a number of pages and reading some, she slammed the book closed and declared, "There is no edification in that book." It was only then that Andreas realized his mother's cool behavior had to do with his learning lessons she believed unnecessary.

She got up and returned to her kitchen project as she considered how her youngest son was changing.

The six weeks went by and before long the young man was joining his father, rowing again toward the dock on which he would sit until the 3 A.M. arrival of the steamer, *Karmsund*. This time Anders sat with Andreas, and later watched the young man board. Anders waited until daylight and then began the slow, one-oared trip back to Stord.

Arriving back at school was nothing like last fall. Except for the few boys who had graduated, the same students took up their same rooms, excitedly telling of their summer adventures. Mrs. Fleum greeted each of them as the smell of fresh cookies drifted through the swinging kitchen door.

"Just take two. We will be eating soon enough," she reminded her charges.

The next day, with school starting, Andreas was thrilled to join the sixth middle-school class. No longer would he need to be privately tutored in the back room where he had spent the entire previous year.

During the first week it seemed everyone was adjusting to life together in the Country Boy's Home as well as in their classrooms. On the following Saturday afternoon, Eric and Andreas decided to take a trek to the southeast side of the Stavanger peninsula. As they walked along a cliff that rose steeply from the sea, they ran into an elderly woman who was dressed in dirty, torn clothes. As they passed her on the narrow ledge, she mumbled something. They stopped and Andreas asked, "Ma'am, what did you say?"

She began to mutter, "I'm going to jump. I *am* boys, you can bet on that. I'm going to jump!"

Stopping in their tracks, they looked at each other with surprise. Eric, the stronger and taller one, spoke first. "You don't want to do that! You really don't. Why don't we all just sit down?"

Andreas took the old woman's arm and helped her to a nearby rock. When he asked her name, her response could not be understood. They kept talking with her between their expressions of surprise and fear.

"Could we help you get home?" Eric asked.

She slowly got to her feet and began walking back toward the city, continuing to stumble along the path, murmuring as she made her way. She led them to a white house on a street not so far from their residence. The old lady took hold of the latch and opened the door. As she walked through, the boys were left on the step until a younger lady appeared and asked gruffly, "Well, what do you want?"

They politely tipped their hats. Andreas, the more talkative one, said, "We found this lady on the cliff. She said she was going to jump, so we sat her down and just talked. Then we asked if we could lead her home. So here we are."

"Oh, she talks like that all the time. She is my aunt, and she knows to come home when she gets hungry. Now she's home early and I won't get anything done, so stay out of our business."

Andreas swallowed hard as the woman slammed the door in their faces. They stared at each other, turned toward the street and walked home.

Back at school the following Monday, the student's excitement centered on Rector Steen's visit. For most of the previous school year, he had been away serving as a member of parliament. When he returned, they would all gather in the lunchroom and listen to his stories of government service. The boys were proud to know someone of such importance.

The rest of the school year of 1885-1886 was quite uneventful, except for the month Andreas spent almost alone in the sick room at the Country Boy's Home. Following a doctor's visit, Andreas was told he was suffering from scarlet fever and immediately had to be quarantined. Staying in an extra bedroom, saved as a sick ward, Andreas wondered how long he would have to be separated from his housemates and endure this darkened, lonely room. By late afternoon that day, he was saved from complete isolation. Since Eric had already suffered from the disease, he offered to join Andreas in the room. The luxury of two boys in a room was something they especially enjoyed. Every afternoon Eric would report on the events at school, delivering Andreas his books and assignments. With winter coming on, their conversations moved from the discovery of caves and playing with salamanders to the sport of ice skating.

It was during his time in the sick room that young Andreas began recording experiences at school in a journal. Although he had to be coaxed along with the other boys to write letters home, this writing project interested him. On the first page of his journal he wrote; "Life at the Cathedral School of Stavanger."

JOURNAL October 13, 1885

I arrived in late summer of 1884. When everyone began school, I was forced to be tutored by Peter Hognestad, who was attending the Gymnasium. He was very kind and helped me through the first year. During that time I visited home for the Christmas holiday and the six-week-long summer break.

I returned for this year prepared to attend class with my friends. I had spent the summer working with father and studying my history and geography book, a book my mother thought was useless. She questions the value of what I am learning.

I spend most of my time with my classmate, Eric. My closest friends are older boys who have taught me much. At the end of my first year, Richard Erikson graduated. At the end of this year, I will have to say good-bye to Peter Hognestad who is going on to school in Oslo.

Chapter 7

Tragedy and Triumph

To the liking of most of the students, the fall turned quickly into typical winter weather. The talk of the house centered on the ice that seemed to be quickly forming on the small lake, just a short walk from the residence. After Mrs. Fleum checked with a neighbor regarding the condition of the ice, the boys were given permission to skate as long as they stayed together. Like a herd of cattle, they ran from the kitchen to the closet under the stairway. There they found a wooden box filled with used skates. Excited about the prospect of their first skating adventure of the year, Gunnar and another boy spilled the contents of the box onto the parlor floor. Each boy scrambled to find skates that might fit. Next came the mad dash up the stairway to get their coats, mittens and scarves. They ran out the front door, into the brisk night lit only by the bright stars and a full moon. Discovering a number of other skaters already enjoying the lake, they sat on the bank and changed from their boots to skates.

While Andreas was quick to show the kind of speed he could attain, his friend, Eric, struggled to catch up. That night Andreas wanted to learn to skate backwards, a trick he had never accomplished. He skated over to an area where he could practice without being teased by the others. As he turned around and began to slowly move backwards, he heard the sound of cracking ice. Terrified, he changed direction. Even so, the cracking became louder and louder. Fortunately he remembered his father's instructions to immediately lie down on the ice. Spreading out his legs and arms, he began to call for help. As the boys skated closer, they realized their own danger. Still lying flat on the ice, he yelled, "Stop, stop."

The boys slowed and pleaded, "What should we do?"

Andreas slowly crawled toward them and as the cracking sound began to subside, he knew he had reached safety. In the meantime, Gunnar skated over to warn others of the thin ice. The boys retreated to the shoreline where they changed again from skates into boots. As they walked up the street together, the retelling of the event grew in seriousness and its possible outcomes.

Eric declared, "I'm not skating at night ever again."

Gunnar, running up from the back of the pack, demanded silence from all. "Don't you dare tell Mrs. Fleum or we will be in trouble."

Everyone promised. Greeting them at the door, the matron asked about the skating. They said they'd had a good time. She then surprised them with freshly baked cookies and hot cocoa.

"Off to bed now, boys!" was her command. "And be ready for church at 10:45 A.M. I expect you to get there on your own and sit in our pew."

Wishing Mrs. Fleum a good night and thinking of the thin ice, Andreas took a deep breath as he climbed the stairs to his room.

The next morning, sleeping later than most days, the boys were treated to the special sweet rolls set aside for Sundays. After breakfast, they left through the heavy wooden front door and walked toward the cathedral. In the middle of the service, the matron realized one of the boys was missing. That was not unusual for Olaf Asseng. He was raised in an unchurched home and was not accustomed to weekly worship. After the service, the boys filed out of the pew and hurried down the aisle toward the back door. As they arrived back at the house, panting and teasing each other, they were surprised to see Pastor Oftedal's serious face as they entered the parlor. Quickly they quieted down and were asked to take a seat. When Mrs. Fleum arrived, the pastor nodded toward the kitchen and the two of them went through its swinging door. As the silent boys looked at each other, they wondered what trouble they might be in now. Had someone told their benefactor about the skating mishap the night before? They could hear only whispering until they heard Mrs. Fleum's scream. After a few minutes the pastor and matron returned to the parlor, Mrs. Fleum with red eyes and Pastor Oftedal looking even more somber. To everyone's astonishment, he shared the tragic news of Olaf, who had not attended church that morning. Deciding to sneak off to the lake, he had fallen through the weakened ice where Andreas had had the close call the night before. The boys all looked at each other, frightened and saddened. A few quickly wiped at their eyes with their shirtsleeves.

Mrs. Fleum broke the silence. "I want you to spend some time in your rooms before the noon meal," she said, "praying for Olaf's family. I do not want any noise."

Once the four boys got to Andreas' room, Gunnar whispered, "Why didn't we tell the matron what happened to you last night? Why?"

"Telling Mrs. Fleum would not have stopped Olaf," interrupted Eric.

Sitting quietly on his bed Andreas wondered if his silence about the cracked ice could be responsible for Olaf's death.

The next morning, he gently knocked on Pastor Oftedal's office door.

"Yes," came the response from behind the frosted glass on the door.

Andreas walked in, removed his hat and said "Pastor Oftedal, I need to see you."

"Yes, son, what is it?" the pastor said in a staccato manner.

Andreas stood there with his head hanging down. "On Saturday night Mrs. Fleum gave us permission to skate on the pond."

"Yes, go on."

"Well, I was in one place where the ice began to crack. My father had told me to fall to my stomach and spread myself out. I did that and then I called for help."

"Did you tell Mrs. Fleum of this?" the portly man asked.

"We thought it was best left unsaid," Andreas confessed.

"Well, Andreas," the former statesman said, "it would have been better for you to have told Mrs. Fleum." Then, after a long pause, he continued, "What happened to Olaf is not your doing. No matter how sad this is, you are not at fault. It is not your doing. Olaf knew of the danger. Is that all, my boy?"

Andreas looked up, with tears flowing down his cheeks and said, "Yes, sir."

"Remember, it was not your fault. It was not. When you are ready, return to your classroom."

Andreas backed out the door, tipped his hat, bowed and went to sit on Pastor Oftedal's bench. Wiping his eyes, he finally returned to his classroom.

During the lunch hour everyone was curious about Andreas' visit to Pastor Oftedal.

Gunnar, sitting at the end of the table barked, "You shouldn't have said anything. Now we won't be able to skate again. That will be your fault!" he cried, pointing across the table at the "guilty one."

The next week the funeral took place in Oslo. Only Mrs. Fleum and Rev. Oftedal attended from the school. That evening, as the boys sat around the kitchen table, a dark cloud hung over them and silence enveloped everyone and everything. Only the ticking clock interrupted the stillness. For the rest of the day, a somber mood continued to permeate the house.

As the weeks passed, a more normal life slowly returned. Everyone was surprised one Sunday afternoon when Olaf's parents arrived at the Country Boy's Home to once again visit Olaf's old room.

"Andreas," Mrs. Fleum called, "Andreas, this is Mr. and Mrs. Aaseng, Olaf's parents. They would like to talk with you privately."

Frightened of what they might say, he replied "Me?" and followed Mrs. Fleum into the kitchen where they all sat down at the table.

Mr. Aaseng began, "Now, son, I was told by Mrs. Fleum that you had almost fallen through the ice the night before the accident."

"Yes, sir," Andreas replied.

"And you felt bad that you had not told her about the ice."

"Yes, sir," Andreas repeated as he sheepishly glanced at Olaf's mother and then at Mrs. Fleum.

"Olaf is, I mean was, always an adventurous boy, and he was known to try things on his own. Mama and I want you to know that you had nothing to do with his accident," Mr. Aaseng continued.

Andreas bowed his head, wiping away a tear. "I am sorry…but thank you," he said.

Although Andreas appreciated the words of Olaf's parents and Pastor Oftedal, his guilt continued to plague him for weeks. As the spring breezes off the sea replaced the winter wind, the heavy mood of the house lifted and the boys looked forward to the end of the term and summer at home.

With the excitement of school drawing to a close, the boys now feared the posting of their grades and the future of their schooling.

Permission to return to the noted Cathedral School was in the hands of the teachers and Pastor Oftedal.

As his second year ended, with his grief slowly lifting, Andreas became more confident, not only in his studies, but in his willingness to defend his honor. He had always received a perfect "1" when it came to behavior. Gunnar's nickname for Andreas was "Mama's boy." Then, at the end of the third grading period, Andreas was surprised to see a "2" in behavior. Knowing that Pastor Oftedal would review his grades, he was frightened this rating might jeopardize his standing in the school or even his ability to return in the fall.

Mustering up more courage than ever before, he walked into Mr. Berg's classroom. He stood politely across the desk from the Latin teacher and asked for a moment of his time. Mr. Berg, known not only for his excellent teaching but his quick temper, looked up from his papers and asked, "Helland, what is it you want?"

"Sir," Andreas began, bowing slightly, "when I received my marks I saw that you had given me a '2' for deportment. Sir, have I changed in any way from the last term?"

"Not really," the teacher replied. "You have done nothing wrong. However I have observed that there is a rogue in you."

Holding his hands to his sides while maintaining a quiet respectful voice, Andreas inquired, "Has this rogue ever come out in the open?"

Mr. Berg grasped the edge of the desk with his hands, as if his temper was coming quickly to the surface, and replied, "No, no, that is not it."

There was a moment of silence until Andreas surprised himself by saying, "Then I think I should be graded for keeping it in."

"That's enough, son. What's done is done. Go now."

"Yes, sir," Andreas responded. He turned and walked out.

Andreas left school that spring still wondering about the nature of "the rogue within," hoping it would not adversely affect the scholarship and housing opportunities he had been given the past two years. Finally, during the short six weeks at home, a letter was received not only encouraging him to return but announcing, "Andreas' deportment has always been excellent." With those words he was able to relax. The daily farm chores were both tiring him and helping to build muscle on his quickly growing frame.

Returning to school in the fall, Andreas joined most of the same classmates. Although he was not excited to see Gunnar, the teasing had mellowed over time. Knowing Eric had returned, Andreas looked forward to the next year.

As classes began, Andreas and Eric had grown more confident in their studies and began to question whether they could complete the remaining three years of studies within a two-year time frame. Because of his childhood illnesses and late start with his formal education, this might be an especially challenging accomplishment for Andreas. Now ranked numbers one and two in the class, they decided to talk with the temporary rector, Mr. Langberg. The rector promised to consider their proposal.

A few days later, the two boys were called into the rector's office. As they walked in, they tipped their hats, bowed and were asked to take a seat.

"I have not made a final decision as yet, but I can give you some advice," Mr. Langberg said.

The boys listened as the rector continued. "It means," he said, "that you would have to cover all of the second year's work during this coming year. Within the two years you would have to study two more languages besides continuing with Norwegian, German and Latin. You would take Greek and either French or English. These additional studies would require advanced text books, except for geography, which you have completed."

Andreas stopped listening for a moment, remembering his mother's disgust with his geography book and her suggestion that its knowledge was not needed.

"Andreas," the boy heard the rector call his name.

"Yes, sir," Andreas replied.

"You would also need to take up a new study, that of church history. You would continue your work in mathematics, as well," the rector said. Mathematics frightened Eric; for Andreas it was one of his favorite subjects.

"Well, that would be the plan. Do you think you can do all of that work?"

"I do," Eric quickly answered.

"Yes, sir," Andreas said quietly.

"Well then, let's try it. Would you like to study French or English?"

The two boys had already agreed that French was the more cultured, dignified language.

"French, sir. We think we would both like to study French," Eric said.

"Good. I have a retired teacher who could tutor you in that subject. Well, that's that then. You had better get started."

They thanked Mr. Langberg, stood, bowed and almost collided as they backed toward his office door. Once in the hallway, they vigorously shook hands and returned to their classroom.

That afternoon, their accelerated course of study began. Mr. Langberg had delivered the advanced texts to their classroom and had told them their French lessons would commence the following Saturday morning. Rather than their sleeping in and enjoying long Saturday walks, the two boys would look forward to French tutoring, extra assignments in mathematics and a shortened hike.

With all of the extra assignments and little time for recreation, by the end of his third year in Stavanger, Andreas looked forward to a slower pace during his six weeks of summer break in Fitjar. He helped his father with the chores, attended the local church and studied advanced texts in preparation for his final year. With all of his siblings still working away from the home place, he spent the summer alone with his parents. Andreas came to realize how hard his father had worked preparing the rocky soil and what was involved in his mother's care for the sheep—the sheering, spinning, weaving, and finally dyeing of her prized woolen cloth. His father proudly told him how necessary Bertha's income had been over the years. Her sale of goods had afforded Andreas the luxury of a store-bought coat, a shirt and even new shoes. This news changed Andreas' attitude toward the confirmation suit he had worn more than a year earlier. Never again, he pledged to himself, would he complain about his clothes.

Reminded again of the struggle of rural life and how lonely he felt even in his own home community, Andreas grew more determined to find a way to limit the time on Stord and continue his education.

With his summer visit complete, he took one of the oars in hand and helped his father as they rowed the ten miles to the steamer. Again, he sat on the dock in the night air awaiting the ship's 3 A.M. arrival in Brandasund. Its timely arrival was expected and, by 8 A.M. the next morning, Andreas had returned to the familiar old house painted white and blue, and the welcome smile of Mrs. Fleum.

As the fourth and final year at the Cathedral School began, both the tempo of study and the excitement increased. There were more than a few students betting that Eric and Andreas would not be successful in their accelerated classes. In addition, certain teachers believed that decreasing the amount of time it took to complete classes served as an insult to the entire educational system. Some were calling this practice a "student factory" rather than a serious school.

When it came to the written examination, both Eric and Andreas proved their naysayers wrong. News of their excellent grades arrived first by telegraph and then through the mail. It was finally time for the final oral exams.

Andreas' last exam was on the subject of church history. The teacher quizzed the five other students before getting to Andreas.

"Helland, tell me what you know about Tertullian."

Prior to closing his church history book Andreas had seen the famous name Tertullian with the number 220 behind it, with a small cross next to the number. In a cautious voice Andreas answered, "He died in the year 220."

"That is correct," the teacher said, smiling. Then followed what seemed an endless pause.

Finally, the teacher continued, "Well, what did he do before he died?" The silence in the room was punctuated with laughter.

"Nothing?" Andreas meekly answered.

The teacher went on to lead Andreas through nearly an hour-long inquisition. When the ordeal was finally over, Andreas stood, knees wobbling and sat down again. A voice cried, "Quickly! Get Helland some water before he faints!" A student ran out of the classroom to fetch the water.

The long days of examination had finally passed, and Eric and Andreas had achieved their goals.

Eric's voice was now filled with confidence, and Andreas had grown from a sickly child into a young man eager to continue his schooling. Both boys had accomplished their B.A.s by the age of 18. On June 12th, 1888, the two friends graduated and moved from the Country Boy's Home. At the graduation ceremony, Andreas received his diploma without the traditional hat and tassel.

Eric moved back home to join his father's business in Oslo and Andreas, lacking funds to continue his schooling, returned to rural life on the island of Stord.

Chapter 8

In-between Times

This time when Anders met his son at the dock in Brandasund, Andreas had with him the painted wooden chest his father had built. With his school years finally over, the chest was coming home, too. The family was looking forward to this homecoming, one they hoped would last their entire lifetime.

Andreas' brothers and sisters still worked away from Fitjar. However, to his pleasant surprise, his older sister, Helga, had returned home to share the chores of the farm. For Andreas, the dry hay had to be carried into the small barn. There was the house-to-house peddling of potatoes in Bergen and a variety of other farm chores. Using the same boat his parents had received as a wedding present, Andreas spent the evenings fishing in the local waters for brown cod. This solitary occupation gave him time to rest, think and dream of the future.

For weeks before his return, Bertha's conversation with her friends centered on her youngest son's anticipated return. When asked what he would be doing while back home, she guessed he might work on their farm or find employment like his brother, Kristen. Within just a few weeks after hearing of his return to the island, the local school offered Andreas a substitute teaching position on a small island just west of Stord. With a meager salary came the use of a rowboat and a small cottage. Andreas was excited about his return to books and school life. He quickly accepted and began to enjoy the role reversal from student to teacher. Though his mother voiced her disapproval and her wish for him to stay on the farm, Andreas packed his belongings and took them to the little cottage. He spent the evenings preparing his lessons. Sometimes he perused a catalogue of correspondence courses from the university in Oslo. The catalogue, with its appealing course descriptions, whet his appetite for future study. Reality presented itself when he saw the cost of tuition.

Andreas left his little island each Saturday morning, rowed to the dock at Fitjar, then hiked up to the Helland farm where he would stay until the next afternoon. He would help his parents with the chores and attend Sunday services. The farm work, combined with the rowing and long walks between his little cottage and his parent's farm, balanced his life as a schoolteacher. Tutoring the young children was a challenge so that, after just six weeks, Andreas began to hunger for adult conversations and reading that would challenge his intellect.

In September of that year, a letter arrived from his closest friend and sibling, Peder. Earlier that spring, Andreas had been bitterly disappointed when Peder announced his intention to take Marie, his young wife, to America. Although Andreas would miss Peder, he was determined to avoid America Fever. To the relief of his parents, he had made his decision quite public when he chose to learn French instead of the more popular study of English.

The family was thrilled to read that son, Peder, having finished school in Oslo, had received a pastoral position in a town known as Racine in the American state of Wisconsin. At dinner, they talked of Peder's good fortune, hoping that once he had been able to pay his school loans and passage ticket, he might come to his senses and return to his motherland.

Well into November, Andreas found a letter on his doorstep, secured by a small rock. Just then, a neighbor ran to meet him. She paused to catch her breath.

"Mr. Helland! The postman asked me where you could be found. I told him you were teaching school and, so, he left this letter for you. He told me he is your cousin from Aga."

"Oh, yes, he is indeed my cousin. Peter is from my mother's family. Thank you."

As the neighbor turned toward her simple wood-framed cottage, Andreas waved and thanked her again. Reading the return address, "Cathedral School, Stavanger, Norway," he quickly ripped open the letter.

"What could this be?" he thought. To his surprise the message was from his former rector, Mr. Langberg.

Cathedral School
Stavanger, Norway
November 17, 1888
Dear Andreas:
*I hope this letter finds you well and content in what you are
doing. I was recently in Oslo and visited your dear friend, Eric
Eriksen. He informed me that you have taken up a substitute posi-
tion in your local school district. Since I spoke with Eric, you have
been a heavy weight on my mind. He gave me your address. Eric
told me of your desire to continue with your studies in the future.
Remembering your excellent progress here at the Cathedral School,
I am offering financial help in the form of a loan for future study
at the university in Oslo. If you would be able to leave your current
position, I believe something could be worked out for your stay in
Oslo from March to early June. If you are interested, please write as
soon as possible. I hope and pray that your teaching is going well.*
Sincerely,
Mr. Langberg, Acting Rector

Still standing on his front step, the young teacher read the letter
over and over again before fully realizing its message.

Once inside his small cottage, Andreas pulled the only chair he
had to the little table and looked at the letter for the fourth time. He
grabbed a piece of stationery and began to write.

November 26, 1888
Cathedral School
Stavanger, Norway
Dear Mr. Langberg:
*I have just received your letter and wonderful offer. I am commit-
ted to continue teaching here until late February on a small island
close to my home. God seems to work in a mysterious way. I have
recently been studying the University's correspondence catalogue of
courses. However, with your kind offer, I could enroll in two of those*

courses immediately! For the classes at the university, I will need to borrow the transportation cost to and from Oslo, if that is possible. I gratefully accept this generous offer and look forward to hearing from you soon.
 Sincerely,
 Andreas Helland

That evening Andreas walked back down the path toward the school and posted his letter at the small post office. His cousin, Peter, would pick it up in a few days. Heading home with a new spring in his step, he hummed a tune. Before the evening grew too dark, Andreas reread the catalogue that yesterday had been just a book of dreams. A new possibility occurred to him. Accustomed to writing letters while in Stavanger, he had attempted to journal only once. He went to his table and lit the kerosene lamp. Taking paper and pen in hand, he began to write.

JOURNAL November 26, 1888
This has been a day of great joy. After a difficult day in school with some children unwilling to learn, I returned home to find a letter from Rector Langberg. My dear friend from Stavanger days, Eric, has told the rector of my activities. Mr. Langberg wrote to offer me a loan for my M.A. degree at the university. I have been paging through the correspondence catalogue yearning to take a class, but I could not put myself in debt. Immediately, I have posted a letter accepting his kind offer, and as I begin this journal, my heart is as light as a feather.

Finished writing, he turned down the lamp wick and went to bed. Unlike late August when he arrived, the straw mattress no longer smelled of the fresh field. On his back, in the pitch dark, he imagined the ceiling above and his thoughts of future schooling kept his eyes wide open. For hours it seemed he gazed into the dark night.

In the morning, still in need of sleep, Andreas rolled out of bed and washed up with the water he had used the night before. He grabbed a piece of bread his mother had baked, a slab of cheese and slowly made his way to the little schoolhouse. The children were busy playing, waiting for their teacher to arrive.

After the traditional opening prayer and scripture reading, Andreas gave the students their first assignment. He sat at his desk staring past the heads of the children, attending to the new dream that had arrived yesterday. He thought he must finish his courses at an advanced speed, as he had in Stavanger. He had mentioned to Mr. Langberg that he could study astronomy and German by correspondence, leaving philosophy, Latin and zoology while in residence at the university in Oslo.

That evening he ate his supper and sat down to the journal he had started the night before.

JOURNAL November 27, 1888

After school today, the need for sleep caught up with me. I must confess my attention was focused on my good news rather than my students. Today I hardly earned the small pay due to me. I anxiously await Mr. Langberg's letter and his loan so that I can order the texts and materials for the two courses I have decided to take by correspondence. Well, feeling sleep coming on, I close.

Andreas' pen nearly dropped from his hand as he retreated to his bed. Before long, his eyes closed and did not open until the next day.

At the end of the week, Andreas was so anxious to share his news with his family that he didn't wait for his usual Saturday morning crossing to the island of Stord. After school on Friday, he filled his carpetbag with a change of clothes and steered his double-bowed rowboat across to the Fitjar dock, arriving at the farm with the sun already set. He told his parents the good news. Bertha was simply relieved that he would not be gone for long. She hoped he would return to either teach or work at the home place. No matter how many times Andreas assured her that he had no intention of ever succumbing to America Fever, the fear of it lingered in her mind and caused her mood to be troubled whenever anyone talked of it.

Chapter 9

On to Oslo

JOURNAL March 5, 1889

Although I promised myself I would keep a journal to record my happenings, my last entry was in late November. With life going so fast and changes happening, I think writing not only reminds me of what I am doing but also serves as good practice for my classes. I have already forgotten so much of what happened while away at school in Stavanger. I want to spend more time writing, if for no other reason than to be able to think about the future.

I have said goodbye to mother, father and my sister who remain at home. Now accustomed to such farewells, my tears have all but dried up. Mother's tears continue to run freely. Her last words are always the same, "I pray for you, Son." I nodded to her and then father, and I rowed the ten miles to the same dock at which he had left me some five years earlier as I first departed for Stavanger. As I sit on the steamer deck today, with a cool breeze whipping up my paper, I am headed first for Kristiansand and then on to Oslo. The fall and winter sessions of school went as well as they could for a teacher with little experience. Christmas, a celebration Father begins to plan in late October, was again a wonderful time. All but Peder were home. We enjoyed reading the letter he had written from his new home in Racine, in the state of Wisconsin, USA. As I write this, I miss him even more. Oh, I wished he had stayed here.

Well, for now that is all. I hope to write again soon.

JOURNAL March 7, 1889

I am doing what I promised. I left the steamer in Kristiansand yesterday for four hours. I wanted to see Miss Thomassen who is now matron of an orphan's home for girls. When I saw her last in Stavanger she had treated me and all the boys like children. Yesterday she saw me as a young man. For these pages only, I must admit she has grown to be quite beautiful, even though many years older.

When I arrived in Oslo, I went to find my schoolmate Eric Eriksen. He had found me a small room to rent. Though I am thankful, I wish the room didn't look out onto the courtyard. I can't see the sun. I look forward to seeing Eric often, though, during these next months.

JOURNAL March 10, 1889

With my rent comes a mug of coffee in the morning and a pitcher of sweet milk in the evening. In a small shop down the street I bought bread and butter for my noon meal. I go to the municipal steam kitchen for my supper. Each day we are given two choices of food, one less expensive than the other. Hundreds of students line up to pick up their meals. Yesterday I was late and stayed until the kitchen was closing. Walking past the alley, I saw another line of children and adults with tin pails. This evening I asked Eric about them. They are children who cannot pay, and any leftovers are given to them at the end of the mealtime. I must begin reading my Latin text.

JOURNAL March 20, 1889

I now have my routine down. I wake up at about 5 A.M. and study until noon. As I have some distance to go, it takes an hour to walk to school. I have started my classes in Latin and chemistry at the university. I have been warned not to miss the chemistry class since the text is inadequate and the professor is quite unpredictable. His name is Peter Vaage but, since he seems only to speak about oxygen, some students call him "Peter Oxygen" behind his back.

My zoology teacher is very stern and when one is called upon, he had better know the answer. Today I was the unlucky one. The teacher asked me to stand and tell him about the ptarmigan. Thankfully, teacher Bahr at Cathedral had told us about this bird and so I answered correctly. As time goes on, he seemed kinder to students who are having trouble and so I have begun to feel less nervous.

My eyes won't stay open any longer.

JOURNAL April 10, 1889

As I begin another week, I will try to write just a little more often. My routine continues to be the same. The meals at the steam kitchen are simple but nourishing. I am studying German by myself. I am reading works by Schiller and Goethe. I have met with the professor once and he seems very pleasant. After I have finished studying, he will give me an oral exam.

Most of my time is spent reading philosophy and particularly logic. Professor Monrad is my teacher. I know this is unkind to think, let alone to write, but I have never seen anyone who looks quite like him. After class one day, Eric said, "Professor Monrad's facial expression convinces me that man did indeed descend from the ape." I laughed and turned to see that no one was listening, no one that is, except for Professor Monrad. Eric and I turned and ran out the door.

JOURNAL April 17, 1889

Another week has passed. When we arrived at philosophy class, I noticed the professor looking strangely at Eric and me. I was nervous all week about Eric's comment but Professor Monrad didn't say anything. I am adjusting to the long days, still getting up at 5 A.M. and not getting to bed until 11 P.M. I fill myself at the kitchen but often need another piece of bread late at night. I am thankful it is warming up. My room has been quite cold and the weather very rainy this last month. Eric and I have been attending his mother's church each Sunday after which she offers us a nourishing meal and sends bread home with us.

JOURNAL May 17, 1889

No matter how much I intend to write, it seems the days are not long enough. Classes are going well and I am keeping up with my private study in German. I am happy now that Mr. Langberg encouraged me to take all five subjects at once so I can complete my education. In three weeks I will be finished. I am no longer cold in my bed at night. Eric has told me he will continue his study in philosophy. He is more of a dreamer than me. As we talk, I am afraid his faith might be fading into some philosophical thought. Imagine this is the 75th anniversary of independence from Denmark. Flags are flying along the streets in celebration.

JOURNAL June 16, 1889

Amen! It is done. I slept late today. I have taken my last exam. I think I have done well. Once my exams are read, I will receive the results by mail. On Monday I will say farewell to Eric, still my best friend except for Peder. We will have a meal with his mother. I have applied for a tutor position with three children in Kristiansand. The father is a civil engineer.

On the following Monday morning, Andreas and Eric said farewell at the dock where Andreas was to catch his steamer for home. Besides a simple farewell handshake, their conversation was all about the test results for which Andreas would wait an agonizing month. Sitting on the open deck, he enjoyed the view of the water and the green islands dotting the area. He smiled as he compared his self-doubt with Rector Langberg's confidence in his gaining an M.A. in such a short time. He wondered what the uncharted future held. As the steamer arrived at Brandasund, he saw his father waving from the dock. Together they rowed back to Fitjar. Bertha, with a letter in her hand, welcomed her son with a warm embrace and smiling, she said, "We have a letter from Peder!" He quickly let go of her, took the letter and began to read.

May 11, 1889
Dear Mama, Papa and Family,
   Last month Marie and I celebrated our first wedding anniversary. On that day we took a leisurely walk together and my dear wife fixed a wonderful meal. We are adjusting to life in Wisconsin, liking it more and more. The church people are very nice but expect to have much more to say in the workings of the church than in Norway. We have had a cold winter compared to Fitjar, and we always wear the wool clothing you made for us, Mama. We do enjoy Racine more than Chicago, which was so busy. Marie's sister, Bertha, stayed in Chicago and so we don't see her very often except when she can save money for a train ticket. I am sure by now you are missing Kristen. We expect him shortly and have a room in the parsonage for him during his stay. It is such wonderful news about his engagement. I think Andreas should consider joining us here and possibly continuing his education. We could help with funds after he arrives. I know he has never wanted to come to America; however, for a short time he might like it.
   We await Kristen's arrival and miss you very much.
   Love,
   Peder

With supper over, they sat at the table and reread Peder's letter. Bertha asked Andreas if he wanted to leave Fitjar. She had hoped he was ready to settle down. "I don't know, Mother. I don't have any offers of employment. I must wait for the results of my tests." During the next few weeks Andreas was kept busy working with his father in the rocky fields.

Chapter 10

America Fever Coming On

JOURNAL—July 2, 1889

I returned home to the smiles of Mother two weeks ago now. She was happy to hear that since I didn't speak English, I wasn't offered the position with the family in Kristiansand. I am now wondering what is next. At the end of the day, after helping my father, I still enjoy taking the rowboat out to fish. I think about Peder and Marie and their new life in America. I think of my friend, Eric, and I wonder when I will see him again. After our talks, especially about philosophy and with Peder's encouragement, I am thinking more about the university course in theology.

Andreas continued to spend part of each day helping his parents with their daily chores. "Would you fetch a pail of water?" his mother asked. Andreas picked up the empty pail from next to the kitchen sink and swung it back and forth as he left the house for a trip to the community well. With blue skies and marshmallow clouds above him, he made himself comfortable sitting on the large rock next to the well. There he sat, thinking to himself about the friends he had grown up with on the island as well as those who had become his closest friends in Stavanger. He couldn't help but feel a bit jealous and even disappointed with himself. While many island boys had already worked for years in their trades, others were joining their father's businesses. Still others were able to continue their schooling. "Here I sit, wondering what is next for me," Andreas mused. Nearby tutoring or teaching positions were scarce. His father could always use his help, yet Andreas knew he was a drain to his parent's limited means. The longer he sat, the more he missed his brother Peder. Always open to adventure, Andreas wondered why he had always been so opposed to those who gave in to America Fever. Suddenly he began to feel a warm presence, a new joy, almost a feeling of contentment.

His thoughts were interrupted by his mother's voice. "Where are you Andreas? I need the water; come quickly!"

Andreas, feeling less confused, quickly filled the bucket and began to run back home with a smile on his face. "Where have you been, Son? Have you been daydreaming again?"

"Just daydreaming I guess, Mother," he answered.

JOURNAL July 10, 1889

While last night was my first good sleep since I left Oslo, I actually dreamed about how I was going to tell Mother and Father what happened yesterday at the well. While sitting on my favorite rock, I realized what I wished to do in the near future. I know this will not come as good news. Everyone will be surprised. Hearing from others on the island that America is the land of opportunity and that wages are much higher, I think I want to spend the next two or three years near Peder, make enough money to pay off my debts and then return home and continue my schooling. I know how disappointed my family will be when I tell them of my plans. I cannot ignore the warm feeling and my change of heart. I am tempted to believe this is what God wants for me.

On July 10th, Andreas celebrated his 19th birthday. He called for a family council meeting for the following evening. "I would like to tell you about the plans I am considering," Andreas explained. Helga wrinkled her nose while his parents, with furrowed brows, looked at each other and simply said that will be fine. The next evening, following a quiet supper, Bertha and Helga washed the dishes. Andreas and his father checked on a sickly goat.

Later, with the family gathered around the kitchen table, Andreas took a deep breath and began, "I am sure this will come as a surprise to you, as it did to me just yesterday. Mother, what kept me at the well yesterday was not just a leisurely look at the fields. I sat down and thought about my future on Stord or somewhere nearby. I also thought about my friends—those who stayed here, and my friend in Oslo who has joined his father's business. I, too, have been praying about what I need to do now that I have completed my schooling. To my surprise, what came to me was the idea to join Peder in America. This thought left me with a warm feeling of contentment. I would join Peder long enough to save money to pay off my school debt. Remember, cousin Nils is one of Peder's boarders. He easily found a job."

"But Andreas," his mother interrupted, "you have always spoken against those who leave their homeland."

"I know, Mother. I did not expect this change of attitude."

As they went on to discuss his passage over, his possible living arrangements and his plan to return, his father and sister appeared to become more comfortable with the possibility. It was his mother who kept shaking her head saying, "But Andreas, I can't lose another son; I just can't."

The young man patiently repeated, "But Mother, it will be only a few years. I will miss you, too. When I return, I will be free of debt. I will write to Peder and ask his blessing."

Helga closed the meeting with a prayer, as was their custom. She asked for guidance for her brother, and comfort and strength for her parents. They closed with the Lord's Prayer.

JOURNAL July 12, 1889
Writing helps me to think more clearly. Keeping this journal is a good habit. I am relieved that Mother, Father and Helga know of my decision and plans. Last night I wrote to Peder, asking for his blessing.

July 11, 1889
Pastor Peder Helland
Bethesda Lutheran Church
Racine, Wisconsin, USA
Dear Peder and Marie,
Thank you for your past letter. It was good to hear all the news. I finished with my M.A. last month and returned home. While

fetching water for Mother a few days ago, a most persistent idea flooded me and gave me a strangely warm feeling. I have decided to go to America. My plan is to work hard enough to pay off my school debts and then return to the university in Oslo to study theology. With your blessing, I would arrive in early October. At the family council meeting last night, I received the family's blessing.

I will now post this and look forward to your answer.

Love, your brother,

Andreas

August 1, 1889

Dear Andreas,

This is very good news! Please do join us here in Racine! If you like, you can stay with Kristen in his room. Marie is looking forward to getting to know you. There are always jobs available here while you work on your English. Kristen arrived safely and I can tell he misses Anna very much. He found work in our mercantile and is happy with that for now. Anna is planning to join him here next year when they will be married. He has asked me to perform the service, which of course will be a joy.

For now, it remains warm but we expect fall to arrive soon. Since our church membership is nearly all Norwegian, I know you will feel at home. The town has a generous mix of Germans, Swedes, Irish and Norwegians.

Greetings to Mama, Papa and Helga,

Peder

August 18, 1889

Dear Uncle Anders, Aunt Bertha, Andreas and Helga,

I am saddened to tell you of our dear Peder's unexpected death. At a church picnic, Peder must have eaten something that made him terribly ill. The doctor said that his weakened heart did not help matters. He suffered for only a few days before his passing. That is all the information we know at this time. Marie asked me to write this letter on her behalf. She misses Peder very much and wishes she was home with her family. The church people are doing what they can to help us at this difficult time. Please continue with your plans, Andreas. Peder was so excited about your coming. Please let us know when you will arrive, and keep Marie in your prayers.

Faithfully, your cousin,
Nils Meling

September 18, 1889
Dear Marie,

We received the news of Peder's death in Nils' letter. I am writing for Mother, Father and the rest of our family. Our hearts are heavy with sadness. You and our family have been included in the prayers that close our Sunday service. You are also remembered in our table prayer at every meal. It is as if the clouds of winter have gathered far too early, yet we have faith that Peder is with the Lord.

As Nils suggested, I have decided to continue with my plans to go to Racine. I hope it will not be a burden for you. I intend to help in every way I can. I will quickly find a job and a place to live. I will be leaving on September 28th and, God willing, will arrive by the middle of October. Hopefully you receive this letter before hearing my knock at your door.

Love, your brother,
Andreas

JOURNAL September 19, 1889
Yesterday I wrote to Marie. As the days have passed, I am getting more anxious about this adventure. I don't look forward to my fare-well, especially in this time of deep sadness. Mother and Father have become accustomed to farewells over the years, starting with Kristen's leaving to begin his own farm work. I keep my mind busy with my preparations. It has been a great struggle gathering the four signatures I need to guarantee my loan that makes this trip possible. The banker was not supportive until I mentioned my return to study theology.

JOURNAL September 20, 1889

Today I bought my ticket for the Domino, *a Wilson steamer that will take me to Hull, England. I think it is the same ship Peder and Marie had taken. I will transfer from Hull to Liverpool where I will board a newer ship, the* City of New York. *I am relieved that the ticket is purchased but keep wondering how I will finally pay my loans.*

On the night before Andreas departed, neighbors arrived at the Helland farm to say their goodbyes. Sunny weather allowed many to visit in the front yard. After a final supper, everyone joined in prayer. While his father remained stoic, Andreas' mother and sisters joined others who were shedding tears.

The next morning, Andreas stood at the dock, his mother clinging to him as if she would never let go. After the long and tearful goodbye, Andreas and his father rowed as they had so many times toward Brandasund to meet the steamer bound for Stavanger. Once he arrived, Andreas climbed the hill to the Country Boy's Home to bid farewell to Mrs. Fleum. She greeted him with a giant smile, a pat on his head and a warm embrace. She invited him to the same kitchen table where he had eaten so many meals, and then brought out a plate of fresh oatmeal cookies. Before the former student could take a bite, a tear formed in the corner of her eye. "I have heard about your brother, Peder. I am so very sorry. Understanding God's will is not always easy, is it my dear?"

Arriving back at the Stavanger dock, Andreas bought some supplies he would need for the voyage, including a narrow straw mattress, eating utensils and a tin cup. On Saturday evening he boarded the Wilson steamer, *Domino*. It proved to be a very old and uncomfortable vessel. Traveling steerage class or what his brother called *Mellomdekk*, made the voyage even more unpleasant. With his wooden chest in storage, he made his way down the ladder, the mattress over one shoulder and his carpetbag flung over the other. He stayed at the bottom of the ladder for a while assisting women and children. When he was able to find a bunk, it was almost the last vacant one. The narrow bunks lined the side of the ship. Women were in another area as well as families traveling together. Arriving in Hull on Monday morning, Andreas carefully climbed the ladder to the open deck where he took in the cool, salty harbor air. Once off the gangplank, Andreas found his way to the rail station where he boarded a train for Liverpool. The train soon rumbled out of the station. Seated next to him was a young man who seemed close in age to Andreas. After introductions, Oscar told Andreas that he had come from Stavanger and was on his way to Minnesota. Oscar could speak English so Andreas decided to stay close to him. Andreas lamented, "Why did I take French instead of English?"

By the time the train arrived in Liverpool, the two had become like old friends. They found a rooming house for the next two nights. They agreed they would spend the next seven days or so looking out for each other. Andreas was thankful for Oscar's command of English, while Oscar was glad to have a travel companion.

JOURNAL Tuesday, October 1, 1889

As I sit on my bed in the Liverpool rooming house, I realize how much has happened in the last few days. My farewell at home was a sad occasion, and yet I feel like I belong somewhere more like Stavanger than Fitjar.

As I write, intense feelings of sadness have flooded over me. I will have to tell my new friend, Oscar, what has happened lately in my life. I catch myself thinking over and over again, "Oh how I wish I could have spent more time with Peder." I still wake up in the morning with a heart that feels like it has been ripped in two. I have never suffered such pain. Tomorrow we will begin the longest leg of our journey. I certainly hope the next ship is more comfortable than the Domino.

JOURNAL Wednesday, October 2, 1889

I woke up early this morning with a great deal of mixed feelings. I am still sad about Peder, but excited and nervous about the transatlantic voyage. Again last night I had to hide my tears from

Oscar. I hear someone in the kitchen so I guess I will wash up and join others for an early breakfast. The hot oatmeal and coffee will taste wonderful.

After two nights in the rooming house, Andreas and his new friend, Oscar, packed their belongings and headed outside. Their wooden chests had already been loaded on the ship. As they approached the crowded dock area they heard, "Have your tickets out and stand in this line for inoculations." Andreas had never seen such a sorry state of frightened men. He and Oscar felt like they were drowning in a sea of people as everyone waited for the command to board. Amid the throng of people, Andreas felt a deep sense of loneliness. Finally it was time to board. Oscar and Andreas took their places in the long line of passengers. A well-dressed gentleman asked in English if they had a second-class ticket. They shook their heads "no" in unison, and the officer hurriedly took the tickets, then ordered them to move on. "Faster! Faster!" This time they were able to descend a stairway to steerage-class level. Unlike the *Domino*, this brand new ship had electric lights and good ventilation. The cabins in steerage had small rooms that held eight men.

JOURNAL October 3, 1889
Our first night on board I awoke only to hear men leave for the bathroom or the occasional snoring. Yesterday, when we left the port, a band played "God Save the Queen." As they lined up along the rails, the people cried and waved their handkerchiefs. I, too, felt sad and yet knew I would be returning in just a few years. Oscar explained to me what two men near him were saying, "That is New Brighten Pier and there is Holy Head over there." Everyone quieted as the ship passed through the Irish Channel.

Andreas enjoyed the luxury of this new ship. With the families in a separate section, the only noise was men playing cards late at night.

Andreas needed to rise earlier in order to escape the long lines for the bathroom. At eight o'clock each morning, Andreas and Oscar walked to the dining room where they were served oatmeal, soft bread and a cup of coffee. Following breakfast, they stood out on the open deck focusing on the churning water below and listening to the variety of languages being spoken.

JOURNAL October 5, 1889

Peder must have felt better about the crossing last year since he had Marie and three others with him. Besides Oscar and a few people I have talked with at meals, I feel so alone. Today, Mother is on my mind. She didn't want me to go to America. She reminded me of my childhood illnesses and was worried I would not only become ill but would get lost in big cities like New York and Chicago. I was told at dinner yesterday, by someone whose brother had already gone over, that the entry point for immigrants in New York is very organized. I wish I would have known that long ago. I could have mentioned it to Mother.

As I stood at the railing, a little boy, about eight years old, ran into me. His mother scolded him, but I didn't understand what she said. He just looked up at me, said something and ran off. A few feet away was a woman speaking to her husband in Norwegian. She would cry, then talk, then cry some more. Today many passengers seem sad. When we left Liverpool everyone seemed to be talking but now many sit on the benches or stand at the railing, not saying a word. I returned to the dining room to read. Dinner was meat, potatoes, soft bread and coffee.

JOURNAL October 6, 1889

A pastor from Oslo led the Sunday service in the lounge. A crewman played the piano. It almost felt like I was at home or at St. Petri Church in Stavanger. We sang two of my favorite hymns, "God Bless Our Precious Native Land" and "A Mighty Fortress Is Our God." I wasn't the only one with tears in my eyes. I felt comforted by the Bible passage and the words of the preacher. Oscar practiced his English by attending an English service led by a Methodist preacher.

Rumor has it that there is to be clear sailing. Imagine them knowing that out here. It is still very calm and sunny yet quite cool. Everyone wears a woolen coat while strolling on the deck. When I tip my hat or try to grin at people, they either greet me in German or English. I am now good at saying "Guten Tag" and "Hello." If it is some other language, I just smile and keep walking.

The men's quarters remind me of the Country Boy's Home in Stavanger. The men are just a little older. I am surprised at the way some of them fight and argue. Some spend every day playing cards and smoking. Others take constant sips from their flasks. Yesterday a man walked right into me, then said something angrily in English and walked on.

I find some comfort reading the Psalms, especially Psalms 23, 130 and 121. It seems every time I get up from my bed I have to wipe tears away.

JOURNAL October 9, 1889

I have missed writing for some days. Even so, nothing new has happened. I spend my day eating, walking the deck, reading, writing in this journal or visiting with Oscar. He is a kind young man. I will genuinely miss him when we finally have to say goodbye. I am glad we are taking the same train from New York, at least as far as Chicago. I keep thinking about my trunk and pray that it is aboard. I am missing Mother and Father. It must be the distance that causes the ache in my heart. I hope this is worth the pain.

I have now figured out the best time to rise and use the bathroom each morning. This ship is much more comfortable than the Domino. It is clean and spacious, even in steerage class.

The staff is telling us we will arrive this afternoon.

Chapter 11

America the Beautiful

October 11, 1889
Dear Mother and Father,
We have arrived safely. The crossing was peaceful with calm seas. I had a comfortable small cabin, which slept eight men. The only challenge to sleep was the snoring of some of my cabin mates. It reminded me of Father's snoring and made me feel at home. The most exciting event has happened in the last 24 hours. We slowly approached what others told me was Long Island. As we got closer to docking, everyone pointed at the Statue of Liberty. It is a beautiful sight. Suddenly the ship shook to a stop. Before long a group of tugboats arrived to free us from a sandbar. That didn't work. Finally other steamers and tugboats came for the first-class passengers and their baggage. We were so close. We in steerage class thought they would come for us later. Instead, we were told to go to bed and wait for morning.

First thing in the morning, those who could understand English, like my friend, Oscar, heard the Irishmen pestering the crew as to what was going to happen. We were told to keep our straw mattresses since we might have to stay on board another night. Many of the men in my cabin, along with others, immediately took their mattresses and threw them into the harbor in protest. The mattresses began to float down the Ambrose Channel and back out to the Atlantic. The only good that came of this was an early supper served in the second-class dining room. What a magnificent room! By 8 P.M., we were told we would be going ashore. We watched as several tugboats came aside. They took us to a warehouse for the White Star Line. We bedded down there. I was fortunate to have kept my mattress but had only my thin blanket to cover me. It was a sleepless, cold night.

At dawn, we were given a small breakfast. Next we boarded a ferry for Castle Garden, the immigrant processing station. Like a large pie, the room was separated into various language sections. My friend, Oscar, stayed close in case I needed his help with translation. He has been so kind. I keep asking myself why I chose to learn French instead of English while in school.

At last we arrived at the front of the line where a doctor checked us for any contagious disease. They rolled back our eyelids with a small hook. I was asked my name, age and destination. The agent looked very tired as he glanced at our tickets, stamped them and directed us to the train. You will be glad to know that my wooden chest arrived safely and a drayman brought it from the ship to the warehouse where we slept. I had to hire another drayman to bring my chest to the train. I will write when I arrive at Peder's home.

Love,
Your son, Andreas

JOURNAL Sunday, October 13, 1889
I arrived in Chicago. Friday afternoon we boarded a "Second-Class" train. The train was already crowded and I was still damp. It had rained quite hard and I did not want to spend $1.50 on an umbrella. We were taken to the railroad station by ferry. I had bought my ticket in Liverpool before the voyage, and so all I had to do was keep from losing it. My friend, Oscar, was on the same train to Chicago. When I got off, he continued on to Minneapolis. It was so much help to sit with someone who knew the language. Like our ship, the train car had people from Ireland, France, England and Poland. I heard all kinds of languages. By now I have just my ten-dollar gold piece and a few dollars I had converted from kroner at Castle Garden.

This was my first time to ride a train. On the platform a uniformed gentleman asked for our tickets. Oscar pointed to the man's hat and whispered to me, "Conductor." Once we found a seat, I kept hearing the conductor shout. Oscar explained that he was saying, "All aboard." My traveling partner pointed to a sign on the roof of our car and said "Pullman." We both shrugged our shoulders and wondered what that meant. There was a gas lamp burning near us. By the time we left the station it was dark except for all the lights in the many buildings. When it cooled down at night the windows fogged over. The seats had very straight backs and when I awoke, many times during the night, I found myself on Oscar's shoulder or he on mine. Being shorter, it was easier for him to find a sleeping position. Every time I got comfortable, the conductor tapped me and said something in a stern voice. I finally understood that he was telling me to remove my legs from the aisle. The clicking of the wheels on the tracks reminded me of a ticking alarm clock one of my roommates had in the Country Boy's Home.

Yesterday morning, I awoke to the smell of garlic, onions, sausages and cigar smoke. At one end of the car, ladies were using the heating stove to cook breakfast. It made me so hungry I pulled from my carpetbag some bread and cheese I had bought before boarding on Friday. Along with the cooking smell was the noise of crying babies, children fighting and mothers apparently telling them to keep quiet. When the train made its first morning stop, a few passengers got off. Vendors ran aboard with all sorts of things for sale—bread, fruit, towels and even cheese.

As I sit here in the Chicago train station, I wish Oscar were still with me to help keep me awake. I don't want to miss the train to Racine. I am almost frightened to see how Marie is doing. Oh, how I wish Peder could be there to welcome me. How can life play such cruel tricks? Could these events really be in God's will? I know I have been taught not to question, but I can't help it.

Andreas' arrival in Racine was filled with mixed feelings. He was now in the town where his brother had spent an entire year. As he looked at the buildings, the fields, even the woods, he imagined where his brother had walked; what wooded lands he might have explored. Andreas told the drayman where the chest needed to be delivered. The drayman's smile suddenly became a frown as he shook his head, remembering the pastor's tragic death. Once the chest was loaded on the wagon, he gave Andreas directions to the parsonage. As the wagon left the station, Andreas stared at his cherished chest and was reminded again of his father's carpentry skills and his mother's artistic painting. He then began to walk the final leg of his journey.

It was not long before he was knocking on the parsonage door and Cousin Nils opened it. Just as they greeted each other, the drayman's wagon arrived. Having only his cherished ten-dollar gold piece, Andreas asked his cousin if he could lend him the 50 cents owed to the drayman.

Laughing, Nil's remarked, "I'll never let you live this down, coming all this way and not even having a half dollar for the drayman."

Marie hurried to the door and gave her brother-in-law a polite handshake and then a warm embrace. Andreas was relieved to see the smile on her face. He was surprised to see that she was pregnant. They went to the kitchen where the traveler was given a large cup of coffee. Fueled by a home-cooked dinner, the two cousins, Marie and her boarders talked late into the night.

The next morning, Marie was already making oatmeal as Andreas walked into the cozy kitchen. Handing him a cup of coffee, they both sat down at the table. Andreas filled her in on the family back home. Once the boarders had gone off to work, the two refilled their cups and retired to the small parlor. Marie began to tell Andreas just what had happened a few months earlier.

"On August 16th, Peder was healthy and fine. It was on Saturday that he began to feel sick. Thinking it was nothing serious, he continued to work on his sermon for the next day. A week later he was gone. He was so excited about becoming a father. I can tell you the rest later; I just can't face it now. I am so glad you are here. It means so much to me," she said as she left the room.

October 16, 1889
Dear Mother and Father,
I arrived safely in Racine. Cousin Nils greeted me at the door and loaned me the payment for the drayman. Marie then came running to me as fast as she could. I need to tell you that Marie is six months pregnant. She appears to have held up spiritually better than I expected. My plan is to find a local job while I learn English.

Eventually I will look for employment that allows me to pay my debts. While I am here I want to assist Marie as much as possible. The congregation and others are still feeding us on a daily basis. For now, you can write at this address. May God bless you.

Love, your son,
Andreas

JOURNAL October 27, 1889

Marie and I attended church today. Everyone greeted us warmly. With Nils, Marie and two other boarders from Oslo, I am surprised how I long for home. Although I don't soak my pillow with tears, it almost feels like my first weeks in Stavanger so many years ago. Today I received devastating news that I must record. This afternoon, as I was reading a local Norwegian newspaper, I heard noise in the kitchen. Knowing it was only Marie and I at home, I went to see what was happening. I found Marie between anger and sobbing. I quickly turned around to allow her to be alone when she turned and asked me to stay.

I was shocked to hear her words. She said the doctor had questioned the cause of Peder's death. No one else at the picnic had become ill. Marie sat at the end of the table and began to whisper, even though we were alone.

She grabbed my arm as if she wanted me to listen very carefully, and then told me the story. "Andreas, my friend Alma Hanson has confided in me that she believes Peder's death was caused in a different way than was reported. Alma told me that the young widow Peder had visited the week before his death had eyes for him. Alma had heard that I no longer wanted to stay in America. Andreas, nothing could have been further from the truth! I like living here; at least I did before all this happened. Peder felt called to this place. I had told the president of the Ladies Aid how much we enjoyed this community.

"Well, you know how everyone wants to feed the pastor? When Peder came home for dinner, he would often tell how much he had eaten that day. Sometimes he was too full to eat the dinner I had

prepared. Alma hinted that poison could have been added to the pie or coffee. Everyone in the congregation knew that the widow did not drink coffee and she certainly is far too thin to have ever even looked at a piece of pie. Peter got sick on the Saturday following his visit, but kept going, knowing he had to finish his sermon."

After hearing about what might have happened, Andreas pleaded, "Marie, we need to tell the sheriff; we must!"

Feeling both helpless and angry, he sat at the table with his hands on Marie's outstretched arms. Confused, and grief stricken, he began to wonder why he had come to this country. The silence was interrupted only by Marie's weeping. "As your brother-in-law, may I have permission to talk with the sheriff?"

"No! I don't want to involve you," Marie answered. "Anyway, the doctor has no proof, no proof at all. Thank you, Andreas, but it would do no good. By now it is too late. I must start to make our dinner now."

As he retreated to the hallway, he stopped, turned and said, "If I can be of any help, just ask. Whatever it might be, just ask."

"Thanks, Andreas. Your being here is a great help and comfort."

Later, in his room, Andreas sat on the bed, staring out of the window. He began to pound his mattress.

Chapter 12

Life in Racine

The front door opened. Nils and the other boarders had arrived home. After their talk, Marie had begged Andreas not to say a word about her suspicions. He promised, and yet he begged her to at least talk with the sheriff about her theory. She just shook her head and insisted it would make no difference. The sobs heard through the walls now had even more meaning. Andreas found it difficult to continue boarding with her. He knew she needed his presence and he had nowhere else to stay. They both admitted struggling with God's will.

Later that night, Marie confided that Peder's substantial debt was also heavy on her heart. She wondered where she was going to live once a new pastor arrived. Currently she relied on her boarders paying her $3.50 each week. Andreas had been successful at inquiring for loans for his own trip and offered to write to the lenders and ask if they could see it in their hearts to delay the pay back or even forgive Peder's debt. She took Andreas' hands, shook them both and then wrapped her arms around him while saying over and over again, "Would you really? Would you? Thank you, Andreas."

Journal October 28, 1889
Tomorrow Nils will introduce me to a shopkeeper who might hire me.

Just three months ago I looked forward to this adventure until, of course, we received the letter from Nils regarding Peder.

America seems to be changing everyone and everything. Oh, Nils confided in me that since coming to America he had changed the spelling of his name to Nels. I think he wants to make it sound more American.

October 29, 1889
Dear Mother, Father, Helga, Martha and Kristen,
I miss you!
I have now been in Racine for two weeks. Yesterday, I received a very warm welcome at church. A strange thing happened. A lady walked up to me and said I looked so much like Peder that I might as well be his ghost.

Nils, who now wants to be known as Nels, told me of a few possible jobs. Even with the current poor economy, there are positions available at three local companies: the Mitchell Farm Wagon Company, the Case Plow Works and the S.C. Johnson Company. The Johnson Company produces beautiful parquet floors. The work at the wagon company consists of taking pig iron from a railroad siding to the furnace. Thank goodness Nels advised me against that position. Without telling me, he went to a local mercantile to ask about a job for me. My lack of English could have been a drawback. When I arrived this morning at the mercantile, a kind Norwegian woman welcomed me. She paid her condolences. After introducing me to the owner, Mr. McKenzie, she acted as my interpreter. In the last several years, he said, Racine has become home to many Norwegians. They are more likely to trade here if we have some workers who speak Norwegian. And, he hired me on the spot!

My first job in America pays $3.00 a week. Until I learn English, I will be working in the back storeroom. When I told Marie that I would soon be able to pay rent, she said I would be her guest until Christmas. In the midst of her needs and sadness, she is so kind. My brother certainly chose the right wife.

I will write again soon.
Love,
Andreas

JOURNAL *November 10, 1889*
I have been working for a week and have a better understanding of what I am supposed to do. My main job is to mark prices on the merchandise in the back room. Without the pressure of paying

rent, I am able to send my first loan payment to the bank. I have sent five kroner to Mother and Father as a Christmas gift.

Although the land is flat as lefse, this town reminds me of Bergen and Stavanger. The population is over 20,000 souls. It sits on a very large lake with docks and ships.

My workmate is a fine young fellow, the son of a German Baptist minister. He is using every possible chance to teach me English. I am paying him back by teaching him penmanship, which I find easy, but he finds very difficult. I am fortunate to have had to write letters for Mother and Father throughout the years.

I continue to room with Nels. He and I share one bed while the two other boarders have another bed. It is getting colder than I had expected this early in the winter. I have read how bitterly cold it can be in this part of America.

We rise by 7 A.M. to eat Marie's hot breakfast. We walk quite a distance to Clark's Bazaar where we begin work at 8:30. At 9:00 sharp, Mr. McKenzie opens the door for the customers. The only thing uncomfortable about this job is when the owner complains under his breath about the lack of customers.

I still encourage Marie to talk with the sheriff about Peder's death but she insists her friend's story cannot be proven unless guilt brings a confession. Knowing that a crime could have been committed makes my nerves raw. I get impatient and angry. When I attend church, I look around wondering which lady might have killed my dear brother. Any worshipful mood is destroyed. Marie has not attended worship for the past few weeks. I don't have to wonder why. The Bethesda members have been wonderful to all of us; nonetheless this uncertainty of how Peder died causes an ongoing bitter taste.

December 26, 1889
Dear Mother, Father, Helga, Martha and Kristen,
As I write this I am still appreciating the kindness of Marie, the parishioners of the Bethesda church and the company of Nels and the other boarders. I am missing you very much, especially at this

time of year. I hope and pray you had a good Christmas. I remember Father beginning his preparations each year in October when he would butcher the sheep. With so many to feed here, we were not able to eat all the mutton we wanted. Even so, Marie, along with church members and neighbors, served a complete Christmas dinner. Did you light the traditional tallow candles? We relied on our kerosene lamps. People brought Marie food even for the Christmas Eve noon meal. I missed our tradition of Molje. From childhood on, I remember taking Mama's flatbread and dipping it in the fat from the boiling meat. Not having that treat made me feel very homesick. I felt better as I enjoyed Marie's rice pudding, of course not the same as Mother's, but delicious anyway. You will be happy to know we sang "Thy Little Ones, Dear Lord We Are" at the Christmas Eve service.

I am afraid that my hope to quickly raise enough money to escape debt and return home is not turning out as I planned. With the economic situation here, I make just enough to live. The good news is that because I have not had lodging expenses, I was able to make two payments to the bank. The bad news is that I will soon have to leave this house because a new pastor has been called. I am very sorry that I have not been able to help Marie with her expenses. She appreciates the letters I have been writing on her behalf regarding Peder's debts. Soon, we hope to hear about our request regarding forgiveness of the loans or at least an extension of credit. She wants to be faithful to her lenders but, with a child on the way and no immediate employment or home, she must conserve what money remains. She often reminds me that all is in the Lord's hands. Please keep us in your prayers.

Thank you for the woolen mittens you sent as a Christmas present. They are used daily. The winter temperatures here in Wisconsin are quite cold.

I pray for each of you and miss you very much. I hope the New Year treats you well.

Your son and brother,
Andreas

February 1, 1890
Dear Mother and Father,

I hope and pray you are well in this New Year. The Lord has begun to bless us richly as I begin with some good news. Marie gave birth to a lovely little girl on January 20. She named her Petra Marie. Pastor Tangjerd will baptize her on Sunday. I have been asked to be one of her sponsors.

As I told you, I wrote letters to those who had loaned Peder money for his education and trip to America. I can report that all but one has totally forgiven his debt, to Marie's great relief. We thank God for that kindness. I have also been able to pay Marie the boarder's fee during January.

Lately, my memories of the mission conference held in Fitjar when I was a child and Mother's interest and constant talk about mission has stirred within me a deep desire to attend seminary here in America before I return. The Lord must have heard all of your prayers, Mother.

I have talked about Pastor Dreyer as well as Pastor Tangjerd with both of you. I got to know them while I attended school in Stavanger. Pastor Tangjerd was one of Peder's closest friends. They all arrived in America around the same time. The two pastors live near the village of Harmony, Minnesota. Knowing of my work in Fitjar, they have graciously offered me a teaching position beginning next month. I have prayed about this opportunity and have accepted their offer. With the help of my mercantile workmate, my knowledge of English has increased. I will be leaving here Sunday, the 20th, following Petra's baptism. In Harmony I will be paid $20 a month. I will have free room and board.

Please greet Helga, Martha and Kristen when you see them. I will write again when I have settled in Harmony.

Love, your son,
Andreas

Chapter 13

Love in Harmony

February 21, 1890
Dear Mother and Father,
    *I am very happy to finally arrive in Harmony and wanted you to
know my address. Your letters are very dear to me and I keep them
in the wooden chest. The celebration of Petra Marie's baptism was
wonderful. It was good having someone I had known from home,
and who was a close friend of Peder, to perform the baptism. After
the service and dinner in the church parlor, it was time to set out for
Harmony. I bid farewell to Marie and her boarders. Nels accompanied me to the train station. He reminded me that this time I did
not have to ask him for a loan to pay the drayman! I do not think he
will ever let me forget it. Here in Harmony I was warmly greeted by
Pastor Dreyer. He and his wife live just outside of the village. He is a
short man with a full beard and neatly dressed.*
    *We loaded the chest and carpetbag in Pastor Dreyer's wagon
and the two of us rode the few miles to his house. His wife, Nellie,
warmly welcomed me, offered me coffee and showed me the room in
which I was to stay. I have a week to get acquainted before I begin
teaching.*
    *The parsonage is quite a splendid home. A square brick structure
with a door and four massive windows on the front. It sits next to a
grove of trees with outbuildings on the side. When I commented on
its beauty, Rev. Dreyer, whose first name also is Peder, told me the
brick came from a nearby kiln owned by a member of his church. I
look forward to seeing the church tomorrow. I have appreciated their
hospitality.*
    Your loving son,
    Andreas

Andreas awoke the next morning to the smell of coffee, bacon and eggs. As they sat at the table, Pastor Dreyer began breakfast with a lengthy prayer. By the middle of the day their new boarder wondered if the pastor talked more with God than he did with anyone else. While the clergyman read throughout the day, his wife talked to Andreas as if starved for conversation.

Following supper, Pastor Dreyer finally began to visit with the new young teacher. He shared his deep concern for his congregation's spiritual welfare. Often quoting scripture, the pastor shared his fear that his congregants were not taking faith as seriously as they should.

To change the subject and learn more about the Dreyers, Andreas asked how they had come to this country. Pastor Dreyer told of his call as a theological candidate. Although the church of Norway did not want to lose pastors in which they had a great investment, the Bishop of the Nidaros Cathedral in Trondheim had allowed a temporary call to America, and particularly to Harmony, which needed a Norwegian clergyman.

Pastor Dreyer had been ordained by Rev. P. A. Rasmussen at Lisbon, Illinois, and had begun his work in September of 1887. Having served now for a little more than two years, Pastor Dreyer believed he knew the spiritual needs of his people. He was very proud that the Sunday school was already 15 years old and the parochial school, in which Andreas would teach, was ready to celebrate its 25th anniversary. Although doctrinal fights had abounded in some of the local churches, Pastor Dreyer had been able to keep his congregation free of splitting. That was also true of the two other parishes charged to him—Henrytown and Fremont.

The pastor ended his one-sided conversation by saying, "Andreas, you are being paid well. Just 15 years ago the teachers were getting $10 a month."

The next day a blanket of snow greeted the three of them as they sat down for a bowl of oatmeal and a cup of coffee. Since the pastor was taking the wagon to town, he offered Andreas a ride in order that he might get to know some of the residents. All the way to town, Pastor Dreyer talked about how modern the little village was becoming. When they arrived, Andreas was not disappointed. Certainly not like the cities of Bergen or Stavanger, this rural town was growing rapidly. Instead of a path in front of each storefront, as in Racine, there was a boardwalk. Each doorway had a metal bar on which to scrape snow or mud from shoes and boots. While the pastor met with some of his more active members, the new teacher took time to introduce himself to a few shopkeepers along the street.

Andreas walked into the Harmony Cash Store and held out his hand to the gentleman behind the counter. "I'm Andreas Helland, the new parochial teacher."

"Welcome. I am Richard Hanson, the owner of this establishment." With a kind smile and soft voice he added, "If you need anything, I probably have it in stock. If not, I will order it for you." Following a short, friendly conversation, Andreas excused himself and walked on.

He hadn't gone far when a man stopped him and asked, "And who are you?"

"I am Andreas Helland, the new parochial school teacher."

"Welcome! I'm Kenneth Olson. I run the drug store." Shaking hands, the pharmacist pointed toward his store. He continued to inform the teacher that his two sons would be in Andreas' classroom. After speaking kindly of Pastor Dreyer's sermons, Mr. Olson shared his concern for the morals of the community. He told the story of two young men who had tried to establish a tavern in town. The community had driven them and their business right out of town.

"We have no need for that kind of sin in Harmony!" he declared, his pride spreading across his face as if he was the authority on the matter.

As he walked along further, Andreas met Mr. Jones. Dressed informally, he said he was the local drayman who had arrived a year earlier from Wales. Upon hearing that Andreas was lodging with the Dreyers, the man's expression changed to one of pity.

Putting his hand up to his mouth he quietly confided, "I don't like the way the preacher constantly hounds me about my need to attend his church. I certainly hope you are a churchgoer or you will not last long in that house."

Andreas felt a bit uneasy walking into the next shop, the millinery store. As he entered, a lady came from behind the counter as if to inspect him. She looked up and down at the newcomer and bluntly asked, "Are you new around here?"

"Yes, I am Andreas Helland. I'm the new parochial school teacher."

"I am Mrs. Anderson. Welcome to Harmony," she said eagerly. "I hope you have brought a wife who will need one of my fine pieces of fashion."

"I am afraid not. I am not married as of yet, Mrs. Anderson."

"Well, I am sure you will be very soon. We have quite a good crop of young ladies right here in Harmony."

Not understanding every word she spoke, he waited for her to pause. She moved into a rapid monologue. Tipping his hat, he simply said, "It was nice to meet you, Mrs. Anderson." He turned and walked out the door.

Once back on the boardwalk, the young teacher noticed the buildings looked brand new compared to those he remembered in Norway that had been built decades if not centuries earlier.

He noticed yet another mercantile. "Imagine, two in one small town," he thought. He was proud to be able to read the sign hanging above the wooden door, "Ralph Harris Dry Goods." Pastor Dreyer's wagon was parked in front of the store. The pastor introduced Andreas to Mr. Harris, who was also new to the community. As they shook hands Andreas said, "I saw your announcement in the Preston Courier."

"We call it an advertisement," Mr. Harris commented.

"Ah, yes, I have much to learn," Andreas said.

"You are doing very well," the pastor reassured him.

Mr. Harris delighted in showing them his newest wares. As they moved toward the door, they heard, "Just remember, I have much more merchandise than Mr. Hanson down the street. Be sure to come back."

On the wagon ride home, Andreas began to list the people he had met. After each name, Pastor Dreyer commented about their church attendance or lack of it. Mr. Hanson and Mrs. Anderson were the most faithful in attendance and, along with the Rockne family, possibly the only ones who could count themselves saved. When Andreas mentioned "Mr. Jones," there was silence and then the pastor's comment that Jones was not to be trusted.

As they neared the parsonage, Andreas realized that his quiet host had not used a single English word in their conversation. Although he felt comfortable using his own language, Andreas wanted to become fluent in English.

After lunch, Pastor Dreyer invited Andreas into his study to show him his most prized possession, his library, much of which he had brought from Norway. Seeing the books brought back memories of Stavanger and Pastor Oftedal's elegant office. The pastor pulled from the shelf his most valued book, a study of the Psalms, written by Oftedal himself, that generous pastor who five years earlier had awarded Andreas a scholarship in Stavanger. The memories of his years in Stavanger flooded back like a river making its way to the fjord. It was as if he held a piece of home and immediately felt the pangs that went along with missing his family, friends and all that he had known in the first 19 years of life. The pastor invited the young man to use the afternoon to read. Looking around, Andreas saw books on prayer written by Bishop Laache, the person responsible for Pastor Dreyer's call to America.

This Sunday the pastor would hold service at the Greenfield Lutheran Church near Harmony. They would not have to be traveling so far for worship. Andreas spent the afternoon carefully rereading Rev. Oftedal's commentary on Psalms.

Although Andreas had seen the outside of the church in Harmony earlier in the week, on Sunday he was able to take in the beauty of the wonderful interior of the building. As he waited for the service to begin, Andreas remembered that in Fitjar, many people came to church by boat. In Harmony, they came from far and near by horse and wagon. Some drove eight to nine miles to attend worship. Since the service was only a monthly event, it lasted for nearly three hours, with the pastor preaching for well over an hour. They began with a hymn, followed by catechism, with children sitting on the floor in front of the first row of pews. The adults sat and waited, appreciating the interest the pastor had for their children.

Andreas felt right at home since the entire service was in Norwegian. He was a little surprised when the pastor introduced him as the new teacher of the parochial school. The one-month session for this location was to begin the very next day.

Since most of the children lived close to the church, the instruction took place in its basement. The building lacked adequate heat and both the teacher and the 12 students wore their coats most of the day. They spent their time with reading, arithmetic, penmanship, geography and a Bible lesson. The day began and ended with prayer. For many of the students, this month-long schooling in Norwegian was an addition to the fall and spring terms in the local public school.

As the month came to an end, Andreas had grown accustomed to Mrs. Dreyer's warm conversations and her husband's quiet and serious nature. As Andreas had noted on his first day, most of the pastor's conversation was with God rather than with his wife or the boarder. Even the wagon ride into Greenfield Lutheran Church was only rarely punctuated with any kind of conversation. Andreas was disappointed about Pastor Dreyer's constant use of his mother tongue and his reluctance to speak English. The only weakness Pastor Dreyer admitted was his difficulty learning the English language. So, during this first month in Harmony, the young immigrant was not able to use his English as he had greatly hoped.

It would soon be time for the itinerant young teacher to move to his next location for another month of parochial classes. He accompanied Pastor Dreyer to a pastoral meeting in a small church just a mile south of the Minnesota-Iowa border. On the way, the pastor pointed out the Rockne home where Andreas would be staying beginning the next Sunday. Pastor Dreyer's usual concern for the spiritual life of many of his families was not voiced when he discussed the Rocknes. "The Rockne family is certainly among the faithful, holding steadfast to the saving arms of God. Possibly one of the few families I can say that about," he added.

After passing the two-story wooden home, they could see the small square schoolhouse in which Andreas would teach. As they traveled south, he wondered what kind of family he would encounter on Sunday.

The day arrived and after Sunday service in the Fremont church, the Dreyers took Andreas to his new home at the Rockne farm. The Rocknes welcomed him with coffee and flatbread smothered with their own rich butter, served up in the parlor. This was a palace compared to the typical farmhouse in Fitjar. The centerpiece of the parlor was the stone fireplace with a hand-carved oak mantel. The rocks had come from the surrounding fields. A bentwood rocker sat in front of the fireplace. The windows were framed with silk draperies. The home was built totally of local lumber, complete with a front porch. Standing to peer out through the window, Andreas noticed the light-green leaves forming on the oak tree that separated the farm from the schoolhouse.

Supper was a typical Sunday night meal of cheese and bread. While they ate, Andreas was busy trying to learn the names of the family members. Five-year-old John sat between eight-year-old Amelia and thirteen-year-old Emma.

The Rockne children were quiet in the presence of their new teacher. Clara, their eldest was nearing adulthood at nineteen. Mrs. Rockne, who quickly informed her guest to call her Anna, sat at the end of the table near the kitchen door. Her husband, Mikkel, assisted Aunt Bertha, Anna's disabled sister, to her customary place at the table. Under Mikkel's graying beard, was a stern face, and yet his voice was kind.

Anna and Mikkel asked about Andreas' home and family in Norway. He did his best to supply answers, but it was not easy with the beautiful Clara at the table. It was during this first meal that Mother Rockne told him she had been born in Stavanger. With a sheepish grin and a humble voice, he admitted that he had attended the Cathedral School there. She beamed with pleasure, reminding her husband that the Cathedral School was one of the finest preparatory schools in all of Norway. As she talked about Stavanger, a wistful glow shown on her face.

The pretty daughter, Clara, sat next to her mother, giving Andreas the added benefit of seeing her frequent smiles while he conversed with Anna. Later in his room, the appreciative young man thought of how wonderful the coming month would be and wondered if it could be extended in any way.

April 21, 1890
Dear Mother and Father,
Since I last wrote I have finished my month with Pastor Dreyer,
whom you know I had been acquainted with back home. Certainly
his kind wife was very cordial. He seemed quite serious about his
mission and disappointed in his parishioners' spiritual growth.

It was good to use some of his private library, especially books
whose authors I knew from home. I enjoyed Pastor Oftedal's com-
mentary on the Psalms again and Bishop Laache's books on prayer.

I visited the three congregations Pastor Dreyer serves and have
now arrived at my second parochial teaching site where I have
completed my first week. I am just south of the village of Harmony,
living with the Rockne family. Mrs. Rockne, a good-hearted lady,
was born in Stavanger and has great respect for the Cathedral
School. Mr. Rockne is a successful farmer with a beautiful new
two-story wooden home. Once again, I have my own bedroom as
I did at the Dreyer's home.

Mrs. Rockne's sister, Bertha, disabled from birth, also lives with
them. I have already noticed how hard she works mending the
clothes and whatever else she is able to do while remaining seated.
She is a generous woman with a strong faith.

The Rocknes have four children: five-year-old John, eight-year-
old Amelia, thirteen-year-old Emma, and finally nineteen-year-old
Clara, the shining star of the family. Amelia and Emma are in
my class. I have learned much about this family as we visit in the
evening.

With my monthly salary and no board and room expenses, I will
be able to pay on my loans and save additional money. Even if I
attend Augsburg Seminary while here, I still hope to be home in just
a few years. I miss you all very much.

I have heard from Marie just once since settling here, but hope to
see her when I have a school break. I continue to pray for her and
all of you. I hope this letter finds you well.

Love, your son,
Andreas

JOURNAL April 30, 1890

*I am not so much confused as I am surprised at what is hap-
pening to me in my time at the Rockne's. I'm finding that if I write
something down it helps to clear my mind. I have enjoyed the din-
ners very much and especially the company of Clara. In the past,
I have admired ladies from afar and have only really heard talk
about them while living in the Country Boy's Home in Stavanger.
Then I just listened and was surprised by those frank conversations.
None of this was ever talked about in my home and, since I have
spent so little time with my brothers over the years, we, too, have
never touched on the subject. Since the very first time I met Clara
I had an urging I have hardly felt before, except in a dream. Come
to think of it, in the past month I have felt as if I have been stuck
in a dream with Clara as the main figure. All I can say is that she
is a beautiful and kind person. I would like to spend more time
with her but sadly I have only a week left.*

*I am feeling a much stronger calling to the seminary. My heart stirs
as I worship and also when I read scripture. Pastor Dreyer has encouraged me to write to Professor Sverdrup at Augsburg Seminary. I will
do that very soon. I must focus now on the 12 students I am teaching.
Most are well behaved, especially the Rockne children—Emma and
Amelia. Olaf, an 11-year-old, is the real rascal. He likes to be called
Ollie. When I am not looking or am helping another student, he likes
to roll marbles on the floor. His reddish hair and behavior reminds me
a great deal of Gunnar at the Country Boy's Home.*

Andreas was delighted to spend May with the Rocknes while
awaiting his next assignment west of Harmony. Mr. Rockne was
done planting and had a bit more time to visit with their guest.
He shared that his wife had come from a very pious family. Anna's
parents had emigrated in 1848. They settled in the Norwegian community of Muskego in Wisconsin. They eventually made their way
to a community called Big Canoe. Anna told Andreas that they
would travel six days a week. Her parents insisted that Sunday was
reserved strictly for worship. Her father, Amund, would lead them

in prayers and hymns and then would read from a sermon book he had purchased. Every time the pious Amund encountered a stranger he would ask, "Are you saved? What is your relationship with Jesus?" Such interrogation often caused all sorts of trouble including a downright brawl with one man. Shaking his head as he continued the story, Mr. Rockne said, "So, trusting in God's power, when Anna's brother was bitten by a rattle snake her father relied only on prayer to heal him. Thank goodness," Mr. Rockne continued, "Anna's mother insisted they see a doctor, and none too soon," he said emphatically.

Andreas thought to himself, "In some ways, my Clara is like her mother, Anna, and my grandmother. She has a devout faith and a great trust in God."

No one had to convince Andreas of Clara's qualities. He had already been swept off his feet for the very first time in his life.

The final weeks at the Rockne home passed quickly. On the last day, the Rocknes complimented Andreas on his excellent job, and hoped he would return again next year. His long-range plans were going to take him to Minneapolis, a city he had only heard about.

The next month took Andreas to still another parochial school a few miles from Harmony. Again he was fortunate to be housed by one family for the entire four weeks. Similar to a log cabin, their house had both an outside and inside wall. On many a night, Andreas was kept awake listening to some critter busily chewing its way in the wall. Waking up, he would check the floor to see that he was not about to step on some rodent.

Nellie and Jon Olson, Andreas' hosts, had two school-age children—Andrew, who was ten, and his wisp of a sister, Margaret, who was just eight and the size of a six-year old. The two of them joined 14 other children in the school. Classes were shortened to allow time for the students to help their parents with chores. They would begin at 9 A.M. with prayer and Bible reading and then go on with other studies until the 2 P.M. dismissal. This gave Andreas plenty of time to prepare for the next day.

When he returned to the small, well-kept house at four o'clock, Nellie was ready with coffee and some home-baked treat for the seemingly famished teacher. At 19, it was as if Andreas was going through another growth spurt, eating a healthy breakfast, a cheese sandwich for lunch, the afternoon coffee and finally a good dinner after the family chores. Although he offered to help Jon, his host limited the teacher's activities to milking their cow and fixing fences.

One afternoon, the lone cow wandered far down the valley below the Olson land. Sent to find it, Andreas searched and searched until he saw a large figure behind a grove of trees. Expecting to discover the spotted Holstein on the other side of a large bush, to his surprise there stood a bull. It was not at all pleased at being discovered. Slowly and carefully, the schoolteacher backed up, looking the bull in the eyes. As the massive animal pounded on the ground and lowered his head, Andreas turned around and ran, searching for a tree to climb. Not far from the point of encounter, Andreas found an evergreen with limbs low enough to climb. The bull quickly followed. It came to a stop just under the tree, sniffing the air, then munching on the grass for what seemed like an eternity.

The bull lumbered away when Jon Olson came over the hill looking for both his guest and his cow. Seeing Andreas in the tree, Jon began to laugh. He wondered if the teacher had ever really lived on a farm. With the bull out of the way, Andreas climbed down and the two of them walked home to find that the cow had returned. That episode was not only the talk of the supper table but also the topic of conversation the next morning at school. Andreas admitted to his audience that this certainly had not been the only time he was challenged by an angry bull.

JOURNAL July 15, 1890

Tomorrow I will be leaving the Olson's and will have a month off before I begin teaching another parochial session. I am getting more comfortable keeping the children's attention and maintaining discipline. Although I have enjoyed this setting and the Olsons have been very kind, I am missing more and more each day the company of Clara Rockne. I look forward to spending the next month at Pastor Dreyer's and being closer to Clara. I will at least be able to see her on Sundays at service. I have never felt anything like this for anyone. While staying at the Dreyer's, I hope to hear from Augsburg Seminary regarding my future plans.

August 1, 1890
Dear Mother, Father and Family,
I know I have not written in a while but was waiting for news about the future. I am pleased to tell you that I have been accepted to Augsburg Seminary in Minneapolis. I will leave this community at the end of September or early October. My heart was warmed when I read President Sverdrup's words to me, "It appears to me that the Lord has led you so far with a merciful hand. He will surely not forsake you in the future." I must hold those words in my heart since I do not know how I will pay for this next step. I did ask to be considered for a teaching position in the preparatory department, but in good conscience, President Sverdrup could not promise a position because this would depend upon the outcome of the union convention and whether or not he remained as president of the seminary.

This means that I will not be returning home as quickly as I had first wished. I know that you understand that when God calls, we must answer. The stirring of my spirit began a number of years ago when we hosted the annual mission conference at Fitjar. What fond memories I have of that time. I remember helping Father build the stage and podium, and then speaking from it in order to find out how far a voice would carry. As we sat on the hillside, I still remember being inspired by the wonderful speakers.

I will not be able to save as much money as I thought since I have a month now without teaching. Thankfully, the Dreyers insist on not charging me for board while I stay with them between my teaching assignments.

During the middle of June, a layman, Arne Kirkeli, invited me to attend the union convention of three Lutheran groups— the Conference, the Norwegian Augustana Synod and the Anti-Missourian Brotherhood. It was held 25 miles east of Harmony at Highland Prairie. They held separate meetings and then came together for a joint gathering. The most blessed event was the com-missioning of a young pastor by the name of Ronning who had been called as a foreign missionary to China. His fiery words of farewell are still burning within my heart.

Pastor Dreyer asked me to return to Harmony to preach on June 15. I must admit that I was thoroughly dissatisfied with my sermon and, watching the faces of the worshipers, I do not think they were edified in any way.

As is true with the children I have taught, there was a common, strange mixture of Norwegian and English used during this conven-tion. Some of the English I was able to understand. The mixing of the two languages sounded at times quite amusing and even ridiculous. There was more than once that I had to cover my mouth to hold back a laugh.

The children here are a mixture of well-behaved, obedient souls and some others who seem not to be disciplined at home. My experi-ence during May was quite difficult with children bringing frogs in their pockets and letting them out during our opening prayer or at other times of serious study. I sometimes wonder if, for some, manners and discipline were left on the other side of the Atlantic. The worst case was when I opened the drawer of my desk to find a garden snake curled up on my papers. I quickly closed the drawer and asked for the guilty party to raise his hand. Everyone looked down with smiles on their faces, but no one admitted to the crime.

I will be teaching one more session near Harmony this month, spending September with the Dreyers and then I am off to Minneapolis.

I feel as if I have been living out of my wooden chest since I left you. I do look forward to spending time in one place once I arrive at Augsburg Seminary.

My hosts have been very kind and I have had the opportunity to help them at times with their chores. These activities certainly remind me of home.

I miss all of you and send my love. I hope and pray you are all well.
Your son,
Andreas

JOURNAL September 30, 1890

Now that I am finished with my teaching assignment, I finally have time to read, pray and think about the future. The Dreyer's parsonage is a wonderful place for this, since the pastor spends most of his time either making visits or studying. If he is on a visit, his wife and I have a good conversation over a cup of tea or coffee. She is a most gracious woman.

I have taken the liberty of asking Clara if I might write her once I leave this area. With a warm smile on her face, she said, "Please do." I now plan on taking the morning train from Harmony on October 4th. Once I say farewell to this community, I know I will feel both excited and heavy hearted, knowing it will be some time before I see Clara again.

Pastor Dreyer, his wife and Andreas took the buggy just a few miles west of town on Friday evening, October 3rd, for the annual harvest festival. The street was filled with people as early as 6 P.M. Thanking the Dreyers for the ride, Andreas made his way through a crowd of children he had taught during the summer. The children were on their best behavior, remembering to tip their hat or curtsy as they greeted him.

At the end of the first block he saw the entire Rockne family walking toward him. Clara's smile was a welcome sight as he thought of his train trip the next day. He greeted Mrs. Rockne, smiled and nodded to Mr. Rockne and shook Clara's hand. His feelings for her swirled inside of him like a hurricane. Wishing they could be alone but knowing that was impossible, Andreas simply joined the entire family as they strolled past the stores. Standing next to Clara every minute he could, the infatuated young man made his leave only when Pastor Dreyer said it was time to return to the parsonage. The only hope he felt was the promise they would both write to each other.

The next morning, on October 4th, Andreas boarded the morning train for Minneapolis. To his amazement, there stood Clara. The family had come to town on an errand. They shook hands, and he boarded the train. He hoped this was not to be his last visit to the little southeastern Minnesota village.

Postcard from the town of Fitjar on the island of Stord, in Norway.

Bertha Helland, mother of Andreas.

Graduation from the university in Oslo in 1889.

Andreas married Clara Rockne in 1893 in Harmony, Minnesota.

Clara, Petra, Melvin and Andreas.

The Helland children: Bernhard, Melvin and Petra.

Andreas married Helen Anderson in Owatonna, Minnesota, in 1905.

The Hellend Family in 1918. Left to right: Petra, Helen, Bernhard,
Beatrice, Winifred, Irene, Melvin, Maurice and Andreas.

Professor Andreas Helland, Augsburg College.

Andreas married Anna Sather in 1921, with flower girl
Winifred.

The younger Helland children, from left to right. First row: Winifred and Maurice. Back row: Beatrice and Irene.

Forest Lake, near Lake Minnetonka.

The cabin at Forest Lake.

Andreas and Anna in their cabin.

The fireplace at Forest Lake, built by Andreas.

Relaxing after church in Minneapolis—
Bernhard, Andreas and Maurice.

Andreas teaching New Testament at Augsburg College.

Andreas typing letters to his missionary children.

The Helland Family in 1941, left to right: Maurice, Andreas, Beatrice, Petra, Bernhard, Winifred, Anna, Irene and Melvin.

Chapter 14

Minneapolis Bound

Andreas stared out of the train window, waving as long as Clara could still be seen. The chug of the steam engine and the click of the steel wheels underlined his pain of separation from a young lady for whom he had grown so fond. As he watched the once-green fields turning brown, and stands of trees going yellow and red, he thought how far he had come in the past 12 months. In his mind he scrolled through the journey, from the island community of Fitjar, across the endless Atlantic, to the smells of meals cooking while aboard his first train. He recalled the exhaustion, loneliness and fear that gripped him while sitting alone in the Chicago depot, and the anxiety of seeing Marie without Peder at her side. As he tried to concentrate on what was ahead, he was comforted by the image of his beautiful Clara who had brought a new kind of love to his life.

Before long, the train stopped in the small city of Rochester, Minnesota. Watching the slow steady line of passengers coming down the aisle, he noticed a young man seemingly looking for someone.

Andreas, raised his hand and asked, "Are you by chance an Augsburg student?"

The young man smiled and said, "I am Oscar Anderson."

"Have a seat." Andreas said, "I believe we are roommates." Looking much younger than Andreas, the other young man explained that he was to begin his second year in the preparatory school. Oscar took his seat, shaking Andreas' hand again. Oscar added, "I am coming late since I needed to help a neighbor with the harvest."

"And I had to finish teaching parochial school," Andreas explained.

Andreas wondered to himself, "Is this boy old enough to work at harvesting? He looks like I did when I began school in Stavanger." While the only other noise was that of people getting settled, Andreas thought there could be some mix up in dorm assignments.

The train left the Rochester depot, making its way past a new multi-story brick building known as St. Mary's Hospital. With a childlike excitement in his voice, proudly Oscar told his new acquaintance of the doctors by the name of Mayo who, along with some Roman Catholic sisters, were establishing the hospital. His story continued with tales of a tornado that had leveled the town a few years earlier.

As Oscar told his roommate about his previous year at Augsburg Prep School, Andreas began to wonder if he was returning to the antics of his school years in Stavanger rather than a place of serious seminary education. Miles passed and Andreas found himself silenced by the melancholy thought of missing Harmony and someone who had so quickly become the love of his life. Between long moments of silence, the two were able to share something about their families—Oscar's love for baseball and Andreas' love of fishing.

Oscar seemed excited to talk with someone who had come from the country his parents had always talked about. His father was a mercantile owner in a little town just west of Rochester, a farming community known as Byron. As Andreas told Oscar about Fitjar, he realized how distant he felt from that life, having spent so little time on the farm or, for that matter, with his family since his departure for the Cathedral School five years earlier.

As the train slowly pulled into the large, steel Milwaukee Road Station, Oscar excitedly pointed in the direction of their final destination. Already knowing the procedure, the young preparatory student confidently told older Andreas that the school's own drayman would take care of their luggage. Andreas smiled as he thought of his experience in Racine. The smile grew as he admitted to himself that it was his own refusal to break his ten-dollar gold piece that forced his cousin to pay the Racine drayman.

Oscar stepped on the seat to reach his luggage over head and began exiting the train. Behind him, Andreas retrieved his carpetbag and followed. Steam seemed to be escaping from under the carriage and enveloped them as if they were in the midst of a morning fog. As Oscar pointed the way, they began to walk down a wide thoroughfare called Washington Avenue. Andreas' melancholy began to fade, replaced with an excitement about his next adventure. Crossing Cedar Avenue, Oscar saw the used furniture store, a destination for the necessary furnishings for their dorm room.

Finding the room to which they had been assigned, Andreas and Oscar were surprised to see it already occupied. Two tall, serious-looking theology students were busy unloading their suitcases.

"If you think this is your room, you've got it wrong," said one in a gravelly voice. The taller student, sporting a full beard, nodded in agreement. They declared that the room had been theirs the previous year and they intended to occupy it this coming year, no matter what anyone else might say. They pointed to the room across the hall, which appeared to be vacant. It had good advantages, they said, like facing Murphy Park and looking east to the rising sun. Surprisingly, even Oscar was not buying their campaign.

He countered, "But, as the sun is rising we are in class and would much rather enjoy the setting sun on the west side. I have a letter informing me of my room assignment and I do not want to go against the administration."

Andreas quickly realized his young roommate could easily become a debater. Both Andreas and Oscar raised their hands as if to say, "We will work this out," and went on to find a janitor. Knowing the two seminary students from the previous year, the janitor simply suggested the two take the other room. Andreas' stubbornness kicked in. "The room the two fine men are occupying is the room the president has assigned to us and I intend to abide by his instruction."

The janitor raised his hands in frustration and answered, "Well, what can I do?"

"Would you please see the president for us, so we can get this issue resolved?" Andreas pleaded impatiently.

Throwing up his arms and sweating from the unusually warm autumn day, the janitor agreed to intervene. When he returned, with head held low, he went immediately to the older seminarians and whispered, "Maybe you had better move across the hall anyway."

Not at all happy, the two used words not befitting seminary students. "It will take us some time to get this &#%! furniture and our belongings moved, so do not plan on settling yourselves until late tonight."

They defiantly refused Oscar and Andreas' offer to help them move.

Andreas and Oscar retraced their steps as they made their way back to the used furniture store on Cedar Avenue. Andreas became angry and told his young roommate how disappointed he was with the unfriendly welcome to Augsburg. Greeted by a kind, elderly gentleman, Andreas cooled down and went about choosing his furniture. In seminary storage, Oscar had a bed and mattress, chair and small table from the previous year. Andreas chose similar furniture and was encouraged when the elderly store owner told him everything could be delivered in just a few hours.

By the time they returned to the basement of North Hall, supper was being served. Although everyone had an assigned seat, to Andreas' relief no one was fighting over places at the table. He sat with other boarding students who were known as the Jacobines' Club, a reference to the worst radicals of the French Revolution. Before Andreas could take his first bite, the student next to him pointedly asked him about his past with question after question. It felt more like an interrogation than the welcome he expected.

Once they climbed the stairs to their assigned hallway, both Oscar and Andreas were relieved to see their baggage had been delivered. They moved Oscar's furniture from storage. As promised, Andreas' furniture had been delivered to the back entrance of the dormitory. Not caring much for the way the first few hours of Augsburg life had gone, they quietly moved every piece of furniture and baggage with no offer of help. It was after midnight when their furniture was finally in place.

The next morning the roommates awoke to the sound of city church bells, ringing in the Sabbath. After a hurried breakfast, Andreas followed his young roommate a few blocks off campus to Trinity Lutheran Church, the "Mother Church" of Augsburg. Trinity was commonly referred to as "Gjersten's Church," after its preacher, who was known for his eloquent sermons. This Sunday afternoon was the last chance for Oscar and Andreas to spend free time without assignments hanging over their heads. The unseasonably warm autumn was another reason for them to enjoy the day. They walked along the Mississippi River bank, chatting and enjoying the rich colors of the changing leaves.

Arriving as they had, two weeks into the semester, the two of them had a lot of catching up to do. First thing Monday morning, Andreas presented himself to the president, Rev. Georg Sverdrup. As he knocked on the office door, he thought of his first visit to Pastor Oftedal's office in Stavanger as a nervous 14-year-old. Now six years older, some of those feelings returned.

"Come in," the president called in a deep, confident voice.

Standing in the open doorway, the young man introduced himself. "Professor Sverdrup, I am Andreas Helland."

"Oh, yes, you have finally arrived," said the older man, a smile crossing his face.

"I was delayed while teaching parochial school in the Harmony area," Andreas explained.

"Yes, yes, that will do. Welcome. I was told there was a rooming problem. Has that been settled? Last spring those boys had asked for another room, but failed to tell us when they changed their minds. I thought I would have to come over and settle the dispute," he explained, shaking his head.

"It all worked out just fine. I actually met you when I was a student in Stavanger, perhaps four or five years ago," Andreas said.

"Oh, yes, I was visiting there in '86. That must have been the time," the professor answered.

"I am wondering if you could give me a list of texts I will need to purchase as I begin class," Andreas inquired.

The professor bit his lip, looked up at the new student and with a serious tone replied, "Yes, I will give you some titles but I must remind you that our primary text is God's own Word. These other books are secondary. I know from your application that you have just finished Latin School at the university. No doubt you are used to many scholarly textbooks but, let me say it again, our primary text is God's Word, and God's Word alone."

"Yes, sir; thank you, sir."

Professor Sverdrup ended the conversation by instructing Andreas where his class was meeting. Andreas gathered up his Bible and writing tools and joined the class being taught by Professor Sven Oftedal.

During the rest of the day, Andreas acquainted himself with the campus buildings, the community around them and with his fellow students.

The next day, Andreas received a note asking him to visit the president's office. The young student wondered what kind of trouble he might have already gotten himself into. But, once in Sverdrup's office, the president kindly offered him the position of teaching history to the preparatory class. The pay of 50 cents per week certainly helped toward his weekly room and board cost of $1.19.

As fall turned into winter, Oscar's health began to deteriorate and he spent many a night coughing. When he was advised to see a doctor, Oscar feared not only the doctor but also the possible diagnosis. Finally Andreas convinced him to visit the Riverside Clinic, which stood on a small, triangular lot facing Riverside Avenue. Andreas accompanied him and rejoiced in the positive news that this was a lung infection that could be treated.

The dormitory was the setting for serious theological debates almost every evening in one room or another. As many as 72 seminary students were in attendance, representing three different Lutheran groups. One group, "the Conference," was a collective body of individual churches. The Conference operated other seminaries, Augsburg being its oldest. Other Augsburg students came from the small "Norwegian Augustana Synod" while still others made their way to Augsburg from the "Anti-Missourian Brotherhood." Each group of students had their own professors. A few, like Andreas, had come from other traditions or other countries. As his seminary experience continued, he aligned himself with the Conference students.

Professor Oftedal, a relative of Andreas' kind benefactor back in Stavanger, was one of his favorite professors. He used the examination method of teaching, constantly asking questions and expecting answers that came from either the Bible or the text. Often, Andreas would couch his answers with, "I should think" or "it is my opinion." After hearing these responses once too often, the professor waved his Bible in the air, exclaiming loudly, "Your opinion is of no importance! What does the book say? We are finished for today."

There was dead silence as Oftedal picked up his papers and walked briskly out of the classroom.

Upon disagreeing with other professors, Andreas would whisper to himself, "I guess I'm still a heretic." He told his classmates that the "rogue" that had been judged to possess him in Stavanger must have finally broken loose and made its way to the surface.

Not every hour was filled with serious theological thought or debate. Without a professor in the classroom, a heavily built student was making his way across the room, carefully walking on each of the wooden chairs. When he came upon Andreas, Andreas gave a gentle pull on the other student's trouser legs. Surprised, the student fell forward toward the rest of the chairs, making a terrible noise. Just as he was getting up from the floor, Professor Sverdrup opened the door, looked at Andreas and said, "Will you please come down with me to the office?"

As he followed the professor, he thought, "What will I do now if I am dismissed from Augsburg?" Feeling both fear and shame, he meekly followed Sverdrup to his office.

The professor took his place behind the desk and, with a voice of authority, asked Andreas to be seated. To the student's utter amazement, rather than asking for an accounting of his behavior, Sverdrup asked, "Helland, would you undertake to teach church history to our deaconesses one hour a week? There is no money in it but I believe they will pay your streetcar fare."

A surprised Andreas answered, "It would be my honor. I would be happy to do that."

Back at the dorm, students were gathered at his door anxious to hear about his punishment. With a smile and an air of nonchalance, he explained, "Oh, he has asked me to teach church history to the deaconesses."

Some students walked away muttering to one another, "I don't believe him. Do you?"

Called again to the president's office the next day, Andreas found Sverdrup in a gloomy mood. "Helland," he said, "I have just been informed that yesterday all of the deaconesses, except one, have left the institution. No teaching will be necessary." Andreas left wondering if the students from the day before would ever again believe anything he said.

As the school year came to a close, Oscar became quite sick. He might not be returning in the fall. Andreas accompanied his roommate as far as Rochester, and then went on by himself to Harmony. He spent the summer teaching parochial school. With every chance that came, he visited the Rockne's and especially his first love, Clara.

Again staying with the Dreyers, Andreas observed that the pastor had become more comfortable having a guest in his house. Conversation was more balanced this time between them. The two were sitting on the front porch of the large, brick parsonage when Andreas disclosed his admiration for Clara. Pastor Dreyer gave his counsel, "If you think you have fallen in love with someone, you should not say anything about it. Instead, return to Augsburg. See if time away makes a difference. See other girls back in Minneapolis."

Between sips of lemonade on that hot day, Andreas thanked the pastor for his guidance while knowing he would take another path.

His last month was to be spent at the schoolhouse just south of the Rockne's where he had been invited to stay. As the household woke one muggy August Sunday, Andreas found his stomach too queasy to keep anything down but a piece of bread and a few sips of coffee. He had been asked weeks earlier to take Pastor Dreyer's place in the pulpit that Sunday, while the pastor and his wife visited relatives in Wisconsin. It had been only the second or third time Andreas had preached and his vivid memories of his first sermon failed to offer him any confidence. The New Testament lesson was from 1 Corinthians 13, and the Gospel chosen was Mark 12:28-34, Jesus' command to love one another.

Wanting to arrive earlier than the congregation, the sick young man borrowed one of Mr. Rockne's ponies to make the journey. Every time a hoof hit the hard gravel road, Andreas felt his stomach churn up, down and sideways. Nearly there, he stopped, dismounted and took a drink from the water jar Mrs. Rockne had sent with him, hoping it would calm his stomach. He slowly remounted and trotted to Greenfield Lutheran Church. He had carefully written down what he was to say on this particular Sunday. When the time came he stepped up to the pulpit and unfolded the paper containing his notes. With his mind wandering, his stomach queasy and while sweating from the humid summer heat, Andreas slowly plodded through the sermon. Every time he came to the word *love*, he became tongue-tied. Parishioners averted their eyes politely, waiting for him to continue.

Once the service was over, he stood at the door while parishioners shook his hand and told him that he had done a fine job. It was only Mr. Rockne who told him the truth. Andreas had valiantly tried to bring the message but still had work to do. Very kindly, Clara's father concluded, "That, son, is why you are at the seminary now, isn't it? Don't worry yourself; it will come. If the Spirit wills, it will come." Surprisingly, those were the very words that made Andreas feel more confident. He regained a sense of hope for the future. At least one person could be both kind and truthful.

It was that matter-of-fact bluntness that Andreas appreciated, not only in Mr. Rockne, but also in his daughter, Clara. Feeling better, he returned to the Rockne home alone on horseback, rehearsing over and over again what he was about to say. Unlike a sermon, this next opportunity to speak was about to change his life, and hopefully, for the better.

The roast pork dinner had been served. The fresh berry pie had been enjoyed. The table conversation had politely centered on topics other than the morning sermon. When Clara and Andreas sat next to each other, Mrs. Rockne would often see her daughter's adoring smile focused on this very special young man. The men in the house left the table to take their place on the front porch, with coffee in hand while the women cleared the table and began to wash dishes.

Mikkel Rockne, as always, began the talk among the men. "You sure can tell when August arrives. The humidity hangs in the air and storms crop up quickly."

"This is such a great front porch," Andreas commented.

"Yes, it is, and the house is an improvement from the log house we lived in for the first ten years. With the size of our family, we are so much more comfortable nowadays."

"As I have told you before," Andreas added, "this is quite a beautiful home and land. You have so many out buildings. In Norway, one small barn is connected to our house. My parents have never been able to build anything like this."

"No doubt we have been blessed and we want to use it for good." Pointing east to the nearby schoolhouse with its stand of shade trees, Mikkel continued, "I was able to give the community the land and my older boys and I helped build the school. On those busy days, my wife kept the workers fed three times a day."

As they sat and sipped coffee, Andreas thought about how lucky he would be to have a father-in-law like Mikkel. He was still "Mr. Rockne" of course. It was hard for Andreas to call Clara's father by his first name.

Back in the kitchen, just halfway through the hot and tiresome task of cleaning up, Mrs. Rockne surprised Clara by saying, "You go now dear. He will be leaving soon and I know you want to spend time with him. You go now."

With a giant smile on her face, and disdain on the faces of her sisters, Clara gladly hung up her dish towel and said, "Thank you, Mother, for the dinner." She walked out into the hot, humid summer day and approached the men's domain on the front porch.

Andreas rose from his rocking chair. "Please excuse me," he said, then took Clara's hand and led her down the wooden steps.

They walked on the narrow footpath that skirted the family garden with its border of alyssum. Moments passed before Andreas spoke. Finally he said, "What a beautiful place this is, Clara. Even on a hot day like this the trees shelter us."

As they turned toward the apple orchard, the Rockne men, still sitting on the porch, silently looked at each other with knowing smiles.

"You will be a fine preacher, Andreas. It is a fact; I know this," Clara began, with an encouraging voice.

"Well, thank you. I hope someday you are right," Andreas responded. "What really matters is love. That is what I was trying to say, and perhaps it did not come out so well."

"You said that just fine. Yes you did."

"Well, what I'm trying to say...and I'm as clumsy as an ox, well, we have spent some time together. We have gotten to know each other. We have talked. Well...well, I am just wondering if, in time... in time, you would be willing to...to become my wife?"

Her eyes beaming, Clara clapped her hand over her mouth, looked up at this tall, lanky 21-year-old and quietly said, "Yes, I would love to be your wife."

The relieved Andreas answered, "Well, that would make me very happy. I'm afraid I don't have a ring now, but we will take care of that when finances allow." Quietly he bent down and kissed her. They embraced, ignoring the humid air that made them cling to each other.

"May I tell Mother and Father and the others?" Clara asked with an excited voice.

"Well, of course, you can. Of course."

The two held hands as they walked through the orchard, looking at the young, green apples. Noticing the dark clouds gathering to the west, Clara reminded, "We better get going; I have something to say to my family."

She let go of her intended's hand and ran ahead of him.

"Mother, Father, Mother, Father, I have good news," she called out. As she ran up the front steps, Mikkel, just finishing his coffee, said, "What is it, Dear? What is it?"

Anna Rockne came running out the screen door and asked, "What's the matter? What is it?"

"Andreas has asked me to marry him. Isn't that wonderful?" Clara bubbled as she hugged her mother and grabbed her father before he could even get up from his rocking chair. Her brothers and sisters ran to join them on the porch, every one of them repeating, "I knew it! I knew this would happen!"

Andreas climbed the steps, a shy smile on his face.

"Mr. Rockne, would you permit me to marry your daughter?" Andreas asked.

Clara looked back at him and asked, "You mean you have not asked my father yet?"

"Well, as a matter of fact, I did not know that was the custom," Andreas confessed.

There was silence on the porch as the proud father held onto the moment.

"Well, let me see," he said as he held his chin. "Well, let me see."

"Well, yes, yes."

Everyone began to laugh as Clara and Andreas stood arm in arm.

In a few seconds, the joyful mood turned somber. "Before we make any plans, I think we had better get to the cellar. Look to the west," cautioned Mikkel Rockne.

For the rest of the afternoon, everyone sat on pails and crates waiting out the high winds and torrents of rain that crashed down above them. Once it quieted, Mikkel made his way up the steep stairway, opened the cellar door and stepped out onto the soggy grass. "It is safe to come out," he said. Usually, this kind of frightening event would be the sole topic of conversation at the supper table. On this particular Sunday evening, the talk was about a future wedding as they ate their bread, meat and cheese. Through the west windows they watched the sun make its way between the clouds as it dipped into the golden fields of wheat ready for harvest.

That evening, Andreas felt more motivated than ever to write a letter home to share his good news.

August 15, 1891
Dear Mother and Father,
I am finally sending a letter filled with good news, news I know you will not only share with the family but also the gaard, or as we call them here, the neighbors. I am happy to tell you that I have asked Clara Rockne to marry me, and she said yes! She is a fine young lady, certainly dedicated to the Lord and will make a wonderful wife. The word of God dwells richly in the Rockne home and I can assure you that Sunday is kept holy.

Clara has seven brothers and sisters; they sadly lost little Julia as a baby. Their farm is well built with orchards and flower beds.

I have been blessed with a home where good fellowship permeates the family life.

You need not worry; Clara and I will not be married until I have completed school at Augsburg. I will have a free month with the Rocknes after my last summer teaching job before I return to Augsburg. While teaching here, I have been given space to stay at the

Rockne home. I will write again when I return to school.
  Your loving son,
  Andreas

For the next month, Andreas taught at the school just east of the Rockne farm and spent the evenings making plans with Clara. Although they wished the marriage could come earlier, Andreas insisted that he finish seminary first.

When the day came for him to return to his studies at Augsburg, the future groom boarded the train in Harmony. He was suffering in two ways. He was sick about leaving his fiancée behind, and he was suffering from a fever and a raspy cough. As the train approached Rochester, Andreas remembered the excitement he had felt the year before, wondering about the identity of his new roommate. This time there was no roommate on the train. Sadly, Oscar's health had continued to deteriorate and he was unable to return to school.

After a number of days back on campus and still suffering from a fever and the cough that kept his dorm mates awake at night, Andreas was persuaded to see a new Swedish doctor known to specialize in lung maladies. As he waited in the doctor's office, Andreas could not help but reminisce on the mad search for a doctor while rowing home from Bergen as a young child. He thought about the months of forced bed rest while longing to begin school. Just as the memories were dragging his spirits down even lower, the door opened and the doctor called him into the office.

Once he had stripped to his waist the doctor declared. "Ja, Ja! Poiken has alls inte mycket kjett paa bena!" or "Well, the boy does not have much meat on his bones."

At the end of the visit, and with some pills in hand, Andreas was told to take rough towels, wash his body in cold water every morning and then briskly towel himself off until warm. Returning to his room, Andreas postponed his studies, sat back on his bed and returned to a journal in which he had only sporadically written.

JOURNAL November 3, 1891

It amazes me how fast the time goes by between my journal entries. I have kept busy with studies, teaching parochial school and of course, courting Clara, whom I am thrilled to write is willing to marry me. As we talked before I returned to school, I could see that she would have liked to become my wife earlier than I thought it possible or at least practical. I look forward to the day sometime in the summer of 1893 when we will be husband and wife. It feels good just to write it.

But, in the midst of the joy, I must admit I still experience times of deep sorrow and even questioning God's working in my life. Again I am suffering from issues with my lungs. Like a constant burden in my chest, they have given me such suffering ever since I was a child. Again this past month, my constant coughing and intense weakness have made life less than enjoyable. Yet, I know God is working out His plan through all that happens. At least, now with pills in hand and a new doctor's orders to bathe and briskly towel off, I have a new regimen that, God willing, will improve my general health.

Part of my melancholy comes from missing Clara. I am also saddened that Oscar is unable to continue school due to his delicate and worsening health.

It feels as if one challenge piles upon another. It has been over two years since Peder's passing. I am anxious to see how Marie is doing in Racine. I still wonder about the cause of Peder's death. I will ask Marie again if she has been able to reconcile what might have happened. I can admit only to these pages that, although it will be good to see Kristen again, I still deeply miss my closest brother, Peder. He was always such a witness to me. Over the years how I wish we could have seen each other more often; how I cherish his welcoming me at the dock in Stavanger when I was so young and guiding me to the Country Boy's Home. I hold onto the memory of just that one short journey and our words to each other.

I had better get back to my studies. I pray daily for my family, for Clara and for my return to health.

Over time Andreas' prayers were answered, his spirits lifted and by December the dry cough had disappeared. Besides wanting to feel better, Andreas was motivated to carefully follow his doctor's orders so that he could return to Racine to see Peder's widow, Marie, his brother, Kristen, and his new wife, Marta. More importantly, he was going to see his Clara, who was visiting relatives in Chicago.

Finally the day came for his visit to Racine. As the train made its way into the depot, Andreas wondered why Pastor Dreyer had ever given him the advice to wait regarding engagement. He could not imagine dating another girl. As the train jerked to a stop, he looked down at the excited greeting party. There stood Marie, his brother, Kristen, Marta, and his cousin, Nels. After a round of hugs, Andreas handed Nels his carpetbag and jokingly said, "I don't need another 50 cents for the drayman, do I?"

Together they walked toward the little house Marie rented when she left the parsonage.

Standing in the front room, Marie declared, "I'm afraid you will need to sleep in Nels' room again. The inn is full."

She smiled as Andreas said, "That will be just fine, just fine."

"Well, you know, we have two newlyweds staying with us and a bachelor, so you get the bachelor," Marie said.

Andreas was relieved to see that her spirit was so much more relaxed than it had been during his first stay in Racine.

Late one night, with only Marie and Andreas sitting in front of the fire, he asked the question that had been hounding him since he left Racine: was there any news regarding the cause of his brother's death?

Marie informed him that months after Andreas left for Harmony, she visited with the local sheriff. Sadly, he dismissed her as a widow grieving her husband's death. She said that the sheriff had been quite brusque and didn't want to take up the matter. He said, "Mrs. Helland, it is too late," he said, adding, "no one else got sick at the picnic. There is no proof that any foul play took place."

When Marie told the sheriff that one particular lady had a crush on the pastor and that he had turned her down, the sheriff asked her if Peder had said anything about that happening. Marie told him that her husband would never have worried her with such filthy business.

As they sat quietly, watching the fire turn to burning coals, Andreas' wondered if there was something he could do to bring the culprit to justice.

Two days later, Andreas boarded the train for Chicago. He was comforted by Marie's positive nature and excited by seeing his brother for the first time since his own farewell party in Fitjar. Listening to the click and clack of the train, Andreas' mind went to the uncertainty of the cause of his closest brother's death. Like a pest, the thought always seemed to sit in the back of his mind. As the train made its way south toward Chicago, he was reminded of Clara's smile and his deep affection for her. He knew that he would see her for only a few days and then be separated until summer.

Most of his time was spent with Clara and her uncle and aunt, Mr. and Mrs. Quales. He roomed for the first few days with one of Peder's closest friends who had moved from Racine to Chicago. Long into the night Peder's friend, Erik, and Andreas reminisced about their dear friend and brother. Andreas told the story of Peder's absence from Fitjar while learning to become a baker in his uncle's shop. Although years separated them, Andreas explained that it felt as if he and Peder had been twins. They had similar interests and abilities. They were both avid fishermen, readers and in time, both would be clergymen. Andreas explained his dream to return to his homeland while he knew Peder was content living in America. He told Erik, "I guess my brother had the America Fever much more than I did."

After Clara left for her home near Harmony, Andreas hiked across what seemed like an endless city to finally see his brother, Kristen, and his wife, Marta. He felt his stomach rumbling as he climbed the steps to the large wood and glass front door. Their apartment was on the second floor. He took the back stairway, which led to another long hallway. He came to apartment number eight, paused, took a breath and knocked. His older brother quickly opened the door, looked proudly at Andreas and invited him in. Marta rushed from the kitchen where she had been preparing supper and stood next to her husband. Kristen introduced her to Andreas and quickly they moved to the sitting room where they spent the entire evening catching up on family, friends and Andreas' engagement news. Later Andreas was given the davenport in the front room on which to sleep, while the newlyweds retired to the one bedroom. While Kristen was at work the following day, Marta shared with her new brother-in-law something about her family back in Norway. Being a comparatively warm December day, they walked along Lake Michigan. Then, home for supper, Kristen and his brother continued to talk about family members and home.

The next morning, Andreas said farewell as he took a trolley to the depot where he boarded the train for Minneapolis. As he waited on one of the beautifully crafted wooden benches, his thoughts went back to his first visit to that particular station on his trip from New York to Racine. He couldn't help but think about all that had happened to him since that October day two years earlier. It could all be described in so few words—parochial school teacher, student and husband-to-be.

"Imagine that," he whispered to himself as he watched a young mother trying to carry a suitcase in one hand while dragging two little children with the other.

Soon the announcement for his departure reverberated through the station. He picked up his bag and set out for the tracks. Once on board, he took out two books he had brought and spent the time reading and enjoying the vast countryside of rolling hills, rivers and snowy fields.

The spring semester passed more quickly than Andreas had ever remembered, and it was not long before he returned to Harmony for another stint as parochial school teacher. Every weekend was spent at the Rockne home with his beloved Clara. As summer turned to fall, not only were the fields ripe with abundant wheat and corn, but the crop of apples was even more plentiful than the year before. Clara and Andreas shared another tearful farewell but found comfort in knowing that, following this coming year, they would finally be together.

The fall semester of 1892 brought a surprise and yet another visit to Professor Sverdrup's office. Andreas wondered what kind of heresy he might be charged with now. Not ever taking the theological disagreements with other students or faculty too seriously, Andreas simply smiled when he thought of the possibilities. He knocked on the professor's door and was invited in. With a warm handshake offered, Andreas was seated.

"Mr. Helland, Professor Reimstad is quite ill. As you know, while many are suffering from typhoid fever, others have contracted tuberculosis. I am wondering if you would be willing to take over Professor Reimstad's teaching load while he recovers. I understand that you will not be able to attend some of your theology classes during this time, but, that would be permissible."

October 21, 1892
Dear Mother and Father,
I hope you received my last letter that I wrote during my summer in Harmony. Although the children in the parochial school at times would misbehave, I kept them busy. Clara's brother, John, and sister, Amelia, attended when I taught at their schoolhouse. I am sure they felt more pressure to behave since I could report their manners directly to their older sister or parents.

When I returned to Augsburg, dearly missing Clara, I was called into Professor Sverdrup's office and asked to teach Norwegian and Latin to the senior class and physiology to the lower classes. Although it is an honor to be asked, and the students are nothing like those I encounter in the summer, I am concerned about my studies for my final examinations. Every hour I am not teaching or preparing for the classes, I am reading in preparation for those examinations scheduled for next spring.

I wish I could see Marie, Kristen and Marta more often, but the distance and time does not allow it. I hope and pray they will be able to attend our wedding, which we are now planning for July 6th of next summer. I know it is impossible, but oh how I wish the two of you and the rest of the family could join us for this very special day. I hope and pray that someday Clara and I will be able to return to Norway, at least for a long visit.

I feel more and more that God is calling me to serve a parish somewhere in Minnesota or Wisconsin, which will very likely be

*part of the United Church. Though I will miss serving the Church
of Norway, yet I see some advantages in serving a congregation here
in America. Here, the pastors have a closer connection to the people.
The clergy do not represent a state church or government.*

*I hope and pray this letter finds you healthy. Please share these
words with family and friends. I remember so well Mother and
Kristen reading letters at the table with friends and family gathered
around. I certainly miss celebrating Christmas with you as we did
for so many years. The Rocknes continue to serve lefse, flatbread
and dried fish, and so I feel somewhat at home while visiting them.
I know Clara will continue our traditions.*

Love,

Andreas

As the time for examinations approached, Andreas was haunted
by nightmares in which he had failed to answer correctly the questions on the oral examination. Once awake, it dawned on him that
the examination week had not yet arrived. As he tried again to sleep,
he felt better, reminding himself that the oral examination was only
20% of his final grade. He prepared late into the night for tests in
Old Testament and New Testament, Church history, Systematic and
Practical theology. He always remembered his welcome to Augsburg,
and being told that what really mattered is the knowledge of God's
Word—and that everything else is secondary.

With the trees budding, the grass slowly turning green and temperatures rising, examination week finally arrived. Once his tests
were finished, Andreas was greeted with the news that he had been as
successful as in the past, even with his teaching load and inability to
attend many of his own classes. On the morning of the closing exercise, he and others tried to pass the time with a game of croquet. None
of them took the game very seriously. What caught Andreas' attention
on that day was the casual announcement made by one of his closest
friends. With a foxy smile, Olav Refsdal came over, took the croquet
mallet out of Andreas' hand and proclaimed to the others playing,
"I would like to introduce the number-one student in our class."

"What do you mean?" Andreas asked.

"Well, heretic or not, you have the number-one rating in the class," Olav announced.

A few of his classmates congratulated him, then continued the game.

With no graduation exercises as he had experienced in Norway, Andreas and his classmates returned from their games to a classroom where they received their diplomas, sang one hymn and were on their way back to their room to either sell their furniture or place it in storage. On the street across from the park there were horse-drawn carts being loaded by fathers and students as they packed to return to their homes.

April 4, 1893

Dear Clara,

I miss you so very much! I am sorry to say that with the scheduling of the United Church Convention in June, I will not be able to return to Harmony until June 17. Let me assure you, I am already counting the days. I have done some arithmetic to find the number of hours but counting the days sounds better.

I was sorry to miss the Easter celebration with your family. This will be the last Easter you and I are not together. That thought brings me a very warm feeling.

I have good news! As you know, Professor Sverdrup recommended me for a call to four little churches in McIntosh. I admit it is quite a distance from Harmony, but only three miles away from the town of Ephriam King, which has the Great Northern Railway Station. In fact, that is how I got there last week for my visit with the call committee. Imagine, I had to preach on Easter Sunday in all four churches since they have no pastor serving them at this time. As you might guess, the town is named after a Scottish man who had come from French Canada. The good news is that the people are friendly. There is a store, a lodge and even a post office near the village. They took no time in offering me the position, and so, by God's grace and your willingness, I plan on accepting this first position. I will explain why the timing is so important when I see you. They have asked me to begin my ministry on the last Sunday of July. I told them that I would be married on July 6th which made them very happy, especially the women. Imagine four little Norwegian Lutheran Churches in an area named for a Scotsman.

Greetings to your father, mother, siblings and, especially, your Aunt Bertha. If I may be so bold, please ask her if she would be willing to mend some of my shirts and pants. I know what an expert seamstress she is and appreciate how busy she might be with your wedding dress.

All my love,
Andreas

Chapter 15

The Big Day

While so many other seminary graduates were greeting their parents and girlfriends, Andreas went about packing up his room. He would remain in Minneapolis for the United Church Convention and his ordination. Today he needed help moving his furniture into storage. Olav Refsdal helped him carry his table down the stairs and into the storage room. He asked Andreas, "Well, was I right? Did he ask you to divide Matthew?"

A few days earlier, like many of the students, Andreas was busy studying for the examinations while enjoying the spring sun in Riverside Park. When leaving the park, Olav, seemingly out of the blue, asked his friend to divide Matthew into the sections Professor Sverdrup had instructed. Tired of studying and talking about academics for so many months, Andreas remembered his response to Olav's questions in a frustrated voice, "I don't know and I don't care."

As the two of them arrived on the stairway landing, Andreas had to admit that the very first question the professor asked him in his oral exam was, "Mr. Helland, how do we divide the Gospel of Matthew?"

"I know, I know, Olav. Thanks for the warning. Because of your question in the park, I got it right—chapters one and two, three to ten, eleven to twenty and twenty-one to twenty-eight." As he kept bobbing his head to properly bow to his friend, Andreas said, "Thank you, Olav. You were right and I'm indebted to you. Now, let's get this table into the room."

Once his furniture was in storage, he spent the day walking along the river and sitting in Riverside Park. With no meals available on campus, he would eat either at Professor Sverdrup's home or at a café on Cedar Avenue. With very little spare change, he would order the cheapest thing on the menu, oftentimes a fried egg sandwich and cup of coffee.

Each night as Andreas awaited sleep, his mind teamed with the activities of the coming weeks—the United Church Convention, his ordination and, most importantly, his return to Harmony to see Clara and await their July wedding, followed by beginning his ministry. From his professors and other pastors, he was beginning to understand the differences between those supporting the very authoritative approach to congregational leadership experienced in the traditions of the Norwegian State Church and those known as "free church" advocates who preferred authority to be kept in the hands of the laity and individual congregations.

Since most of the students had vacated the dormitory, Andreas felt as if the walls of his room were closing in on him. He remembered feeling much like this on the steamship. He was lonely, and he wondered what the future held for him and his new bride.

JOURNAL June 14, 1893

I attended my first church convention during these last three days and must admit that I am sorely disappointed. The convention is certainly not a uniting event or a holy atmosphere, as I believe it should be. I firmly stand on the side of the minority when it comes to the polity of congregations, pastors and the larger church. I thought America stood for freedom, but all I hear from the majority is their desire for the larger church's control of each parish, thus each pastor.

I was deeply saddened to witness the resignation of both Sverdrup and Oftedal as professors. Sverdrup has served as a mentor to me these past three years, and Oftedal is a constant reminder of the brother who allowed me to attend the Cathedral School. Meaning no disrespect but at times I must admit I feel like I have as much connection to Stavanger as I do to my home in Fitjar.

I have been so disappointed and so confused that this afternoon, at this very late hour, I went to Pastor Sverdrup's office to ask if I should present myself for ordination. I understand it would mean disappointing the congregations in McIntosh, to which I have been called, and yet I can't agree with the United Church's belief that more authority rests in the synod than the individual congregation. Again, his advice was helpful. I want to remember his every word.

I think he said, "You had better use the opportunity when you have it. It is difficult to say when you will have another." After my visit, I admit I still question the future and wonder if I can be a clergyman in such a church but, God willing, people will come to their senses. I will do what he suggested. So, with mixed feelings, tomorrow I present myself for ordination.

JOURNAL June 15, 1893

Well, at least today was a much more peaceful meeting of the United Church. I was ordained and now look forward to what is next on my mind—seeing Clara again and looking forward to our wedding. These last four days certainly tired me out and, although I am happy to be ordained, I hold onto a bitter disappointment in the behavior of many of the United Church pastors and lay people. These past days I have felt like I did rolling over the waves on some of those rough days off the dock in Fitjar. What a simpler life it would have been, staying in Norway, but I guess God has other plans. May His will be done.

Early the next morning Andreas awoke to a sunny, dry Saturday. The school drayman arrived to take Andreas' wooden chest to the Milwaukee Road train station. Andreas stuffed his sheet and blanket into the carpetbag, left the key to the room on the bed and looked one last time out of the window toward the park square. Its young trees were filled with vibrant light-green leaves. He made his way down the stairs and out the door, where he ran into Professor Sverdrup. They shook hands and Andreas thanked him, then shared his disappointment regarding the professor's resignation.

"I thought I must, Andreas. God will lead us," Sverdrup assured him. "I'm glad you were ordained and will begin service in McIntosh. You will do well, and do not worry about me. Both Oftedal and I will do fine. God has a plan for us."

They shook hands again, and Andreas walked on with Sverdrup's parting words, "You will do well, Helland. Do not worry, you will do well."

Encouraged and yet still anxious about the future, Andreas trekked down Riverside Avenue, across the tracks at Cedar Avenue and on to Washington Avenue and the train station. With plenty of time before the arrival of his southbound train to Rochester and on to Harmony, he opened his journal to continue what he had written two nights before.

JOURNAL June 17, 1893

I have just said farewell to Professor Sverdrup. This past week and the events of the convention do cause me to wonder about the church and my part in it.

I hope and pray Clara is pleased with our first call. It is a long way from her family, but at least it is on a rail line.

My first impressions of McIntosh stay with me today. The town has very few frame homes, with most people living in log houses, and even some made of sod. The town church and two others meet in converted schoolhouses. Another church meets in a log building. The entire area looks very primitive but quite interesting. As I wrote Clara, at least there is a mercantile, boarding house and post office, with the rail station just three miles away.

Before accepting the call, I was surprised to hear Professor Sverdrup share his concerns regarding my delicate health and the rigorous climate in that area. I will never forget that in the same breath he shared his distaste for students who were busy trying to control the Holy Spirit by what he called "fishing for a call."

My own questions and confusion did not center on the right call but the realization that I had always wanted to serve in missions in Madagascar. I wondered if God was calling me there. Sverdrup's advice was to wait until the mission issues are cleared up with the United Church. He also reminded me that my lung issues were still problematic. I remember his last words regarding the subject. He said, "You are still young, you can bide your time." So, I take his counsel.

Andreas boarded the train, walking through its great steam clouds that billowed up from under the locomotive. Placing his heavy carpetbag on the luggage rack, he sat down with only his jacket, pencil and journal.

JOURNAL continued, Saturday, June 17, 1893
Well, finally on my way. Not easy to write with the train leaving the station. I am lucky to have this seat to myself. This is going to be more of a challenge than I thought. Two small children are fighting in the seat ahead of me. They look back at me asking over and over, "What are you doing, mister, what are you doing?"

For a number of miles, Andreas closed his journal and simply looked at the scenery while being forced to listen to the tussling children. It was only after the train began to roll south through the countryside that the children were given something to play with to stop their warfare.

JOURNAL continued, Saturday, June 17, 1893
As I look out at the countryside, I think about how I can catch up with sleep after my examinations and the convention. I want to help Clara with wedding preparations and hopefully help Mikkel with his work.

As the green fields of crops passed by in a blur, Andreas thought, "Oh, to see Clara again! I can't wait!" In Norway the barns and houses were painted red with white trim. The farmhouses in southern Minnesota were all white with only the barns painted red. Many buildings had not been painted at all.

Traveling past the new hospital in Rochester and on to the station, Andreas thought again of his first-year roommate who had dropped out of school for health reasons. He had always liked Oscar and his willingness to show Andreas around the school and the shops on Riverside and Cedar Avenues. He had not heard from Oscar since he left school, but hoped he had finished preparatory school or was working in his father's mercantile in Byron.

As the train sped on, the green, rolling hills caught Andreas' attention. He compared the wide-open spaces with the small plots of land farmers kept on the island of Stord. He also compared the beautiful Rockne home with the small cabin-like house in which he had been raised. As he pondered both present and future, he was reminded of his professor's comforting words, "Let God do the guiding."

Arriving in Harmony, his concerns evaporated when he saw Clara waving and her father's broad smile.

Sunday, June 18, 1893
Dear Mother and Father,
I hope and pray all is well with the two of you and my sisters. When I last wrote, I don't think I told you of my thoughts during the service of ordination. As I stood in front of Professor Sverdrup and the others, I was reminded of the mission festival in Fitjar when I was about 12 years old. I remember, Father, how we built the platform and lectern and you encouraged me to try out my voice in the wide-open spaces. I must admit, I felt sort of like a preacher then. I remember thinking, "Someday I might be given the opportunity to preach God's word." I want to thank the two of you for your constant encouragement in the faith and, especially, for your prayers.

I arrived at the Rockne's yesterday. It is a home bustling with people preparing for our wedding. I have been politely asked to stay out of the way and help Clara's father with his chores. The crops have been planted and are bursting out of the rich soil. Here there are not as many rocks to pick as we always had on the home place.

A funny thing happened to me at the church convention. A middle-aged man walked up to me and asked if I was Andreas Helland. I said I was and he introduced himself. It was none other than Nils Saterbo. He has changed so much. He is much heavier, and bald with just a fringe of gray hair. You certainly remember him. I was but a child when he immigrated to America. I do remember that one time he hired me to shepherd his sheep up in the hills above his gaard. I was working only a short time. I remember the gift his brother gave me. It was an arithmetic book I treasured for years. He and his family continue to be as kind and giving as I remember them to be back home. He even offered me a loan for school but, since I had seen the end of that adventure, I told him it would not be needed. He asked me to send you warm greetings.

When we are settled in McIntosh I will be writing again. Oh, how I wish the two of you were able to be with us. I find comfort in knowing we are in your prayers. Our wedding trip will take us to Racine so we can see Marie again. We will not get as far as Chicago to see Kristen, but I hope to see the two of them another time.

Greet those to whom you will read this letter.

Your son,

Andreas

The days between Andreas' arrival in Harmony and July 6th went as slowly as pouring honey in the winter. Yet when the big day finally arrived, everyone was greeted by a hot, sunny muggy morning. The groom kept busy with farm chores while the bride and her sisters prepared the parlor and changed into their wedding clothes. The dress Clara's aunt had made was a true piece of art. The temperature of the house continued to rise as the neighbors prepared the dinner. Flowers from the Rockne gardens, and those of the neighbors, graced every corner of the parlor. As the early afternoon passed, the blue skies began to turn a strange color of gray.

When the many invited guests stood facing the front door, the bride, groom and attendants entered. While Pastor Harbo performed the wedding ceremony, Mikkel Rockne's attention was focused on the western sky.

Following the ceremony, the guests entered a tent that had been put up on the side lawn for the wedding reception. With everyone at their tables, the guests were welcomed with the father-of-the-bride's customary speech. It was not only shorter than usual, but spoken in an unusually quick tempo. Just as the meal was served, the winds began to shake the tent, the flowers in the corner fell to the ground and everyone scurried into the house. Guests and cooks alike quickly gathered up the food and ran inside. By now it seemed everyone's attention was on the clouds to the west. The next hour passed with people balancing their plates of food while standing or sitting on a few parlor chairs. Once the winds died, the clouds opened and the guests began a mass exodus through the mud to their buggies, hurrying to check on their own farms. It was not until the next day, on the train bound for Racine, that the wedding couple heard of the tornado that had devastated an area just south of the border in Iowa.

Rather than spending a traditional honeymoon alone as a couple, they journeyed to Racine to visit Peder's widow, Marie, and Andreas' brother, Kristen, who had traveled by train from Chicago. The small town was filled with excitement when a Viking ship sailed up Lake Michigan from its World's Fair mooring in Chicago. For several hours on a summer afternoon, the bride and groom searched every nook and cranny of the authentic-looking vessel.

Two days later, they hurried back to Harmony to pack and prepare for their new home. They treated themselves to a two-day stopover in Minneapolis to pick up the books Andreas had left behind. Taking his bride to the Augsburg campus for the first time, Andreas struggled with the disappointment of a campus missing the heart and soul of the place, Professor Sverdrup. On the afternoon they arrived, Andreas looked forward to introducing his new bride to a couple who had hosted him while attending school, Pastor Nils Iversen and his wife. Andreas had felt especially close to the Iversens since the pastor had been Peder's predecessor in Racine. Added to the excitement for Clara was her first ride on a streetcar. When the two boarded a streetcar on Washington Avenue, Clara was surprised to see how small it was compared to a rail car. Following the ride, they walked the rest of the way to Iversen's parsonage. Andreas warned his young wife of the many moods that he had seen the pastor display. Mrs. Iversen, Andreas explained, had always been cheerful and kind, even while enduring the poverty that came with her husband's calling and the struggle of raising a family of six children. Arriving at the modest home, it was Pastor Iversen who greeted them.

"Oh, Andreas, it's you. Come in," he said with his tone clearly suggesting it was no time to visit.

"We have stopped by in order that I might introduce you to my wife," Andreas said.

"Yes, of course. Well, nice to meet you...ah," the pastor said while looking at the floor.

"It's Clara," Andreas chimed in, "My wife's name is Clara."

"Yes, well, come in and let me get Mrs. Iversen."

With his shrill voice, he shouted, "Borghild! We have company." There was silence.

"Borghild," he repeated, impatiently.

Finally, the three of them, still standing in the foyer, heard a muffled sound. "Come up; I cannot come down."

Quickly offering to return another time, Andreas turned to lead Clara out the door when the pastor stopped them, insisting they follow him.

With puzzled faces, the visitors looked at each other and slowly followed their host up the stairs, Andreas protesting with every step he took, saying, "We can return at a better time."

"Nonsense," the pastor replied.

As they arrived at Mrs. Iversen's bedroom door, her husband knocked. They heard a weak, "Come in," and Pastor Iversen opened the door.

"Andreas is here with his wife. You wanted to meet them, didn't you?"

"Oh, yes, I guess so," she said, inviting them in. "Is it Clara?"

"Yes, Ma'am," Clara respectfully responded.

"As you can see, I am not feeling well," Mrs. Iversen continued in a whisper.

"Well, we can return at another time that would be better. We are leaving tomorrow for my first call in McIntosh," Andreas said.

"Oh," Mrs. Iversen said. "Well, I am quite sorry to hear that."

"Borghild!" her husband said with a sharp tone. "You knew Andreas had accepted that call. What are you saying?"

Looking straight at Andreas, Mrs. Iversen continued, "Yes, but still,

I want to warn you. It is not an easy calling for you, or especially your wife; not at all. People expect so much from me. That is what tires me, and why I am confined to bed. I just can't take it."

There was silence until Andreas again insisted they return another time.

"Well," Mrs. Iversen said, "blessings to you, but I do not think you will like this life at all."

Andreas took Clara's hand and led her back through the bedroom door and into the hallway. Pastor Iversen followed. No one uttered a word until they bid each other farewell at the landing.

"We will see ourselves out. Goodbye, Nils. I hope your wife feels better soon," Andreas said in a hushed tone.

Once the couple left the house, they walked in silence, back to the corner where they boarded the streetcar.

"I have never seen her like that, Clara, never. She has always been filled with joy when I visited. She must be ill," Andreas offered.

Once they made arrangements for Andreas' furniture and books to be picked up and delivered to the station, they set out for the depot. This massive granite building was certainly the most magnificent structure Clara had ever seen. Tired from the frantic activities of the day, they hoped that once aboard they could get some rest.

Chapter 16

First Call

It was on a cool morning, the last Tuesday in July, when Andreas and Clara arrived in the little community known as Ephriam King, located just a few miles from their new home. Both Andreas and Clara could not help but feel the excitement of a new adventure, and yet they were tenuous about what this first stage of married life and ministry would be like. Mr. and Mrs. Thompson, two members of the church whom Andreas had stayed with back in April, were waiting for them.

Andreas introduced his wife to the older couple as they rode the three miles to the Thompson's country sod house. Once inside, they sat around an old pine table. The chairs squeaked even under Clara's diminutive body. The breakfast of eggs, bacon, pancakes and fried potatoes was a welcome sight for the two travelers who had not eaten since noon the day before. Mr. Thompson and Andreas talked about the community and their need to purchase two sturdy ponies and a buggy while the two women sat silently. Clara's questions of the hostess were answered in one-word replies.

"I keep to myself pretty much. I like it that way." Mrs. Thompson explained when asked about any community activities. The longer they sat in this damp house, the more Clara began to wonder what lay ahead. "Did Andreas' positive spirit exaggerate how pleasant the parsonage might be?" she thought.

Finally, the host suggested they get on their way to show the young pastor and his wife their new home. As they left the sod house, Clara took in a deep breath of fresh air, turned and thanked the hostess. She took her husband's hand and stepped onto the buggy that held all of their worldly possessions. Mr. Thompson drove about a mile to the parsonage. From a distance, Clara's nerves calmed as she realized it was indeed the kind of wood structure Andreas had described. Her first impression was, "dry and small, but livable."

Certainly this was not the two-story brick home to which she had been accustomed. From the entrance, she saw a small sitting room and, behind it, the wood stove and kitchen area. She noticed the plastered walls and the braided rug in the living room. To the left she found the one bedroom. With a relieved smile on her face, Clara turned back to Andreas saying, "Yes, this will do." By the time she had spoken, Mr. Thompson had unloaded the few pieces of furniture, suitcases, three wooden crates and Andreas' sacred wooden chest. Everything was in place, ready to be unpacked. Andreas reminded Mr. Thompson, "Can you take me to the person selling the horses and buggy?"

"Oh, yes, of course, Pastor, come aboard," he said.

As the two rode off, Clara thought to herself, "It is as he promised; a wooden home. Small but dry. In the bedroom there is a bed and mattress."

Mr. Thompson and Andreas drove to the home of another local pastor who had a pair of ponies and a buggy for sale. Pastor Roberts, warmly greeting Andreas, immediately began listing the qualities of his two ponies. "I hate to say goodbye to them. They have served me well. I have been called to a congregation in Seattle, Washington, and must sell the ponies, buggy and some furniture items," he said. As he listed the qualities of these two fine animals, his wife stood shyly at the open door, listening in. The expression on her face reminded Andreas of Mrs. Iversen back in Minneapolis. As carefully as he could, without knowing much about horses—or in this case, Indian ponies—Andreas inspected them, asking about their health.

"Oh, they are in perfect health. I would not say anything that was not true. You might know that, Pastor," Roberts said acting as if he had been insulted.

"Yes, of course," Andreas said, then taking a careful look at the worn buggy. He realized it might be all he could afford. As they discussed the price, Mr. Thompson whispered to Andreas, "I don't know of any other horses available at this time." Tired from the long trip, Andreas agreed to Pastor Roberts' price.

Andreas expressed his thanks and stepped onto the buggy. He took the reins and spoke affectionately to the two ponies, Prince and Polly, and they followed the trail back home. Andreas arrived to find Clara busy unpacking their few possessions.

By late in the afternoon, everything was in its place. They sat at the new kitchen table that Clara's parents had given them as a wedding gift. With staples already stocked in the one cupboard, they were ready to visit the grocery store when their first guests arrived. Up to the front of their little cottage came a couple on a wagon. They introduced themselves as Ole and Anna Olson, explaining that their custom was to provide milk for the pastor's family. Politely Clara and the young clergyman thanked them, inviting them in for a cup of coffee. Clara poured the rich cream that had settled at the top of the milk bottle into her coffee. "The milk is even cold!" Clara exclaimed.

That week, other church members arrived with meat, vegetables, fresh bread and even feed for the ponies. If the congregation continued to be this generous, the young couple realized they would not be visiting the village grocery. As time went by, the fresh produce was replaced by leftovers and, rather than fresh, young chickens, tough grandma hens were left at the door. In the fall, hunters would stop by with pheasant, duck and deer meat.

The first year of ministry passed quickly, and Andreas began to learn what it meant to serve a congregation. In school he was taught scripture, theology and church history, but now the young pastor was learning how to care for his flock. Although well meaning, his parishioners were not as consistent in their worship attendance as he had hoped. While kind to his face, he knew that behind his back they openly questioned if he was old enough to care for their souls. With homes having only one or two rooms, his visits, especially with the sick, took place with other family members standing nearby. Private conversations were rare, and individual confessions were almost impossible.

When Andreas arrived at a home without communion elements, the families chalked it up to his inexperience. But failing to bring the sacrament the first time did make it possible for him to suggest a second visit. Meanwhile, Clara kept up with the cooking, sewing and visiting with the women of the parish while Andreas prepared sermons, made home visits and constantly fixed the aged buggy. Andreas thought, "The pastor did not tell me the buggy was in good shape; he just said it worked fine." What bothered Andreas the most was Pastor Robert's interpretation of a healthy pony. Andreas thought it peculiar that the ponies had been declared healthy in view of Prince's weak back and Polly's faulty kidneys.

With fall came the celebration of confirmation. Four young people had studied with the new pastor for some time and were to be questioned in front of the congregation. On this particular November Sunday, snow blanketed the ground outside the log schoolhouse. Horses and buggies seemed to surround the small building. The confirmands, their families and friends crowded together on long wooden benches.

Andreas stood facing the two boys and two girls who made up his very first confirmation class. He had insisted they memorize the Catechism and a number of Bible passages. Fear and worry were written on their young faces as the questions were asked. Slowly but surely they began to relax when they realized a wrong answer did not mean failure but just a bit of embarrassment.

Bjorn, the star student, was asked to recite the Apostles' Creed. He started out confidently, but nearing the end he looked worried. "I believe in the Holy Ghost, the holy Christian Church, the communion of saints, the..." and then he stuttered. He tried again by backing up, but to no avail. Finally, Andreas prompted, "Bjorn, the forgiveness of sins."

"Ah, thank you, Pastor; the forgiveness of sins, the resurrection of the body and life everlasting. Amen."

Andreas turned to the crowd, "Isn't that true? That's what we often forget—the forgiveness of sins."

The other three students relaxed and confidently answered the questions asked them.

As the closing hymn was sung, Andreas reminisced on his own confirmation Sunday in the beautiful church right off the harbor in Stavanger. He thought of how fortunate these children were to have their parents, friends and family in attendance. He wished the weather in McIntosh was closer to that of Stavanger and that sea breezes would replace the bitter, snow-whipped winds. "Oh, to be home again," he dreamed.

By the time the service ended, the blowing snow was piling up. Andreas had to get on the road for the evening confirmation service some 20 miles away in Maple Bay. As the wind stung his face and the snow gathered on his mustache, it was not long before he was wishing for a sleigh rather than his unpredictable buggy. He questioned the wisdom of continuing his journey, as the three young people who had studied for this special day flashed in his mind. Prince balked at the job he was being asked to do as Polly slowly plodded along.

With the wind gusts throwing the snow, visibility worsened. Ahead, Andreas could make out a deep ravine with an old wooden bridge crossing it. Arriving at one side of the narrow passageway, he stopped and jumped off into knee-deep snow. He knocked the ice off the ponies' hoofs and took hold of Prince's bridle to lead the two ponies across the bridge. As they made their way, the creaking of the wooden structure sounded like a cat yelping in the night. With every step he took, Andreas knew he could slip off the side and into the ravine. Just as they approached land on the other side, a gust of wind blew the back wheel nearly off the bridge. Grabbing the bridle while shouting his command, "Go, go, Prince, go!" the ponies lurched forward, the buggy straightened and a sturdy foundation of frozen ground welcomed them.

Hours later, with snow now covering half of the wheels, Andreas safely made his way to the school building in which the service was to be held. Posted on the door was a sign that simply read, "Confirmation service postponed due to weather." With it soon getting dark, the tired and famished pastor visited a member's home where he spent the night. With the wind subsiding at daylight, the sun glistened on the fresh, white snow. Taking his time, as well as a detour around the ravine, Andreas finally arrived home to a wife who waited, hoping and praying he was still alive.

Almost daily during the rest of November and into December, the community awoke to a new coating of snow. For the first time in her life, Clara was to face Christmas without her immediate family nearby. Clara and Andreas had decided to combine their sacred family Christmas traditions. In October, like his father, Andreas had begun to collect the tallow to make Christmas candles. Clara asked the local grocer for the thick-cut pork chops her family had always enjoyed on Christmas Eve. The young couple's holiday season was filled with the special Christmas service and visits from parishioners carrying boxes of lefse, flatbread and sandbakkels as well as gifts of mittens, hats and small, decorative items for the tree.

By now, Andreas realized the disappointing fact that Prince and Polly were not the quality ponies the pastor had described. Prince was almost uncontrollable while Polly was quite slow. Wrestling with one to slow down and the other to speed up was a constant challenge. Along with the ponies, the carriage also needed constant attention that, thankfully, Andreas, as a capable carpenter, was able to handle.

In the middle of their first January, now very accustomed to the bitter-cold winds of the prairie and the deep snowdrifts, Andreas was called to the home of a family some 12 miles away. With snow blowing against the open buggy the entire way, Andreas finally arrived at a one-room sod house. Greeted by a visiting neighbor, he was told of the tragic circumstances. The young mother had just died from postpartum blood poisoning. A week earlier she had given birth to twin girls. The grief-stricken husband, who was now father of four, demanded to know where God was now. He then asked that the babies be baptized as quickly as possible. As the man paced the floor, swore and pounded his fists on the table, Andreas listened.

Later in the evening, the two infants were baptized in the sod house, with the neighbors serving as baptismal sponsors. Andreas poured a bit of water from the kitchen pail into an old china bowl. He used a ragged dishtowel to wipe the babies' foreheads in place of the usual linen baptismal napkin. With the sacrament completed, the now-quiet father sat down, slurped a cup of coffee and stuffed cake into his mouth. His older sons came out from the corner where they had been playing and tried to wrap their short arms around him.

As time passed, the church community surrounded the young family with loving care. Often the little house bustled with activity. Helpers came to cook, to clean, and to wash clothes, while others, like Clara, took care of the children.

During the winter and spring months, Andreas continued to settle into his ministry. By now, his parishioners had come to know him better. A mutual trust developed between him and those he served. During the late fall and early winter, it became apparent that Clara was expecting her first child. The congregation rejoiced with the news that the Hellands would become parents in May.

Clara felt grief over the tragic death of the young mother, concern for the twins and now anxiety about her own quickly approaching due date. Winter's thaw gave way to spring and a parade of well-wishers. Weekly, someone would arrive with a new hand-sewn piece of clothing or a quilted blanket. Some brought seeds for the garden. Finally, on a warm Friday afternoon in May, while her husband was preparing his weekly sermon, Clara's water broke and she began to feel her body's attempt to bring completion to this part of the life cycle. By Saturday morning, the pains of childbirth were in full bloom and screams were heard in the garden where Andreas was busying himself planting his favorite vegetables.

On that very afternoon, Saturday, May 26, 1894, the midwife opened the door and called out to Andreas, who now was pacing between the house and the stable, "It's a nice little girl! Come see your little girl."

Within the month, the proud father stood in front of his congregation saying, "I baptize you, Petra Jeanette Helland, in the name of the Father, and of the Son, and of the Holy Ghost. Amen."

As the smiling father returned to the lectern to begin his sermon, Clara gently patted the baby's back and returned to her seat in the front row.

June 3, 1894

Dear Mother and Father,

Much has happened since I wrote to you. The biggest news is that Clara gave birth to a beautiful baby girl last Saturday afternoon. A very kind local midwife aided Clara. In worship this morning, I baptized her Petra Jeanette. We wanted to name her after our dear Peder, and Clara's sister, Julia, who died a number of years ago at the age of three. Petra Jeanette has reddish-blond hair, was estimated at eight pounds and appears very healthy. Clara is getting accustomed to getting up at night to feed our little dear and so must rest during the day. Members of the parishes have been bringing more food than we can eat. Thank goodness, the garden we planted will not be bearing fruit for quite some time. Last Saturday was about the first warm day we have enjoyed this spring. As I have written before, the winter months are longer and much more severe than I experienced at home, in Stavanger or Oslo. It is even colder than where Peder lived in Racine. I must admit I miss the water, the fish, the fjords and the mild climate.

The people continue to be kind, but Clara certainly misses her family as I do mine. Clara can visit her family by taking the train, which stops just three miles from our parsonage.

Greetings and love from Clara, Petra and your son,
Andreas

By the end of July, Andreas was finishing his first year of ministry and a daughter had been born. He had gotten to know his members and had learned some of the practical lessons of ministry. Never worrying about their next meal, Andreas had kept track of the payments he had received. His Letter of Call had stipulated a salary of $500 a year, plus the offerings from three holy days. By the end of the first year, Andreas had been paid only $210.

Besides the birth of Petra, the other special event in the life of the parish was the visit by L.O. Skrefsrud, a missionary from India. Once Andreas picked him up at the train station, there was constant talk of the missionary's experiences and Andreas' dream of someday serving a foreign mission. He shared with Skrefsrud the vivid memory he still had of the mission conference at Fitjar as a twelve-year old. Andreas described the setting, the crowds and his own handiwork in building the stage and podium with his father.

Just as they were about to arrive at the small parsonage, the missionary surprised Andreas with the words, "Well, I suppose now you will be moving to Minneapolis."

Andreas stopped the ponies, looked at the visitor and asked, "What?"

"I said, 'I suppose you will now be moving to Minneapolis.'"

"But, what do you mean?" Andreas asked.

"Well, you do know that you have been called to St. Olaf Church, don't you?"

"I do not know anything of the sort," Andreas said with a surprised look on his face. "How did you hear this?"

"Oh, well, you will soon find out," the visitor confided. "I was in Minneapolis a few days ago and while talking with one of their members, I mentioned I was making a stop to see you and speak to your congregations."

There was silence for the rest of the ride. Arriving at the house, Andreas introduced Pastor Skrefsrud to Clara and excused himself to put the horses in the stable. As Prince reared while being led to the stable, Polly, as always, allowed her master to lead the way. Adding feed to their trough, Andreas wondered if the visitor's news about a call was meant for someone else. As he walked toward the house, he thought to himself, "We have grown accustomed to this community, the people and my ministry. I have gotten through my first confirmation service, my first personal crisis of a mother's death and my first round of visits to my members. I am enjoying sermon preparation and we have a baby daughter. This is enough. I wish he wouldn't have said a thing."

Before he opened the door to the parsonage, he quickly prayed, "Lord, let us stay here for a bit longer. I'm not done here, you know that. But Your will be done. Amen."

He walked into the kitchen where little Petra cooed at the visitor as she lay in her borrowed crib. Immediately Andreas' mood lightened as Clara invited the two men to the table for coffee and cookies. They chatted about the most recent church news from Minneapolis. Skrefsrud filled Andreas in on the United Church's issues with mission outreach and especially his mission post in India.

At the first lull in the conversation, Andreas quickly finished his cup of coffee and said, "Excuse me; I have an errand. I won't be long."

The missionary rose from the table, walked back over to the crib and asked if he might rock the infant. As Andreas opened the door, he heard Clara say to the guest, "Of course! It seems you have a real knack with babies."

"Well," the missionary announced, "my wife and I have three

children under the age of five, so I have had a lot of practice."

Andreas walked as fast as he could to the local post office at the general store. As he approached his mailbox, he grew anxious, hoping that if there was a letter, it was from Norway or from Clara's parents. Seeing an envelope through the little window, he realized it was larger than a normal letter. As he opened the small door, he immediately saw the return address:

St. Olaf Lutheran Church
1400 Bryant Avenue North
Minneapolis, Minnesota

Andreas took the envelope from the box, closed the door and left without saying a word. As he walked to the side of the building where there was a wooden bench, he felt as if his head was spinning. Seeing no one nearby, he carefully opened the envelope and pulled out the letter. It read:

After prayerful consideration, St. Olaf Lutheran Church of North Minneapolis has voted to extend you the call to serve as our pastor. Following the recent departure of Pastor Nils Iversen, an Augsburg Seminary student, H. A. Urseth, is now serving us on a temporary basis. We hope and pray, if God wills, you will return your answer, accepting this call to ministry.

Yours truly,

Mr. Hoyme, Congregation President

As the sun beat down and sweat rolled off his forehead, Andreas read the letter again. He carefully folded the letter and envelope, tucked it in his pocket and returned home. During that evening, the missionary took great interest in Andreas' activities in his four small churches. Thankfully, the conversation kept Andreas' mind off the letter.

The next day, the entire community came to listen to Skrefsrud, a fiery preacher whose passionate stories of India were second only to his concern for the salvation of his listeners. Without insulting them, he compared the childlike faith of Indian converts with the lackluster nominal faith of most Americans.

After the two-hour sermon, the people gathered around the visitor, busily telling him they were either from the preacher's hometown in Norway or claiming to be related. He would respond to all this adulation by holding his hands up and announcing, "If you are a child of God, we are not only distantly related, we are brothers and sisters." They smiled and clapped in response. Waving his hands to get their attention, he continued, "But, if you are not a child of God, any other relationship means nothing to me." To that pronouncement, some of the adoring crowd looked surprised and turned away as if they had been rebuked.

Following the afternoon meeting, Andreas and Mr. Thompson took the missionary to the railway station. As they drove home, Mr. Thompson commented, "Now, Andreas, that was a fine sermon and no doubt he preaches those same words everywhere he goes, but you offer us a new word every week. We are blessed to have you." For an entire year, there had been handshakes after each service but no one had ever complimented his ministry or his preaching. Mr. Thompson let the young preacher off at his home. They shook hands and Andreas thanked him for his kind words.

Andreas opened the parsonage door and Clara put her hand up to her mouth as if to say, "Shush, the baby is sleeping." With coffee cups on the table, the two sat down. Clara rested her arm on the table. Andreas laid his hand on hers and murmured, "I have something to show you." With surprise on her face she whispered, "What is it?"

Andreas rose from the table, walked into their bedroom and returned with the envelope he had received the day before. "I have received a Letter of Call from another church."

"Oh, Andreas, we have just gotten settled. We can't move yet!" she said.

"I understand, but I need to talk with you about it. I did not want to say anything while Pastor Skrefsrud was here, but the first thing he told me when he arrived was that I was going to receive a Letter of Call."

"How did he know?" Clara asked.

"Because the call is back to Minneapolis, to St. Olaf Church,"

Andreas continued.

"St. Olaf, but that is where Pastor Iversen serves," she said.

"He has recently left," Andreas confided.

"But, we like it here for now at least, don't we?"

"Yes, dear, I do like it and Mr. Thompson just told me that the congregation feels blessed to have us here."

"Well, it's about time they say something. And, with the condition of our personal finances, it's also about time they start paying us what they promised."

"Oh, I know that but we certainly have not starved."

"When it comes to a train ride to Harmony, I don't like to rely on my father for buying the ticket," she continued.

"I know, dear, I know," he said as he continued to softly pat her arm. "Well, I want to think about my sermon for tomorrow," he concluded.

As he left the table, he noticed the worried look on his wife's face.

From that day on, for almost a month, the two talked about a possible life back in Minneapolis. Remembering the needs in McIntosh and knowing they had been there for only a year, Andreas had mixed feelings about the possibility of leaving. He had written Pastor Iversen, asking his reason for leaving St. Olaf. Surprisingly there was no response. Andreas grew worried that something was wrong with the Iversens or with the congregation. He certainly wanted to avoid serving a church that had been unfair to their pastor. As August ended, letters of encouragement arrived from members of the Minneapolis church. Andreas' favorite seminary teacher, Professor Sverdrup, encouraged him by writing, "If you are fearing the lack of ability to serve a larger congregation, remember that God provides. If you are successful in the country, you will do just fine in the city." Clara and Andreas began to think in terms of moving as part of God's will.

With the encouraging letters and Clara's realization that little Petra would be much closer to her grandparents, aunts and uncles, Andreas and Clara left McIntosh the last week of October 1894. Unlike their welcome by only two people 15 months earlier, this time there was a large group of congregants seeing them off. One of those at the farewell was Hans Nielsen, one of the most educated members.

Even so, he had difficulties holding his liquor. On this particular day, his voice was louder than usual and what he said embarrassed everyone. Mr. Thompson tried to usher Hans back to his buggy, but refusing to move, he asked, "Pastor, did you get paid everything you were promised?"

Not wanting to embarrass the members, Andreas simply said, "Don't worry about that, I have been treated well; look at my stomach."

"Well, Pastor, did we pay you more than we agreed?" Hans continued.

"Well, as a matter of fact, no," Andreas answered. By this time, many lowered their eyes and stared at the ground. Andreas thought to himself, "Well, at least Hans is asking the same question Clara brought up a few months earlier."

While another member, with thick and powerful arms, took Hans off the platform, the troublemaker shouted, "I'm an Augsburger; I'm an Augsburger," which only embarrassed the departing pastor more.

Mr. Thompson whispered, "Andreas, we will be sending you what we owe, when we take it in, rest assured of that."

As they left, the members in their native tongue began to sing "God Be With You Till We Meet Again."

Chapter 17

To Minneapolis and Beyond

On the trip to Minneapolis, the young couple talked about the advantages of a larger city. Clara's health had become a concern in the past few months. They both suffered from weakened lungs and were relieved that more specialists were available in Minneapolis. Clara smiled to herself as she thought of being closer to her family, just a few hours south in Harmony. Andreas wondered about the challenges that a larger parish could bring. He thought, "I'm just getting used to preaching every Sunday, and now I wonder who will be seated in the pews." Unlike the few farmers who would attend the four small churches in the McIntosh area, this was a city church. He shook his head and prayed, "Lord help me."

Conversations with professors during the past four years, and personally witnessing impassioned churchmen at conventions, Andreas questioned if he was up to all the politics involved. It seemed so much simpler in Fitjar, where members accepted the pastor sent by the bishop. But now, as an adult and an ordained minister, everything for Andreas was different; everything was much more complex. Complicating the politics as well as the theological fights were his own human frailties, and the realization that his gentle spirit at times did not stand up to the brash behavior of some of his colleagues. On the other hand, it was his quick temper that caused others to step back and question his maturity. Andreas sat back, thinking how he might best fit into the larger church body and into the congregation to which he had been called. Growing more and more concerned, if not depressed, he gazed at his wife, patted her hand and looked into the eyes of their little Petra. Staring out of the window, he noticed the trees already bare in mid October. As they continued south, leaves appeared in brilliant reds and oranges.

Alone in his thoughts as the train rambled on, Andreas remembered his most recent trip to Minneapolis. He had brought greetings at the banquet celebrating the 25th anniversary of Augsburg Seminary. He winced as he thought of how he had looked and felt while plagued by infected eyelids. He recalled the expression on the faces of people meeting him and the excitement he felt about soon returning to live among the people, and the anxiety of his questions and doubts. In the midst of that uncertainty, he was convinced he could help resolve the differences between the two existing factions of the church. One side prized the traditions of the State Church of Norway, where the authority was placed with the bishop and synod, while Andreas sided with those who believed that more authority resided within the individual congregation. He wondered just how long these battles might last.

His questions, doubts and excitement piled up like the stacks of luggage on the wagon next to the tracks as they headed into the Great Northern station. Having sold their ponies and buggy, for the time being they would rely on walking, the kindness of others and the few streetcar lines available to them.

Clara gathered up the sleeping baby in her arms and Andreas guided them down the steps onto the platform. There, waiting for them, were Mr. and Mrs. Melby. Andreas had visited with the short, rotund balding man just a few weeks earlier. His wife was three inches taller than her husband and as thin as a three-penny nail. His broad smile was tempered by her rather severe, serious expression.

Mr. Melby was the first to speak. "You will be staying with us just a few days until you are able to purchase your furniture and get settled." Mrs. Melby politely shook their hands and pointed them toward the buggy. While Clara, Petra and Mrs. Melby sat in silence, Andreas and Mr. Melby talked of the weather while waiting for the luggage. Once it arrived, they drove to the Melby house, just south of the parsonage. With the buggy parked, the horses in the stable and the five of them sitting in the living room, Clara broke what seemed like a long silence with the request, "May I see the parsonage?"

"Of course," Mr. Melby replied, "Let me take you right over." "Mother," he said to his wife, "these two must be starved. Let's have dinner together when we return." Without saying a word, she went to the kitchen. The others walked out the front door and over to the Helland's new home. Short of breath, Clara handed her daughter to

Andreas as they stood to look at the front of the house. It was a bit larger than the home they had just left. Clara was thrilled to find a separate living room, dining room, kitchen, bath and two bedrooms. She marveled at the simple-but-beautiful woodwork that decorated the living and dining areas. Two small piano windows highlighted the built-in hutch and the oak floors looked nearly new. After returning to each empty room, they went back to the Melby's for a quiet dinner.

The young couple awoke the next morning relieved that little Petra had not cried during the night. In the morning, the few pieces of furniture they had brought from McIntosh were delivered and Mr. Melby, Andreas, Clara and little Petra set out for the used furniture stores in the area. Purchasing what they could afford, Andreas and his host negotiated a loan from one furniture store. With the business concluded, the furniture was stacked on the wagon and brought home. Clara was especially proud of the almost-new dining room table. It had four wooden chairs with woven wicker seats. As the final pieces were unloaded and carried into the parsonage, Clara remarked, "This house is just a smaller version of the one I grew up in. It's beautiful." By the next day the Helland family was home.

In the next few days, the usual expressions of welcome were delivered to the parsonage: cakes, pies and tea towels sewn by some of the ladies of the parish. The following Sunday was a cold and windy November day. Andreas was installed at the morning service, followed by a coffee-and-cake reception. One of his mentors, Professor Sverdrup, attended. In the sermon delivered by Professor Blegen, Andreas was reminded that there could be times when he would be tempted to give up; times when he would want to say, "What's the use?" As a response to those temptations, the professor encouraged him to "keep close to the Savior in prayer and meditation, and through it you will receive strength." Those words were to be a valuable counsel in years to come.

Feelings of disappointment came to Andreas and Clara within the first couple weeks of their arrival. There was no one bringing milk each day, or weekly offerings of meat, potatoes or canned goods. They quickly realized that city folk were expected to be self-reliant.

Because they were being paid less than in McIntosh, every penny would now need to go to the local grocer and meat market. It was Grandma Rockne who kept busy sewing for both her granddaughter and daughter. Andreas continued to wear the few suits he had brought with him, many dating back to his earlier time in Norway.

As the windy days of November turned to the bitter cold of December and January, Clara began to wonder if her fatigue had to do only with the tiring task of moving. Her cough became a constant companion. It was on a Friday afternoon that Andreas arrived home early to find both Clara and Petra fast asleep.

Later that evening, after supper, Andreas thought about the challenges of this relatively young congregation. Along with the rest of the nation, his members were enduring high unemployment commonly referred to as "the depression of '93." As in other churches, these financial struggles created the need for many to rely on something besides their own strong work ethic. Slowly but surely, a spiritual revival began to make its way to congregations like St. Olaf.

August 5, 1895
Dear Mother and Father,
As we have written, our adjustment to city life has gone quite well. We do miss the friendships we gained in McIntosh when members would stop by and visit. This does not seem to happen in a city church. With so many people surrounding us, it is surprising that we feel lonelier than when we were in the country. I do not want to get your hopes up, but I have begun talking with Clara about my return visit to you possibly next summer. I have missed you so very much. We felt like Americans as we celebrated their Independence Day last July 4th. My memory of Peder's summertime death does dampen my celebratory spirit. Caring for Petra, who began walking quite early and is now running around the house, keeps Clara busy. She often becomes quite tired. I have encouraged her to take daily naps along with our little one.
In June, I had the opportunity to help Kristen, Anna and their two children pack up and move from Racine to Harmony where

Clara's father found employment for him, at least during the harvest season. We thank God for this opportunity. So, once again, Kristen is a farmer. It is good to have them closer to us and fun to visit them when we make our way to Clara's family home. Clara and Petra will spend the rest of the summer in Harmony. I will soon join them for a week. I look forward to the quiet of the farm and possibly seeing Pastor Dreyer again.

As I have gotten to know the pastors in the area, I realize how careful I need to be. Emotions are running high between the conference churches and what are becoming known as the "Friends of Augsburg." Although my father-in-law is a staunch supporter of the conference congregations, my congregation is truly committed to the Friends of Augsburg. I fear it will not be long before we will need to separate ourselves from the very conference into which I was ordained.

Please continue to pray for Clara and her lack of strength. I hope and pray this letter finds the two of you, and others, well. Please send greetings to all.

Your son,
Andreas

Before long Clara explained to Andreas the reason for her fatigue; she was pregnant for the second time. Again, Andreas wrote his family back home with the good news. It was on a cold January day in 1896 that little Melvin Andreas Helland was born in the St. Olaf parsonage. Like Petra, his name was carefully chosen, this time in honor of his grandfathers; his first name, Melvin, for Grandpa Mikkel Rockne and his middle name, Andreas, in honor of Anders, his grandfather in Norway.

Baby Melvin spent days lying in his crib or on blankets in the corner of the kitchen. Petra would busily make her way to the corner to plant a big-sister kiss on Melvin's forehead.

Chapter 18

Family Reunion

With the activities of the church and keeping up with two children, there was little time to plan Andreas' dream of visiting Norway. But, just 16 months after Melvin's birth, Andreas began his journey. For three months, Clara survived Andreas' absence by moving with the children back to her family farm. She would sit and rock on the front porch as Petra ran through the apple orchard and Melvin stumbled behind. With Grandma and Grandpa Rockne always there to babysit, Clara enjoyed her summer sewing and reading. She eagerly awaited the arrival of her husband's precious letters.

Andreas' traveling partner was Nils Halvorson, a good friend who served a church in Fargo. Following their three-day, second-class rail trip, they boarded a steamer in New York. The accommodations had not improved much in the seven years since Andreas had last crossed the Atlantic. Having to pay a substitute pastor his entire salary, Andreas had little money to spare. Just prior to boarding, they were able to purchase straw mattresses from passengers who had just disembarked. Carpetbags in one hand and mattresses slung over their shoulders, they made their way up the gangplank, across the deck and down many flights of stairs into the lower realms of the ship.

Assigned a windowless cabin that slept 14 other men, they each selected a bunk, laid down their mattresses, stored their luggage and returned to the deck to wave farewell to Lady Liberty. As the ship steamed toward England and on to Bergen, their days were spent reading, writing and standing in line for meals. In the large third-class lounge, it was often difficult to concentrate with children running and mothers shouting commands. Andreas was relieved by not having to struggle with language. Now fluent in English, he could converse with many of the passengers on board. It was in the cool air, walking the deck that he experienced mixed feelings. Though missing Clara and his two little ones, he was anxious to see his two sisters and his parents. He wondered about the condition of his 72-year-old father and his mother, now 63. In their letters, they never complained about life over the years. He wondered just how they might have changed. On his voyage to America, he had never imagined being away this long. The last time they saw him, he was a young, strapping 19-year-old. Now he was returning as a husband and father of two. He wondered about his sister, Helga, now a mature 40-year-old woman he hardly knew. Andreas was very excited about seeing Martha. She had played the role of big sister and substitute mother. Besides his dear brother, Peder, she was by far his dearest sibling.

The ocean trip was over as the steamer docked in Bergen. A neighbor had rowed the 40 miles to meet Andreas. With choppy seas, they immediately got on their way. It wasn't but a mile into this last leg of the trip that Andreas realized how weak he had become after eight years away from rowing. As they approached the island of Stord, Andreas was again able to see the little village and the hills where he had been raised. While they tied up in the harbor of Fitjar, Andreas found it difficult to even lift his carpetbag out of the boat. Walking up the path toward home, he could hear the neighbor's jovial laughter and a gentle tease, "Will you make it up the hill, Andreas? Do you think you can make it?" Trying to ignore the comment, the tired traveler put his luggage down, looked back and simply said, "Yes, yes." He picked it up again with the other hand and continued on, slowing with every step.

With the Helland house in sight, he saw Martha running toward him, "Andreas! Andreas! You are home!" As she ran into his arms, he dropped his bag and gave her a long, warm embrace. They walked together up the path and to the house where his life had begun 26 years earlier.

His mother, with her short, plump body, limped toward him, revealing a shy smile. A glimmer of joy shown in her eyes. With the aid of a cane, his father approached slowly and carefully. Andreas knew his plans for spending extra time in Stavanger and Oslo were dashed. The mortality of his parents hit him like the worst of a winter gale. Covering his feelings with a smile, he hugged his mother and shook hands with his father. During the coming weeks he worked with his father in the field and with his mother in her garden. Evenings were taken up with visits from neighbors, extended family and friends.

June 15, 1896
  Dear Clara, Petra and little Melvin,
    I am glad to tell you that I have arrived safely in Fitjar. Oh, how I wish you were with me. I hope you received my postcard telling you of my safe arrival in New York. The seas were mostly calm and we arrived on time. I left Nils in Bergen and will meet up with him again for the return trip. I find Martha in good health, and this coming weekend I will be seeing Helga, meeting her husband and children for the first time.
    Everyone marvels at how my mustache has grown. They tell me I look so much older. Both father and mother are slowing down, so I am happy to take over the chores and help with the fieldwork. The visits I had so looked forward to in Stavanger and Oslo will be very much shortened.
    I admit my arms are no longer as strong as when I was a 19-year old accustomed to rowing. Thankfully the aches and pains are slowly subsiding. I am lucky not to suffer from any lung trouble.
    Greetings from Mother, Father and Martha. I will write again.
  Much love,
  Andreas

The summer passed quickly, and it was time for Andreas to leave the island. This time there was no promise of a future visit to his parents and sisters. It was a heavy load to bear—the thought of never seeing his parents or dear Martha again. No matter how much he missed Clara and the family, in those last few days he caught himself wondering why he had listened to the voice at the well, saying, "Why not go to America and stay there for three or four years and make money?"

He chuckled when he remembered the words "and make money." Along with so many others, Andreas, too, had believed that mistaken notion about America.

The last day of his visit arrived and, as if morning fog had swept its way up the hill and into the Helland cottage, sadness hung in the air. It was only his mother who could say what was on everyone's hearts and minds. "If not here, then in glory we will meet again," she said, dabbing her eyes. Fixing breakfast, at their daily devotions and again at supper, she kept repeating the same litany, "If not here, then in glory we will meet again." While she and Andreas talked, Anders stared beyond them, as if this moment was too painful for words.

The next morning, Bertha and Anders stood at the gate to their modest farmstead as Helga, her husband and children, and Martha accompanied Andreas slowly down the path toward the small harbor. There, the same neighbor was ready to row the prodigal back to Bergen.

Andreas stood one last time on the dock, looking up toward the field where he and his father had built the stage and lectern for the annual mission conference 14 years earlier. His mind flooded with memories of the strong preachers and the overwhelming sound of hundreds of people singing. He stared up at the school where he had gotten such a late start. Glancing to the right, he saw the church building where he had been baptized. Many pastors had come and gone in this humble parish. Trying to smile, then unfolding his handkerchief, Andreas looked into the moist eyes of his sisters. Over and over again he said, "Takk for sist" or "Thanks for the last time." Finally he turned and, with his well-traveled carpetbag, Andreas boarded the small boat, now heaped with potatoes bound for the Bergen market.

Between rowing and waving, it was not long before his family lost sight of the small boat. Andreas was on his way home again. The only relief from the grief he felt was knowing that the next few days would be filled with visiting friends in Stavanger and Oslo, and then finally returning to Clara, the children and his ministry.

JOURNAL August 20, 1896

We boarded our ship in Bergen. Between there and Hull, the seas were quite choppy and now, on the open waters, they seemed to have calmed. What a wonderful-yet-difficult visit. During the last few days, I was able to see my friends in Oslo and Stavanger. Although Mrs. Fleum is no longer the matron at the Country Boy's Home, I was able to revisit my room and even enjoyed another cookie right out of the oven. In Oslo, I visited my old friend Eric Eriksen. He has become a professor and now holds a doctorate of philosophy. He showed me one of his latest publications. Seven years ago, he had great interest in spiritism, and for that matter many other isms, but I was thankful to hear of his return to the Christian faith.

I have enjoyed traveling with Nils Halvorson. We have talked of our challenges and joys in parish life.

I think I will close for now. The sea has become quite rough and writing is difficult.

Chapter 19

Sorrow Visits

When he returned home, Andreas was reminded of how much he had missed Clara and the two children as well as the congregation. He was amazed at how Melvin had grown, and how fast Petra had discovered the world around her.

Coming home to north Minneapolis, the parsonage, and the church brought mixed feelings. Andreas knew how much Clara enjoyed rural life and seeing her extended family so often. On the other hand, he was grateful for their warm and quite-modern home. It was a sharp contrast to the small farmhouse in which his parents had lived all their married life.

Although Andreas considered some of his congregation to be "confessing Christians," he was concerned for the majority of members who appeared to be less dedicated. There was also a visible tension between the two groups. With the constant balancing act of faithfully serving every member of the congregation, those faithful and those not, Andreas was blessed with having to deal with only a few whom some called "bad apples" within his membership. They would quietly complain about the general membership or about specific individuals who placed their own selfish desires above that of the congregation. At the congregational annual meeting, these men would ask some mean-spirited questions about issues out of the pastor's control.

During the winter of '98, a most pleasant event took place in the life of the congregation. Covenant and Lutheran evangelists began the year visiting the city and caused a spiritual revival that Andreas only attributed to the work of the Holy Spirit. While, thankfully, it did not create spiritual radicalism or spiritual confusion, it did bring a new surge in worship attendance and sober spiritual growth among the members of St. Olaf.

Just as the spiritual revival bore fruit, so it was with Andreas' family. Early in January, the word in the pew and on the street was how much the pastor's wife was "showing." Their third baby arrived in late spring. The three children had been born in a span of six years. This time it was a large baby boy—Bernhard Alvin. His name honored his two grandmothers, the "B" in Bernhard was a tribute to Bertha Helland, and the "A" in Alvine was for Grandma Anna Rockne.

During that year the family flourished, with Melvin now discovering the world around him. Baby Bernhard seemed to grow faster and taller than the two other children had. While Andreas carried on with his ministry during the summer, Clara and the three children spent another summer in Harmony with Grandma, Grandpa and Sophia. As the summer ended, Clara's mother noticed her daughter's weakened condition. When Andreas arrived in Harmony for his annual vacation, Mrs. Rockne insisted that when they returned to Minneapolis, Clara should see a lung specialist. He agreed although Clara balked at the idea, explaining that her fatigue and cough was only the result of caring for three small children.

Clara would say, "I'll be just fine, Andreas; I'll be just fine."

As late summer turned to fall, the leaves dropped along with the temperature. Clara's health still concerned Andreas. Christmas passed and as the Hellands entered the last year of the century, the young mother came down with a serious case of influenza. She was finally forced to seek medical treatment. The doctor dismissed her persistent cough as harmless. As spring arrived, Clara's condition had worsened. To their complete surprise, she was prescribed a treatment that included sleeping in a tent in northern Minnesota.

Leaving the children in Harmony, Andreas and Clara spent a number of weeks up north. Every other Sunday, Andreas returned to Minneapolis to lead worship and care for the sick. As the summer passed, Clara's hopes grew and she felt somewhat stronger. Returning to Minneapolis in September, they prayed that more treatment would allow Clara to rest and Andreas to return to his normal duties at St. Olaf. Their visit to Dr. Bell caused both relief and disappointment. Although Clara's lungs seemed better, she was told that the only long-term cure would be to winter in a very dry climate. The doctor suggested Arizona. Concerned for his wife's health and his growing congregation, Andreas consulted with the doctor as well as his church board. The spiritual revival from the past year inspired widespread concern for the pastor and his family. There were no naysayers with regard to the temporary absence of Andreas from his pulpit.

It was decided that while the two of them tried Arizona for the winter, Auntie Sophia from Harmony would move into a small apartment in Minneapolis to care for Petra and Melvin. The baby, Bernhard, would live with his grandparents in Harmony. Andreas' past years of service and kindness to others was returned with offers from local pastors and seminary students to cover his church duties at no cost.

On October 3, Andreas and Clara boarded the train for Phoenix. They were both buoyed by the doctor's recommendation, yet felt pangs of sadness, already missing their three children.

October 10, 1899
Phoenix, Arizona
Dear Grandma and Grandpa Rockne,
I am writing to assure you that Clara is doing fine. She is very tired from the long trip. With the salary still coming my way, we rented a small cottage a distance out of town. This is a city of about 15,000 souls where we have already found a kind Methodist pastor who will check in with us from time to time. There are no Lutheran churches in these parts. You will note that I am already using the local vernacular. Here they always refer to "these parts."

As we are adjusting to our new surroundings, we are missing the three children so very much. I pray that Clara's sadness will not get in the way of her healing. Sophia may have told you that we were able to rent a small apartment for her during this time, renting out the parsonage and placing many of our possessions in storage. This arrangement has helped financially. As we traveled west, all Clara could talk about was the children and her wish for another summer on the farm. We are so thankful for your constant hospitality.

Well, I must take another lesson in cooking so that my dear

Mother *can rest. Already we cannot imagine a Christmas without our children. Still know that God will be faithful.*
 Love,
 Andreas

Before long, Andreas noticed a great improvement in his wife's health. In written form at least, he began to call her *"Mother"* rather than by her name. He would write *"Mother* is doing better" in his letters to Harmony, Sophia, his family in Norway and the congregation.

Christmas came and was about the only cloudy day they had seen in months. Clara sent small gifts back to the children. The couple decided to forego gifts and simply enjoyed each other's company. Rather than lefse, for this one year, they ate tortillas. To surprise Clara, Andreas visited a local meat market and bought pork chops for their Christmas dinner.

The dry climate was healing one of Clara's lungs and, as the first days of the New Year passed, there were moments of real hope. For the caretaking husband, the days were filled with theological reading and letter writing. Clara spent her time knitting, sewing children's outfits and with occasional visits to the doctor. As the days passed, they learned that the creosote she religiously took was killing germs yet damaging the lining of her stomach and intestines. Her fear of the future was overshadowed only by her intense homesickness and grief at not being the mother she had dreamed of becoming. Her heart broke every time she gazed at photographs of her children. Hours of weeping were interrupted by long spells of coughing. Often Andreas joined her, feeling his own sense of despair. Their hopelessness was somewhat relieved by worship in a local Methodist church and the visits of its pastor.

While the low humidity felt good, they both longed to return to the life they knew. One sunny winter morning found them once again in the doctor's office waiting for his latest diagnosis. Following a test, the doctor walked back into the examining room with a morose look on his face. He sat down behind his desk and spoke in a gentle, kindly voice.

"From what I see, I believe your digestive organs have begun to fail."

Clara stared at him in silence. Alarmed, Andreas moved to the edge of the chair. "What does that mean? What must we do now?"

"I'm afraid there is not much we can do, Pastor. I think you had better return immediately to Minnesota to see your family."

"For a visit, you mean…and then we should return here?" Andreas asked.

Clara cleared her throat and continued coughing. Andreas kept trying to understand what the doctor had said. His words seemed not to make sense.

"Pastor, you will not be able to return. This is all we can do."

"But, I think we can rent the cottage next year."

"No, Pastor, you do not understand," the doctor repeated. "This is all we can do for Clara. We do not have any more treatments for her condition. The medicine has broken down her digestive system."

As they left the office, politely thanking the doctor, Andreas began to think, "What am I thanking him for? He is taking my wife away."

Once back at the small cottage, Andreas arranged to purchase the tickets back to Harmony.

"I want to see my children," Clara kept on saying. "I want to see my children."

"Once we get to Harmony, I will find another specialist. I have heard there are good doctors in Rochester. We can try there," Andreas said in an encouraging voice.

While Clara rested, her husband of seven years took a walk. Sweat poured off his forehead as he noticed a thermometer on a post that read 91 degrees. While he mopped his forehead, tears began to flow more easily than ever before. Andreas had lost his brother and now was he actually going to lose his wife?

Andreas immediately packed for their journey home. Not known for his cooking, Andreas did the best he could to prepare what was left in the icebox. Following supper, he went to the owner of the cottage to announce their plans. The owner's kind words of support caused Andreas' eyes to again swell with tears.

Four days later, Andreas and Clara stepped off the train in Harmony. The temperature had dropped 109 degrees since they left the Arizona heat. Though the sun was high in the sky, the thermometer read 18 degrees below zero. Instead of a four-mile trip to the Rockne farm, the two were bundled up in a buggy and delivered to Andreas' brother's nearby log home. With warmer weather the next day, Clara was brought to the Rockne's farm house where she was reunited with Sophia, Petra, Melvin, Bernhard and the rest of her family. Even Andreas' brother, Kristen, rode through blowing snow to be there. In the next few days, Clara became bedridden in her childhood home.

As energy began to escape from her already-weakened body, she began to lapse in and out of consciousness. When she could be understood, her mumbling messages were about visiting angels. As the family sat around her bed, Andreas could feel the slight breath escaping her mouth and hear her say, "Oh, but it is beautiful over there!" With those words, the ever-so-slight breath simply stopped. There was silence, then tears, followed by a husband laying his head upon her breast while saying in a pleading voice, "Oh, Clara, Clara." The wooden floor softly creaked as those gathered slowly walked down the stairs to the parlor. Church members had gathered in the kitchen with their gifts of baked goods and loving presence.

On a cold, sunny day, in the same church where she had been baptized and confirmed, Clara's life was remembered with love. Pastor Dreyer, who had warmly welcomed Andreas to the community so many years before, officiated at Clara's funeral. Members of St. Olaf Church had traveled from Minneapolis to support their Pastor Helland and his young family.

February 15, 1900
Dear Mother and Father,
This is one of those letters that no one wants to write. I must tell you that my dear Clara died just a few days ago. We had arrived back from Arizona where the doctor had informed us that she would not survive this terrible disease. Her lung problems seemed only to grow worse. While the medication killed the germs, it ate away at her stomach.

On the day she died, Kristen and I took a walk down the road in front of the Rockne farm. In the midst of great sadness, my visit with him was so very important to me. Our talk of personal matters encouraged me. The two of you were also in our conversation. I have boldly requested a loan from a member of St. Olaf in order to purchase a ticket for Kristen's return to visit you and help with whatever plans you may have for the future. If you are going to move this year, as you well know, it must be done in the spring. If you choose to take Helga's offer to live with her, the land will revert to its owner and Kristen will help in the sale of the house and anything you are unable to take with you. I hope these plans for this visit come as good news. He will leave around Easter time, arriving in Fitjar 10 or 11 days later. He will be able to stay for two or three months to help you.

I also need to quickly make plans for my future. I am wondering if sister, Martha, might be able to come here to care for the children. Clara's sister Sophia has been so much help these last months but she is also needed in Harmony.

Please pray for me. It will be difficult to return to my parish without my dear Clara. Still, I must carry on. In the meantime, Sophia will be helping me with the children.

Love, from your grieving son,
Andreas

Once Andreas' parents received his letter, they began to make arrangements for their move to Aga and a new life with Helga and her large family. When Kristen arrived at the Helland Farm, he sold the little cottage, the old plow, the cow and sheep and the few belongings they would not need at Helga's home.

On moving day, 75-year-old farmer, Anders, with cane in hand, insisted on walking the path down to the boat landing. He stopped and looked across the field where he and Andreas had built the stage for the mission conference so many years ago. He and Bertha, hand in hand, made their way past the schoolhouse, the new church and finally to the dock. When the elderly couple got settled in Aga,

Kristen and his sister, Martha, sailed to Bergen, on to England, and then to America. Only a few days before their sailing, Andreas received Martha's letter telling of her decision to come to care for his children.

Sophia had been a great help, but later it became evident that she had been stricken with tuberculosis. With Martha's arrival, Sophia returned to Harmony.

JOURNAL July 5, 1900

I received good news today—a letter from home telling me of Martha's decision to come and help me care for the children. What a gift! What a relief!

I have not been able to keep up with this writing, but thought it was time to put into words my feelings and experiences since Mother Clara's death. Without her at my side, I simply do not have the energy to continue the pace at St. Olaf. Members are whispering about my health, afraid that I, too, am suffering from tuberculosis.

My sleepless nights, filled with tears and shivering, remind me of the days when Clara was so sick. Shivering together, we would cross our feet to warm them. Together, in the middle of the night, we would pray our Lord's Prayer. If we were not able to sleep, I would read to her one of her favorite Psalms. Even in the suffering, we had such a good life.

Now, I shiver alone in my bed. There is no one to pray with me. Oh, how I miss her. What a trial this is.

Tired and trying to balance work and time with his three children, Andreas was finally convinced to visit a Norwegian lung specialist who said, "Pastor, you are suffering from kidney disease and, yes, your lungs are also affected. But I think we can treat your problems with a drug I will prescribe."

Andreas thanked him and asked him for the bill. He paid the $2 for the visit, purchased the prescription and walked back into the summer heat.

A week passed and Andreas' symptoms had not improved. He decided to visit Clara's doctor whose clinic was in a triangular building on Riverside Avenue, just a block from Augsburg Seminary. Following the examination, Dr. Bell told Andreas that, although he looked poorly, he did not have tuberculosis.

"Your lungs are very weak, but they are not infected. I know you cannot leave your work, but you must let go of those things others can do for you. Although this is a condition you will battle for the rest of your life, I do not see it shortening your life by even one day," the doctor assured Andreas.

Thanking the doctor, Andreas turned toward the door. The first smile in a long time appeared on his face while a tear of joy ran down his cheek. He felt a new spring in his step as he walked out into the sunny day. "That is the best news I have heard in years. Dr. Bell is a gentle soul. Thank you, Jesus, thank you," he said to himself.

Opening the parsonage gate, Petra and Melvin were full of smiles for their papa. Andreas thought, "With Martha's help, I can do this." And, there she was in the doorway, carrying a plate of fresh cookies just like the ones he had enjoyed at the Country Boy's Home in Stavanger.

The days and weeks marched on. It was not long before Pastor Sverdrup called Andreas into his office. The professor asked if Andreas would be interested in spending a year or more at the Norwegian Mission Center in South Africa. Tempted to immediately say *yes* to escape the responsibilities of the congregation, Andreas agreed to at least pray about it.

A week later, he and Professor Sverdrup spoke again. Andreas began, "You know how much I love adventure and I do have a deep and enduring call to missions. Yet, I have already been away from my congregation for eight months and have three children to look after. I would love to take you up on your offer, but I must decline."

With Doctor Bell's encouraging news and Martha's help, Andreas began to see the sun make its way through what had been months of dark clouds. Just as that glimmer of hope appeared, a letter from Norway arrived.

Dear Andreas, Martha and Family,

I am so saddened to tell you that Father, dear Anders, died not long after he and Mother arrived to live with us. Although he was weaker than Mother, we thought he had taken the move quite well. I had just served them fresh bread and a morning cup of coffee when he slumped over and fell from his chair. I had a neighbor go for the doctor, but when he arrived Father had already begun his life in glory. Following the funeral service he was buried in our church cemetery. I am sorry to have to give you this news so soon after dear Clara's death and Martha's arrival.

Mother is doing as well as she can after being with Father for so many years. They had a difficult but joyful life together. I don't know of anyone who began to prepare for Christmas quite as early as Father. He was the quiet one, but certainly the far-better singer.

Please write when you receive this letter so that I know the sad news was delivered. Our daily prayers at the table include all of you. Please keep Mother in your prayers.

Love, your sister,

Helga

The news came as a sudden shock to all. Far from being over the death of Clara, the only ray of light for Andreas came from the joy his children brought.

As months passed, Andreas found some solace in his work at church and his involvement with Augsburg Seminary.

It seemed new opportunities would keep coming. By now the Lutheran Free Church had been established and was becoming even more closely linked to Augsburg Preparatory School and Seminary.

Chapter 20

A New Life

In his first 31 years, Andreas wrestled with every challenge imaginable. He spent summer days helping his parents on their small farm; in the evenings he fished for brown cod. He also had convinced his parents to allow him to attend boarding school. He received a B.A. degree from the Cathedral School in Stavanger, an M.A. degree from the university in Oslo and served as a substitute teacher on an island outside of Fitjar. One might think that was enough to accomplish in the first third of life, but that all happened by the age of 19. Always an adventurer, he succumbed to America Fever, which took him on his first transatlantic voyage. Once in America, he stocked shelves in a general store, taught parochial school, graduated from seminary, served as pastor of two congregations, married, fathered three children and, by the age of 31, had already lost his wife to lung disease.

Now it was difficult to focus on anything but getting through the immediate demands of his ministry and the needs of his children. Thinking of the future was like looking into a midnight darkness. Tormented by sleepless nights, his heart ached for Clara. He questioned how God could allow anyone to feel such loneliness. "Why, Lord, why?" he would pray. He never dreamed that Clara would be the first to go home to her Heavenly Father.

Sitting at his black Underwood typewriter late at night, he tried to write, wanting to preserve his memories of life with Clara. He thought of the long talks he enjoyed with his father-in-law, Mikkel, while sitting on the Rockne's big front porch. Each time Andreas would share the story of his coming to America with Mikkel, there seemed to be a new detail emerging from his memory. His stories would prompt Mikkel to share his own immigration story. Andreas was captivated by Mikkel's search for quality farmland which led him to the Dakotas, to Iowa and finally to Minnesota. Along with the story came the pride in Mikkel's voice and joy on his face.

"You know, Andreas, we were able to purchase the land for $150, using five $10-gold pieces as a down payment. For the pair of oxen and harness, we paid $63 to a hard-driving merchant. I remember Anna insisting that I not make an offer on the Sabbath, so we waited until Monday. She had been taught that Sunday was intended only for worship. Even between two farmers, business can make room for the Lord's Day. Clara had a lot of her mother in her, you know. The first spring we dug up 12 acres using only a hoe and spade. It was back-breaking work."

Andreas longed for the sunsets he had witnessed while sitting on the Rockne porch, and the view of the green fields, ripe with corn.

Those late-night memories brought both comfort and pain. With his white handkerchief always ready in his pocket, Andreas would wipe his eyes, trying once again to begin writing a sermon or letter.

As the weeks grew into months, Professor Sverdrup presented a new challenge for Andreas, hoping it might give him a new lease on life. To his surprise, his next opportunity to serve the church came through a formal election. Nominated by his mentor and supported by many others, Andreas was elected Augsburg Seminary's treasurer. Although the opportunity meant some travel, he would no longer be at the beck and call of congregational emergencies and the weekly responsibilities of serving a large parish. Obediently, and with as much joy as he could muster, Andreas accepted this new position. With no one able to serve St. Olaf until a new pastor arrived, Andreas filled both positions for some time.

Finally, with the arrival of Pastor Elias Harbo in May of 1902, Andreas was able to resign from St. Olaf Church. He was pleased to know that the role of treasurer included putting to use another one of his passions, that of fundraising. Whether raising funds for a family, church or institutional budget, Andreas had always taken great interest in finance. He also enjoyed the added assignment of teaching in the preparatory school. He confided to Professor Sverdrup that it was these new challenges, as well as his duties at home, that kept his spirits from sinking any deeper.

Over the years, Andreas had learned the challenges of church politics and the disappointments that came with them, but soon he would experience the full force of such dividedness. It all began with an ending. The day following the dedication of the new Augsburg Seminary building, the beloved Professor Oftedal surprisingly resigned from his teaching duties. A group of congregations known as the "Friends of Augsburg" had formally organized as the Lutheran Free Church in 1897. Wishing to sustain the close connection between congregations and their seminary, both the churches and the seminary desired to have a say regarding the selection of professors. By the end of the spring term of 1903, there were three worthy candidates to fill the position. One of the names was that of Augsburg's treasurer.

In early June, a prominent layman, Ole Johnson, made an appointment to visit with Andreas.

"Pastor Helland," Ole began, "I want to tell you what a fine job you are doing as Augsburg's treasurer and fundraiser. You are a very well-liked pastor within our church and also an effective treasurer. As a layman, I appreciate that very much."

"Thank you," Andreas said, waiting for the man to continue.

"Well, getting to the point, I would hope that you stay on as treasurer. As you know, names are being circulated regarding Professor Oftedal's position. Along with many others, I might say, I believe Oftedal's position would be best filled by Dr. Evjen."

Surprised by Mr. Johnson's blunt approach, Andreas turned his desk chair and gazed out his office window.

Mr. Johnson continued, "It would be best for everyone if you would publicly state that you will not run nor be available for the open position. As I said, I know many people who appreciate your work as treasurer and have desired for quite some time to see Dr. Evjen in Oftedal's position."

Andreas turned back to face his visitor once more and said, "I see."

For a time both sat silent while sipping their coffee. "I am sure you know, Andreas, that Pastor Laurhammer does not have the votes to be elected and, if you choose to do what is best for Augsburg, you will also be doing what is best for the church and for yourself."

Again, Andreas swiveled his chair and stared out the office window. "I see," were his only words.

"I pray and hope that today you might make your decision known in order that all of this can be cleared up. As I said," Mr. Johnson continued, "you are so well liked as a pastor and are doing such a fine job as the treasurer. I believe this approach may very well be God's will."

Following a few more sips of coffee, Andreas turned his chair to face his visitor and began, "Ole, you and I have known each other for many years now. Let me say this: I am not so simple minded as to declare publicly or privately that I will accept something that has not yet been offered. I do not consider myself in some race for a position. I refuse to make myself the laughing stock of the conference."

"Well, I am saddened we could not come to an agreement on this most important topic," Ole said.

He quickly shook Andreas' hand, excused himself and left. Johnson's remark had effectively raised the young pastor's ire. In a few minutes, Andreas also left the office to walk in the tree filled park across from the campus. The park always calmed his spirit.

This important position would remain open for some time. While the possibility of teaching as a full professor lingered in the back of his mind, Andreas spent the last half of 1902 and all of the next year busy raising funds for the new seminary building. With the help of a well-known Minneapolis attorney, Mr. Ino Archtander, the fundraising activity was seen as a great success.

Life for Andreas, Martha and the children had finally calmed down. The intense grief was slowly subsiding and Andreas could again begin to look toward the future. By 1903, Petra, Melvin and Bernhard were thriving under the care of dear Tante Martha. Her constant care gave Andreas the opportunity to continue his ongoing work at Augsburg.

By the time the 1903 conference of the Lutheran Free Church took place, the faculty and board of directors at Augsburg, to the disappointment of Ole Johnson, had recommended Andreas for a scholarship in graduate study in New Testament and church history at the university in Oslo. Of course, the decision to accept this scholarship, and the position of professor following it, meant a great deal of sacrifice, especially for Martha and the children. They would not be seeing their brother and father for some 18 months. There was one other person for whom this departure also hurt a great deal. In the months prior to his leaving, Andreas had been seeing a beautiful lady by the name of Helen Anderson, a member of the St. Olaf congregation. After moving from her home in Owatonna, Helen had worked in the Minneapolis area for some time.

It was on a cold January day that friends and family gathered at the Great Northern Station to bid Andreas farewell. Following repeated hugs and kisses for his three children, he planted one last kiss on the lady who was by then no stranger to the Helland household. As he said goodbye to her, other ladies from St. Olaf were abuzz as to what it meant for the future, not aware yet that Helen had said "Yes" to Andreas' recent marriage proposal. Martha, and of course Helen, knew the pain Andreas was feeling leaving his fiancé behind. As the train slowly made its way out of the Great Northern Station, his children waved wildly at their father while many on the platform were talking only of "the last kiss."

Finally in Bergen, Andreas took another steamer toward the island of Stord. His brother-in-law, Nils Aga, Helga's husband, was waiting with his boat at Fitjar, to take Andreas to his island home. Before boarding Nils' boat, Andreas quickly walked up the path from the dock to visit his schoolhouse and church. As he opened the door to each of the wooden buildings, memories of childhood flooded back.

With the wind increasing and the waters quite choppy, Nils shouted, "It's time we go or we might be stuck here. Come on, Andreas."

As Nils grabbed his brother-in-law's hand to help him aboard, he declared, "I guess we had better try it in Jesus' name!"

At times the water splashed over the bow and they felt as if they were in a little boat being played with by a child. Luckily the wind caught the sail and quickly brought them to the island on which the Aga family lived. They were relieved to have made it across the choppy waters. The storm continued to rage for the next two days. Andreas felt great comfort and calm as he visited with his mother, still spry though 70 years old. She looked so much better than he had imagined. Helga's children kept his mother's hands busy knitting and sewing.

Friday brought calm seas, and Andreas was again forced to say goodbye to his family. From the dock, after arriving safely in Bergen, he looked up at the city in which he once peddled his father's potato crop as a 12-year old. Unlike his home in Minnesota, in this last week of January, he was able to enjoy the budding hedges and greening vegetation. The warm weather seemed to create a new bounce in his step as he walked the streets of Bergen, awaiting the steamer bound for Oslo.

January 30, 1904
Dear Helen,

I must begin by saying how much I already miss you and the children. I can find comfort only in knowing we have made our plans for the future. Both the train trip to New York and the steamer voyage were uneventful. I was able to spend much of the time reading and writing. In fact, I began more than one letter to you but never seemed to finish them and so now I sit down in my rented room in Oslo to write you.

I was able to find lodging in a large home where an older couple rents rooms to students. We are conveniently close to the university. Included in my rent are two meals a day—breakfast and supper. Even before I brought my belongings to my room, Mrs. Stensgard offered me coffee and fresh cookies. Of course, they did not come up to the baking you have done for the children and me.

I am glad to report that my mother, Helga, Nils and children are in good health. I look forward to seeing them at least a few times before I return to America. The short boat trip from Fitjar to Aga was a challenge. Nils prayed that the good Lord would bring us through the rough seas. Once again, God protected.

I am being called to supper and so will say farewell for now. My love to you. Greet Martha and the children when you see them. I pray this time away will speed by. I am already awaiting our life together.

Love,

Andreas

The next day Andreas and his housemates walked to the local

church. The rest of the day was spent getting acquainted with the other university students.

> *February 1, 1904*
> *Dear Martha,*
>   *I hope that Helen will share my letter with you and so I will not offer the same information I sent to her. I encountered no danger during my entire journey except for rough seas out of Fitjar. Nils, Helga and Mother send you warm greetings.*
>   *Please give Petra, Melvin and Bernhard my love with long, warm hugs. I thank God daily for you and your four-year-long errand of mercy. What a saint you have been, giving up so much of your life for the needs of others, especially for your rogue brother who has left you again with three little ones. I would never have taken on this challenge without your encouragement and blessing.*
>   *Today I visited Professor Odland. I was happy to receive his advice regarding my course of study. I look forward to hearing the lectures in New Testament, church history and pastoral theology. Regarding church history, he advised me to purchase certain current German texts. I am reminded how much time I will be spending with my reading lamp. Regarding my New Testament study, I will need to purchase Theodor Zahn's two large volumes—*Introduction to the New Testament. *I have been so blessed with financial gifts, making these purchases less of a burden.*
>   *Well ,that certainly is enough about me. I hope and pray this letter finds all three children enjoying their studies and behaving for you. Enclosed you will find my address. By God's grace, this is where I will be staying for my entire time in Oslo.*
>   *Your thankful and loving brother,*
>   *Andreas*

It was not a surprise that some of Andreas' holiday visits were spent with old friends who had decided to return to their homeland from America. One such couple was the Johanssons, with whom Andreas had a special bond. He officiated at their wedding at St. Olaf Church just a few years earlier. Although spending his first Easter away from home was painful, Andreas appreciated his time with the Johanssons, whom he had grown to know quite well. Sitting in their small parlor and watching their child play, his heart ached as he longed to see his own children and tried to imagine how they might be growing.

Returning to Oslo for the spring semester, Andreas was able to attend lectures on Old Testament and systematic theology, which he found interesting and challenging. At times during late-night studies, he would think, "Just give me the scriptures, the Catechism and my hymnbook. That is all a Christian really needs." Yet by the next day, in the middle of another lecture, he would enjoy soaking in the rich bath of deep theological and historical study. Intellectual thought came naturally to him.

Although he longed to be with Helen and his three children, time went by quickly as he kept busy with lectures, his writing and reading.

Andreas enjoyed the summer of 1904 relaxing with his family in Aga. There he was able to share memories with his mother, sister Helga, brother-in-law Nils and their family. Many evenings were spent fishing in the fjord for brown cod. During the summer days, Andreas helped Nils with the chores on the small Aga farm. Weather permitting, the family would board Nils' boat each Sunday to worship in the sanctuary in which Andreas attended services as a child. At the end of the summer, Andreas began to think about his studies. Saying farewell to his aging mother was especially painful. He hoped this farewell was not the last.

By early September, Andreas was on his way to Oslo for his final set of courses. Although he had hoped to continue living in his original residence, previous reservations prevented that from happening. Fortunately he was able to stay with Mr. and Mrs. Tyedte, a couple he had known from Fitjar. Long into the night, he and his hosts would talk of the religious publishing business Mr. Tyedte owned and operated.

With his studies completed by Easter of 1905, Andreas began the final step of his 18-month-long sojourn. Intending to meet the authors of the texts he had studied, his final journey was a seven-week adventure to Copenhagen and on to cities in Germany. Honoring his Lutheran heritage, he visited Wittenberg, Eisleben and other historic places of the Reformation. One such site was the Colburg Fortress, in which Luther stayed during the Diet of Augsburg in 1530.

By staying in Y.M.C.A.s and traveling third class, Andreas was able to keep the costs very manageable. Although he was with people constantly, the journey was an especially lonely one as he longed for home. With his final voyage home approaching, Andreas became more and more anxious to return to Helen and the children. Letters from Helen were filled with details of the simple wedding that would take place shortly after he returned.

Following a two-day rail and ferry trip seated day and night on third-class wooden benches, Andreas finally arrived in Oslo on Pentecost Sunday, June 10th. Although very tired, once he arrived at worship at Our Savior's Church, a simple announcement quickly caught his attention.

The clergyman climbed the stairs to the pulpit high above the congregation and read, "I have been asked to make an announcement that will reverberate through every sanctuary in our beloved nation. On Thursday, June 7, of this year, 1905, the Norwegian Parliament voted to dissolve its union with Sweden. This day we will pray for our nation."

Andreas remembered the Norwegian history he had been taught at the Cathedral School. He thought to himself, "This is quite a historic day. Imagine not being connected with Sweden for the first time since 1814."

From Oslo, Andreas departed for his sister Helga's home in Aga where he would once again spend the summer. This summer would be bittersweet for Andreas. In August, he would return to America, not knowing if he would see his mother again, or how long it would be before another trip to his homeland. The day before his departure from Aga, he noticed his mother quietly humming her favorite hymns, including the tune to "God Be With You Till We Meet Again." On the next day, she looked at him with tears running down her cheeks as she said, "If not here, in glory we will meet again." Andreas shed tears of joy and sorrow. He feared never seeing his mother again. At the same time, he was filled with the joy of finally returning home. Before Nils and Andreas pushed out to sea, his mother and sister stood at the door of the Aga home singing together the hymn "God Be With You Till We Meet Again."

1. Gud vær med deg til vi ses igjen,
på din reise deg bevare,
skjerme deg mot nød og fare.
Gud vær med deg til vi ses igjen.

[Refreng]
Til vi ses igjen, til vi ses,
til vi ses i fredens hjem,
til vi ses igjen, til vi ses,
Gud vær med deg til vi ses igjen.

After the one verse and chorus, Andreas' mother went on singing.
2. Gud vær med deg til vi ses igjen.
Om du møter store prøver,
stol på ham som hjem deg fører.
Gud vær med deg til vi ses igjen.

By now the sniffles were getting in the way of the singing, but insisting on all the verses, as Lutherans seem to do, Helga and Bertha kept singing.
3. Gud vær med deg til vi ses igjen.
Møtes vi ei mer i livet,
vi skal ses i paradiset.
Gud vær med deg til vi ses igjen.

Tekst: Jeremiah E. Rankin, 1828–1904
Musikk: William G. Tomer, 1833–1896
2 Tessalonikerbrev 3:16
4. Mosebok 6:24–26

Courage mysteriously strengthened each of the singers as they continued.

[Refreng]
Til vi ses igjen, til vi ses,
til vi ses i fredens hjem,
til vi ses igjen, til vi ses,
Gud vær med deg til vi ses igjen.

Stoically, standing at the boat landing, the two women continued to sing as Andreas and his brother-in-law navigated their little boat out of the harbor. The two men overheard each other humming Bertha's tune all the way to Bergen. In Liverpool, Andreas boarded one of the largest and fastest ships of his day—the *RMS Oceanic*—part of the White Star Line.

The big vessel was packed with anxious, grief-stricken Norwegians, Swedes and Germans who had caught a later case of America Fever. Andreas, now fluent in more than one language, was able to answer the questions of many who were filled with fears and misconceptions about their destination. Andreas would spend time consoling and encouraging young and old.

Right on time, the tugs began to push the sleek liner out to sea. Once under way and following a simple supper, Andreas went to bed.

The next morning, Andreas woke to a ship that appeared to be stalled at sea. The engines were quiet. Someone in the next bunk asked if there might be some problem. Andreas answered, "I am sure not, but I will go and check."

Climbing the three flights of stairs to the deck, he walked to the rail to find the ship sitting as if it were a toy bobbing in a bathtub. He asked a crewman, "Why do you think we are not moving?"

Angrily, the young man said, "Go back to the deck where you belong and don't worry about it."

Surprised at the answer, Andreas ignored the command and walked to the bow of the ship. Staring west, he longed for Helen and his children. Walking back to the stern, he noticed no churning water or wake from the ship. Looking back to the east, he noticed another ship quickly gaining on the *Oceanic*. A crackling voice came from the ship's speaker system.

"This is your captain speaking. I want you to know there is no problem on board the ship as long as I am in charge. A few troublemaking stokers have decided to sit down on the job. Rather than putting up with this problem, I have asked the Navy to come aboard and bring justice to the guilty. You will note the naval ship coming beside us. We will be on our way as soon as this inconvenience is dealt with. Thank you for your patience."

The passengers looked worried and even fearful. The British Navy came aboard with guns drawn and the word quickly spread that some kind of work stoppage had taken place. Days later, the ship finally arrived in New York. It was only once everyone had disembarked that the real story came out in the New York *Tribune*. In large letters the headlines proclaimed, "Mutiny on the *RMS Oceanic*." Andreas took change from his pocket to purchase the paper. He read about the refusal of the stokers to keep working once they had left the Liverpool Harbor. Andreas thought, "No wonder the ship was sitting still on the second day of the voyage." The article described how the captain had sent an SOS to the British Navy and told of the attempt by the disgruntled workers to capture the guns on board. Andreas was thankful there had been no bloodshed and everyone had arrived safely.

Once processed from the ship, Andrea was able to pick up a letter from Helen, which confirmed their wedding date. With the letter came a surprising request.

July 25, 1905
My dear Andreas,
As you receive this letter I am hopeful it finds you healthy and safe. I am so looking forward to our life together. Let me begin by saying Petra is such a beautiful young lady. Melvin is so looking forward to seeing you. He adores you. And dear, seven-year-old Bernhard is the one getting into all the trouble. He is very tall for his age. Martha is the same saint she was when you left.

Dearest, I do have a great favor to ask. I am wondering if we could celebrate a double wedding along with my sister, Bertha. It would help my parents as well as all of us in the preparations. As we have discussed, we will be married in our home in Owatonna. Rev. Harbo will perform the service.
  Bride in waiting,
  Helen

Andreas, remembering the history of his parents' wedding, simply smiled and thought the more, the merrier.

Boarding the same train he had taken to New York 18 months earlier, Andreas spent the next two days reading and rereading the letter his dear future wife had written while counting down the hours until he would be home.

Chapter 21

Home Sweet Home

Andreas arrived home with only a few days to spare before the wedding. The time was spent reacquainting himself with the children. Visiting his office for the first time, he was surprised to see painted on the door.

Rev. Andreas Helland
Professor of New Testament

Andreas arrived at Helen's home in Owatonna the weekend before the big day. It seemed everyone was busy with preparations. No one was more excited than the children.

On Saturday night, August 18th, everything changed, especially the joy that had filled the Anderson home. A man arrived at their home and asked if he might come in.

"Certainly, sir. I hope there isn't any bad news," Mr. Anderson said.

"Well," the visitor continued, "I'm afraid there is. I am saddened to have to tell you that Johan Jensen, your daughter's fiancé, has lost his life in a hotel fire."

Mrs. Anderson quickly joined her husband asking, "What is the problem?"

The gentleman repeated himself and was on his way. Once Bertha had been told of the tragedy, all the joy evaporated and, for a few days, Helen and Andreas wondered if they should postpone their wedding plans. Once the funeral was held for Johan, they decided to continue with their wedding. Bertha traveled south to be comforted by a girlfriend in Iowa. Despite the cloud hanging over the long-awaited event, on August 24, 1905, Miss Helen Anderson, a former parishioner of St. Olaf, married her first love. Following a short honeymoon to Duluth and on to Minong, Wisconsin, to visit Andreas' brother, Kristen, the two began their life together near Augsburg College.

As Andreas began his new career as Professor Helland, he joined only two others—Professors Sverdrup and Urseth. While Sverdrup taught Old Testament and systematic theology, Urseth's responsibility was teaching the art of practical theology. That left New Testament and church history to the younger professor. The two more experienced faculty members showed Andreas understanding and kindness.

Andreas was also elected as a member of the corporation of the Lutheran Board of Missions. This appointment fulfilled a passion inherited from his mother that had remained with him since his early days back home. While Andreas' fragile health kept him off the mission field, he would say to his colleagues, "This is a way I can keep my toe in the water."

It was late November of 1906 that Professor Sverdrup again called the young colleague into his office, this time asking him to write an article for an upcoming publication on the mission work in the country of Uganda. Rarely refusing his mentor, Andreas ran back to his office to rummage through his books. Finding his atlas, he quickly searched maps of the world to find the country Sverdrup had mentioned.

As it is with most institutions, no matter their size, when crisis hits, politics bloom. That, too, is what happened following the sudden death of Andreas' mentor, hero and the school's president, Georg Sverdrup. With the void of leadership came two possible solutions. While the younger students were campaigning for Professor Urseth, the older ones were suggesting that Andreas take the lead. As is often the case, the various supporters failed to ask the candidates for their opinions. Andreas made it very clear that his natural gifts, training and temperament would not fit the position of president, and he would not accept such a calling. With that being said, interim leadership of the institution was put in place while Andreas added to his teaching responsibilities those of the dean for the seminary as well as secretary of the Lutheran Board of Missions.

In addition to his tasks at Augsburg, there was a crisis on the home front. Both eight-year-old Bernhard and ten-year-old Melvin had developed appendicitis. In both cases, Dr. Eitel suggested a wait-and-see approach. Much relief was felt and prayers of thanksgiving were offered as the pains slowly disappeared in both of the brothers.

The family grew quickly with the birth of a daughter in 1907, another in 1909 and a son in 1912. Clara Irene was named after Clara, whose memory was still alive in Andreas' mind and heart. Two years later, Thelma Beatrice came along. Continuing the tradition of naming children for family members, Thelma was named in honor of Helen's mother, Thuri. Three years later, Maurice joined the family. Again, remembering Helen's side of the family, the newest child's name honored her brother, Moses.

While life at home was now anything but calm with six young Hellands, back at Augsburg there was more turmoil. A popular professor, Wilhelm Pettersen, had crossed state lines, becoming active in the fight between the Republican Party and the Non-Partisan League of North Dakota. Challenging the strongly held traditions of the Republican Party did not go over well with many of the Friends of Augsburg. While Pettersen's speaking tours began to conflict with his teaching responsibilities, his debate topics brought the most criticism. Suggesting full suffrage for women and state ownership of banks, mills and grain elevators was unacceptable to the city and rural school constituents. His request for time off to accommodate his speaking schedule was denied by the college, which resulted in his letter of resignation. Confident of his outstanding skills as both a teacher and orator, he expected the letter to be refused. To his surprise, and the deep disappointment of his students, his resignation was accepted.

Again, more responsibilities were given to Andreas. One such task was the unenviable job of teaching Pettersen's freshman college history class. Students loyal to their former teacher were angry. Wanting to start on the right foot, Andreas simply admitted he had not been given enough notice to prepare adequately for the class. He announced that they would begin with a review of what Professor Pettersen had covered during the first few weeks of the term. One of the students, incensed at what had happened to his favorite teacher, raised the question of their need to review material they had already covered. To this complaint, Andreas simply reiterated that he had been given no time to prepare a lecture and was honestly rusty on the topic. It seemed this simple admission took the wind out of the protester's sail. Those students who had crossed their arms in defiance seemed to relax and accept the situation.

The difficult challenges of daily teaching were blended with an opportunity to reconnect with Andreas' homeland. The first experiment of inviting a visiting professor from Norway to teach for a short time at Augsburg had been a great success. And so, a second Professor, B. A. Stoylen, was invited to teach practical theology. For Andreas, this connection was stronger than he could have ever imagined. Just prior to his return to Norway, Stoylen was invited to the Helland home for dinner. Once all the children had eaten and Helen was busy putting them to bed, the men made themselves comfortable on the two rockers that graced the living room.

"You know, Stoylen, your dialect reminds me of someone I haven't thought about in many years," Andreas said. "Back home, in the Fitjar parish, I knew a blacksmith. In fact no one called him by his name. They just referred to him as "the old blacksmith." He was a strange kind of man, not terribly friendly, but a good craftsman. My father would go to him. He lived up the hill from our home. The strange thing was that without any notice, he would leave for weeks. I must confess that his funny dialect and strange mannerisms made him a laughing stock in the community."

As Andreas spoke, his visitor stopped rocking. Listening very carefully, Stoylen finally put up his hands as if to beg the storyteller to stop.

"What is it? Stoylen, what is it?"

"I know the story," the guest replied. "You see, I knew this man. When I was young, I attended school in Hardanger, you know about 50 miles from your home. I was about 14 and I had not found peace with the Lord. Once a year, the old blacksmith arrived in our community and would hold meetings in our school. He answered some of my questions and he brought peace to my soul."

"Really?" Andreas interrupted. "That strange old man?"

Stoylen continued, "Yes, and I was so moved by what he taught, that when I returned to school I began to lead some boys in Bible study." Taking his watch out of his pocket and showing it to Andreas he continued, "At the end of the first year, the boys gave me this timepiece. I've had it for so long, it now acts like it has rheumatism."

Pulling another gold watch out of his other pocket, he added, "So you can imagine the surprise and appreciation I felt when your school gave me this handsome new watch."

With a smile on his face, Andreas said, "So we knew the same old man?"

"Yes," and while fingering the old watch Stoylen said, "No matter how slow this one might go, it is indeed a precious keepsake. I'll just keep it in my other pocket."

"What happened to the blacksmith?" Andreas inquired.

"Oh, he died some time ago now. I don't know who is doing his work in the area; I don't think he ever had a family."

As the two men sat listening to the creaking of their rockers, Andreas thought of how visitors, like this one, brought him back to the precious memories of home.

Chapter 22

A Century in the Making

Within Norwegian circles, the years proceeding 1914 were filled with talk and plans regarding the centennial year of Norway's Independence. The date of May 17 was circled on everyone's calendar. Since the current president of the Lutheran Free Church, Pastor E. E. Gynild, was unable to travel, Andreas had been chosen to represent this church body at the celebration in Oslo. With his sister Martha now living in Washington State, his trip left quite a burden to Helen. It was only the help of the older children that made it possible for Andreas to leave the three younger children behind. Knowing of his need to see his mother and family again, Helen supported Andreas' desire and encouraged him to take advantage of this historic event.

In preparation for the trip, Andreas had written a short book on the endeavors of the Lutheran Free Church. In Norway, the short volume was of such interest that it was sent from Oslo to every bishop, theological professor and pastor in the country. A beautifully bound copy was presented to King Haakon VII.

Along with the other three Norwegian church bodies in America, the Lutheran Free Church was invited to construct a display showing a bit of the church's history. The exhibition would include framed pictures of Lutheran Free institutions, its leaders and the church buildings and parsonages.

This time, rather than going third class, Andreas, along with the other church leaders, had been given first-class cabins by the Norwegian American Lines on the newly built *SS Bergensfjord*. As they sailed directly from New York to Bergen, Andreas was struck by the speed of the ship and the comfortable accommodations. As he enjoyed the luxury of his cabin and the beautiful china and food in the finely appointed dining room, he recalled his earlier voyages, traveling third class and having to carry on his shoulder his own straw mattress and utensils.

Among the passengers were the representatives of the Norwegian

Synod, the United Church and the Hauge Synod. In unison, the four would represent the American Lutheran churches with Norwegian roots. Arriving first in Oslo, Andreas was told he was expected to attend a private audience with King Haakon. Realizing the three other representatives were still in Bergen, he quickly sent a cablegram informing them of this most important event. They boarded the night train from Bergen and, thanks to the youngest delegate, arrived just in time. Excited about the privilege, yet humbled by the honor, Andreas and the Hauge Church representative agreed that the other two older delegates would lead the conversation with the King. Andreas was surprised to find the King to be not only very personable but also quite informal.

On Independence Day, Sunday, May 17, 1914, Andreas, regaled in his traditional student cap from so many years ago, walked to Our Savior's Church, the cathedral of Oslo, where the first celebrative worship service took place.

The only time the cordial relationship between the four church leaders became strained was just before the opening of the displays each church representative had brought with them. Andreas arrived at the appointed hour and requested to set up his display while the United Church, by far the largest synod, had ignored the exhibition's instructions. Awaiting the arrival of the others, the organizer finally informed Andreas he could choose any space available. He immediately placed his display in the most prominent site that faced the main entrance. When the United Church delegate arrived, he complained vehemently about the only location remaining. Andreas held his ground as the organizer simply shrugged his shoulders and reminded the disgruntled representative of the instructions they had all received. The representative's anger subsided only days later when Andreas was able to negotiate complimentary tickets to a regal dinner.

The following week, on Ascension Day, services were held in four of the largest Trondheim churches. Andreas was honored to be the preacher at the Lademoen Church. The service concluded with a postlude that brought tears to many an eye. The organist carefully wove together the tunes of "A Mighty Fortress Is Our God," the Norwegian National Anthem, "Ja, vi elker dette landet—Yes, we love this country" and "The Star Spangled Banner."

Andreas was again met in Bergen by Nils, his brother-in-law, who brought Andreas to the family home in Aga. Along with long talks with his mother, he and Nils enjoyed fishing together. Two days later, Andreas had to say goodbye to his family. Again, in a much-weakened voice, he heard his mother say, "If not here, in glory we will meet again." In his heart, Andreas knew this would be the last time he would hear his mother utter those words. Missing Helen and the children, he was more than ready to return to what he now knew to be home.

Almost a month before his departure from his homeland, the Norwegian newspapers were packed not only with the descriptions of the centennial celebrations but also news of the current political crisis in Europe. On June 28, Arch Duke Franz Ferdinand of Austria was assassinated. As Andreas set sail for home, he felt relief and prayed the United States would stay out of what many considered a European skirmish. Following two months of constant travel, Andreas enjoyed the peaceful setting of his first-class cabin. Rarely had he ever enjoyed the kind of elegant dining afforded him.

Enjoyment of the luxurious surroundings as well as Andreas' excitement of returning home was dampened one evening while still at sea. His usual charming smile absent, the captain rose from his chair to speak. With a serious look on his face, he began, "I wish to tell you of a cablegram I received today. On this day, July 28, I am saddened to announce that the Austro-Hungarian forces have initiated fighting with the intent of invading Serbia. Our plan, of course, is to continue at full speed toward New York. We have been assured that we are in no danger. I tell you of this so that gossip might not prevail. As captain, I ask you to remain calm and continue to enjoy your dinner."

As he sat, conversation quickly followed regarding the possibility of future American involvement in the conflict. At Andreas' table, there was full agreement that the United States should remain neutral and not become involved in the hostilities.

Three days later, on a foggy morning with the Statue of Liberty just coming into sight, passengers stood on the various decks, loudly cheering their arrival. Once through customs and about to board his train, Andreas cabled Helen to announce his safe arrival. As he walked past the New York Times building, he noticed the placard calling Austro-Hungarian reservists to return to their home country immediately. Andreas whispered a prayer of thanksgiving for his safe arrival and another prayer for those who might become involved in the conflict, now an ocean away.

Two days later, Andreas arrived in Chicago and took the Great Northern to Minneapolis. He thought of how his children might have changed. He was excited to see Helen again and return to a normal routine. In those two months, Andreas had missed three of his children's birthdays. As the train approached the Minneapolis depot, he saw Bernhard waving. Bernhard had not only just graduated from Augsburg Academy, but had grown another foot. Holding tightly to his mother's hand, little two-year-old Maurice was jumping up and down with a childish delight. Andreas gave the younger children hugs and Bernhard a firm handshake. He then took Helen into his arms for a long embrace. Bernhard looked embarrassed while the other children pestered their father by asking, "Papa, what did you bring us?"

Andreas answered, "Let's go home and you will see!"

Back at the house, the constant begging came to a stop when Andreas gave each child a small souvenir and a woolen toy or set of mittens from Grandma Bertha, known affectionately to them as *Bestemor*. When each child had something to hold, the family sat down for their first meal together.

Returning to his academic duties, the years passed quickly as Andreas taught, served as the Secretary of the Lutheran Board of Missions and helped Helen raise the children. A child, little Martha Winifred, was born four days before Norwegian Independence Day, on May 13, 1916. Martha Winifred was named in honor of two aunts, Martha Anderson and Martha Helland. Her second name was chosen simply for its beauty.

Now and then, there had been repeated requests for Andreas to visit the mission field in Madagascar. Plans for such a journey were scuttled by America's involvement in what began to be known as *The*

Big War. There would be no opportunity for such travel.

Just as tragedy visited those who lost their loved ones in combat,- for the second time, heartbreak visited Andreas. In 1919, his dear pregnant wife developed toxemia, which took her life on February 11 of that year. With the four younger children at his side, Andreas had to search for time to spend alone in his grief. Again, as she had done after Clara's death, Martha returned to care for her brother's children. This time Martha came from her work at a children's home in Poulsbo, Washington.

As time passed, Andreas was comforted not only by his sister but also by Helen's old friend, Anna Sather. Anna became a frequent visitor to the Helland home, helping with the children as well as with daily chores. It was to no one's surprise that just two years after the death of his second wife, Andreas married Anna. His youngest child, Winifred, proudly took the role of flower girl at the June 4, 1921, wedding.

The joy of the wedding day was followed one week later by the news that Andreas' dear mother, Bertha, had died on June 11th. His profound grief was compounded by his inability to share his sadness with his siblings and children, now living in far distant lands. Petra, the oldest, following a year teaching school near the Rockne family in southern Minnesota, had married Ralph Mortensen and the two were on the mission field in China. Melvin, completing his seminary education, had taken his wife Emily to the mission field of Madagascar while Bernhard, newly married, was on his way to the Santal Mission in India with his wife, Muriel.

As the years passed, Andreas spent many hours late into the night typing carbon-copied letters to his three oldest missionary children. Closer to home, the younger children grew to love and enjoy the little lady they quickly began to call *Mama*.

Chapter 23

Fagerheim

Over time, there was one place that brought Andreas joy and relaxation. It all began with a group of friends and fellow Augsburg professors who had purchased a 40-acre piece of land on what became known as Saga Hill. Situated west of Minneapolis, on an arm of Lake Minnetonka, was a large hill that faced a much smaller body of water known as Forest Lake. While some professors purchased land as early as 1885, Andreas was not able to do so until 1909, when a close friend made part of his lot available to him. Fred Paulson sold Andreas a hillside plot facing Forest Lake and across the road from the Lutheran Deaconess Cottage. The deaconess cottage was home to a group of single women who worked as hospital nurses. Because Andreas had rented apartments or lived in parsonages, he and Anna took great pride in owning their own property.

While Fred was the expert carpenter, Andreas had worked with wood since his childhood in Fitjar. He would humbly admit that once in a while he actually hit the head of the nail. With Fred's guidance, the college professor became an excellent carpenter.

By the end of summer 1909, high upon a hill overlooking Forest Lake stood a simple, wood-frame cabin. The Helland's named their retreat *Fagerheim*, which means "Peaceful Home."

Getting to Fagerheim was no easy matter. Andreas and the family would take the Riverside streetcar, and then the train to Spring Park. From this little community, Mr. Bergquist would generously take them in his beautifully crafted wooden launch to what was known as the "company dock." With baggage, boxes and children in hand, they would trek across the highway, down "Lovers Lane" and back up the steep hill on which sat their pride and joy.

On Sundays, the family worshiped with the Lutheran Deaconess Sisters at their large, white-frame summer home just across the highway. The women had named the house *Solbakken* or "Sunny Hill." It was a welcome spot not only for Sunday worship, but it held a daily source of freshly baked cookies for any of Andreas' children able to sneak away.

The worshippers sat on the screen porch while the organist played the reed organ just inside the living room door. As the children became bored with the sermon preached in Norwegian, they listened for two sounds. The first was Captain Deering's steamboat horn. The second came from the cuckoo clock hanging just over the organ. Anxiously they would await the 12 shrill cuckoos, which signaled the end of the service.

During the week, in typical Norwegian fashion, Andreas wore shorts and an undershirt as he sat in a lawn chair, taking advantage of the warm summer rays. Gathered with others, he discussed the events of the community. Daily chores, reading, rowing and occasional fishing took up the summer days. When they expected company, Andreas fished for dinner as he had done back home in Norway. In the waters of Forest Lake, he would catch sunfish, crappies, black bass and the strange-looking catfish. The only means of refrigeration was the wooden icebox, visited weekly by the iceman. Andreas spent one summer building a gray rock fireplace in their newly enlarged living room. This was to be one of several beautifully crafted fireplaces he built over the years.

Once a week, Andreas would make the complicated journey back to the Augsburg campus to catch up on correspondence from the variety of mission fields for which he was responsible. Sitting on his desk was his motto for living, words he learned from his mother, "You will never know the joy of Jesus unless you feel His burden for the world."

Before returning to Fagerheim, Andreas would check on their apartment. Opening the door, he would be greeted by the odor of aging books lining the walls in the entry. He would carefully water the houseplants and wind up his beloved seven-day clock. Returning from Minneapolis in the evening, he would place near the heads of his sleeping children the stamps he had collected from his correspondence from India, China and Madagascar. The next morning the children would awaken to the little treasures. Following his stamp deposits, Andreas would join the community of professors and their wives who gathered around the fire to share the latest campus news and perhaps play a friendly game of croquet.

Andreas and his family loved the summers at Fagerheim. The children spent their days swimming, and playing on the bench swing that hung between two tall butternut trees. On rainy days, they played in the tent their father had purchased. When playing house, cardboard boxes served as furniture, with acorns as cups and saucers. Dolls were hand crafted of corn husks. When returning from their illicit visits to the Deaconess house, the children would bring generous peace offerings of freshly picked gooseberries, currents and red raspberries to their slightly irritated mother. In the evening they would gather around *Papa* as he read to them from "The King's Book," a story of King Haakon. Following his reading of the book, Andreas would remind his children of the day he walked through Frogner Park in Oslo and was personally greeted by the very same king. No matter how many times he read the book or told the story, his children would say in utter disbelief, "Really, Papa? You really saw the King? Really, Papa? He talked to you?"

It was a simple reality that visitors would arrive, uninvited, every Sunday during the summer. Some guests came by train and others by automobile, but always just in time for afternoon coffee or supper. Accustomed to the constant flow of guests in their small apartment during the school year, the Helland family had learned to always have bread, meat, cheese and a newly baked cake waiting. When friends were actually invited, Andreas would announce their arrival by raising both the American and Norwegian flags.

As time went on, even this peaceful environment was invaded by conflict. There had been a gentleman's agreement that the Hellands, as well as other neighbors, could use a gravel driveway constructed by a neighborhood family. Returning one day from a rare family outing, Andreas discovered a large hole where his driveway began. Thinking it might have been some strange force of nature, like a sinkhole, he climbed the hill to the neighbor's cabin. Knocking on the door, he heard the man's shrill voice from inside, "So, what do you want?" Surprised by his manner, Andreas simply asked if he knew of the problem at the end of the driveway.

"Yes, I know of it," the neighbor replied. Not knowing the cause, Andreas asked if he would be able to help him fill in the hole so he could get to his own cabin.

"I don't think so," the neighbor said angrily. Stepping away from the back door, Andreas returned to his family, told them to make their way around the obstruction and asked 18-year-old Bernhard to help him fill in the mysterious hole.

It was only after a number of attempts to talk with his angry neighbor that the truth was told. He had actually dug the hole and the matter had to finally be settled through legal action. It seemed the family had resented the group who so many years earlier purchased the 40 acres that had surrounded his tranquil piece of land. He had decided to take his bad feelings out on Andreas. Following this encounter, Andreas came as close as he could to swearing by saying "He's such a fool, such a fool."

Signing the legal document, the Hellands agreed to keep their children off the neighbor's land. The angry neighbor insisted that while playing near the lot line, the children must remain quiet as church mice. Over the years, the two families remained polite but certainly were never friendly.

As the summers passed, Andreas continued to build and rebuild, even adding a smaller cabin near the shoreline. Another outside fireplace was built and inscribed with the word *Evenrest*.

There was to be only one more major disappointment in their life at Fagerheim on Saga Hill. Raised on the intercoastal waters of Norway, Andreas had always dreamed of building a small launch. Although he did much of the work himself, he took advantage of the skills of his friend, Fred Paulson, and the general labor of Melvin and Bernhard. The summer in which Andreas was busily completing this major project, there was road construction taking place just up the hill past "Lovers Lane." The construction of a new bridge was completed just before his project was done. Andreas was disappointed when he tried, for the first time, to sail out into the larger West Arm of Lake Minnetonka. By just a few inches, his pride and joy, the commissioned *Rajan*, was too tall to make it under the bridge. Wishing the water levels would sometime fall, he hoped someday he would be able to cruise the huge body of water. Taking the situation in stride, Andreas simply made fun of himself and quipped that at least they had a ferry for little Forest Lake. He would welcome his family and guests aboard, and they would make their short trip around the small lake while listening to the chug, chug, chug of the small gas engine that sat at the rear of the boat. He would comment to his friends back in town, "Well, I have a lake-locked launch, but at least it hasn't sunk."

Chapter 24

Soul Care

Over the years, Andreas became a popular teacher due to his well-prepared lectures and the stories he would tell about his life experiences. As the years passed, his dark hair and bushy mustache slowly turned to silvery gray. While students appreciated all of the time he spent soberly answering their many questions, his sense of humor often came through.

A young prepper—a student preparing to enter the seminary—knocked on the professor's door. "Come in," he heard. Cautiously, the student turned the knob and opened the door to an office lined with shelves of books. Seated on a wooden swivel chair at his desk, the professor smiled and repeated, "Come in. And who might you be?"

The young man introduced himself as T.O. Burntvedt.

Gesturing to a straight-backed wooden chair, Andreas invited his visitor to have a seat.

"What might I do for you, T.O.?" Andreas inquired.

Nervous and seemingly confused, the young man began to talk in circles. Finally, the professor took charge of the conversation and asked, "So are you trying to say you would like to teach parochial school?"

"Yes, sir, if I could; yes, sir," the young student stuttered.

"Have you any experience in teaching?" Andreas inquired.

"Well, not really, sir. I just thought I could serve the Lord this way."

"Well, do you preach?" the professor continued to ask.

"Well, no sir," Burntvedt answered.

Quickly the student realized how foolish he was, as well as gullible. It was his school buddies who had convinced him that anyone could teach the ABCs, Catechism, Bible history and such.

The kind-hearted professor continued to smile, giving the young man a searching look. A serious expression came across Andreas' face as he looked his guest in the eyes and declared, "One must be right with the Lord to be given an important assignment like this."

Burntvedt looked around the office as if searching for words. He replied, "I do pray and read scripture, and I think I could pray and give a testimony in front of others. But I confess, I have never really done it."

Following an extended conversation, by the time he left the office, T.O. Burntvedt was assigned to teach eight weeks of parochial school in a South Dakota congregation and four weeks in another, with no expectations to preach.

Throughout the years, as the professor taught, no matter what the topic might have been—the mysterious Gospel of John, church history, practical theology or the art of preaching—his overall lesson was always focused on the care of the soul. Again and again he would remind his students of the motto he lived by, and that was displayed on his desk, "You will never know the love of Jesus unless you feel his burden for the world."

Whether Andreas and Anna, along with their children, were confined to a campus apartment or were enjoying a larger home, people were always coming and going. A neighbor would often ask one of the children who was playing on the front sidewalk, "So, how's your ma? How's your pa? Have any company?"

And after the professor allowed himself to purchase a Model T Ford, he often used it as a free taxi. As he picked up the Deaconesses for Sunday services, he would gallantly open the car door and announce, "As for me and my Ford, we will serve the Lord." Every time he said it, the saintly Deaconess ladies rewarded him with laughter.

Mixed in with the busy days of teaching, traveling on behalf of the college and the Lutheran Free Church, raising children and loving his dear Anna, there were occasions that felt like the chill of a Minnesota winter. Those times seemed to visit him too often, including the anniversaries of Clara's and Helen's births, their wedding anniversaries and the dates of their passings. At those times, Anna would gift her husband with even more compassion and understanding. Other professors, friends and his local pastor were always carefully attuned to his mood, whether it was joy filled or melancholy.

The most joyous times for the family were spent during the long summer breaks at Fagerheim on Saga Hill. The long hours of relaxation, rowing, fishing and motoring in his homemade launch seemed to restore Andreas as well as his family. It was especially during these breaks that Andreas found time to type the lengthy carbon-copied letters to his grown children.

Chapter 25

A Life Well Lived

Through his many years of teaching and traveling, retirement finally came for Andreas in 1941 after nearly 40 years of serving Augsburg College and Seminary. He and Anna began to enjoy even more time at their favorite spot on earth—Fagerheim. Summer was filled with visits from professors, administrators, family and friends. Children and grandchildren began spending more time at the upper cabin while Papa and Nanny lived in a lower cabin near the lakeshore.

Finally, the century hit its halfway point. Just one year into its second half, Andreas began to experience what he thought would happen so many years earlier.

His grandson, the author of this fictionalized memoir, was about to begin his own educational career at Bancroft Elementary School just a few blocks south of the Helland home in Minneapolis. Labor Day evening of 1951, Papa and Nanny moved into their youngest daughter's home. Feeling weaker by the hour, Andreas rested in bed. Andreas heard his five-year-old grandson scurry around getting ready for his first day of kindergarten. Before young Philip left for school, his mother reminded him to say goodbye to his grandparents. Running into their new bedroom, he jumped onto Grandma's side of the bed. Slowly his grandfather turned over, smiled and drew from under the sheet a crisp, new one-dollar bill. He handed it to his grandson, bent over and gave the boy a kiss. "Now you have a good day, Flip."

Later that day Papa made two requests of his daughter, "Could you please send my good suit, the black one, to the cleaners, and then call Pastor Olson?"

By Thursday, Andreas was transferred to Deaconess Hospital where he was cared for by the very same nurses who rode in his car to worship, and who during the summer months would offer the front porch of their Lake Minnetonka cabin for area worship services. These were the same nurses who would sneak freshly baked cookies to Andreas' children and grandchildren. It was Saturday, September 8, 1951, that his wish to finally be outlived by his wife was fulfilled. After losing his dear Clara in 1900 and Helen in 1919, his dear Anna now outlived him.

On the following Tuesday, Anna (Nanny), the family, colleagues, and friends said farewell to their husband, father, grandfather, scholar, prolific author, editor, teacher and passionate missionary. Many were reminded of the two phrases his mother had shared with him: "If not here, then in glory we will meet again." And, "You will never know the love of Jesus unless you feel his burden for the world."

Epilogue

Though Andreas Helland's life on earth has ended, his values have lived on through the generations that have followed. As I spent more than two years researching and writing this labor of love, I have grown closer and closer to a grandfather I barely knew.

Throughout this project, I have come to appreciate the words of Phyllis Theroux—"Being a writer does not have the global reach of being a canonized saint but, at its best, writing is a deeply spiritual act that can have a profound effect upon the practitioner." It certainly has for me.

Philip "Flip" Formo

In Deepest Appreciation

I would like to first thank my wife, Jean, for encouraging me so many years ago to take advantage of writing classes. At the Loft Literary Center, I met fellow students—Kathy Haley and Diane Rifkin—who have inspired me to continue this endeavor.

I am so appreciative of the teachers and students at the Iowa Writer's Festival from whom I have learned so much over the years. I would also like to acknowledge my parents, Jerome and Winnie Formo, who encouraged me with their own memoir writings.

Finally to my co-editors, Jean Lingen and Jean Formo, for their endless hours of reading, re-reading and research—many thanks. Much appreciation to my daughter, Carrie Peterson, for serving as webmaster and social media guru. An eternal debt of gratitude goes to the one who inspired me through his own memoir, my grandfather, Andreas Helland, affectionately known to his family as *Papa*. He authored many books, including *Georg Sverdrup—The Man and His Message*, pamphlets and papers, all focusing on his first love, Christian missions, as well as his beloved Augsburg College and Seminary.

Although most of the material in this book reflects Andreas' own memoir, I have chosen to fictionalize this writing with conversation, letters and journal entries.

About the Author

Philip J. Formo, former special education teacher and retired pastor of the Evangelical Lutheran Church in America, is the grandson of "Papa." Educated at Pacific Lutheran University, St Cloud State University and Luther Seminary, Pastor Formo served parishes in the Minnesota communities of Austin, Roseville, Rochester and Bloomington. He is the co-author of a number of volumes of *Augsburg Sermons for Children*. In retirement, he continues to serve as a clergy coach and enjoys writing and traveling. He and his wife, Jean, live in Savage, Minnesota. They have two grown daughters, Carrie and Krista.